A Sociology of Knowledge of European Integration

This book addresses the important but understudied question of how social scientific knowledge is entangled in the process of European integration. More specifically, it provides the first systematic introduction to a sociology of knowledge approach to European integration and demonstrates the value of such an approach through empirical illustrations.

Drawing on new research in the intersection of sociology of knowledge and political sociology, the book is the first to analyse the entanglement of social scientific knowledge and the development of the EU. The contributors provide the first systematic mapping of the relations between social scientific knowledge and particular aspects of European integration such as the Euro and monetary governance, constitution- and treaty-negotiation, education policy, enlargement and foreign policy. The book imports key ideas from the sociology of knowledge, sociology of science and political sociology to cast new light on the field of EU studies and its relation to the EU polity. The result is a fresh account of European integration, shaped – in often surprising ways – by relatively small groups of people and their particular ideas about economy, law, culture and politics.

This book was published as a special issue of the *Journal of European Integration*.

Rebecca Adler-Nissen is Associate Professor in the Department of Political Science at the University of Copenhagen, Denmark. Her research focuses on international political sociology, diplomacy, sovereignty, security, and European integration. She is the author of *Opting Out of the European Union: Diplomacy, Sovereignty and European Integration* (2014) and editor of *Bourdieu in International Relations* (2012).

Kristoffer Kropp is Associate Professor in the Department of Society and Globalisation at Roskilde University, Denmark. He is interested in the relations between political institutions and social scientific knowledge production. He is the author of *A Historical Account of Danish Sociology* (2015, forthcoming).

Journal of European Integration Special Issues
Series editors:
Thomas Christiansen, Maastricht University, Netherlands
Simon Duke, European Institute of Public Administration, Netherlands

The *Journal of European Integration* book series is designed to make our Special Issues accessible to a wider audience. All of the themes covered by our Special Issues and the series are carefully selected with regard to the topicality of the questions addressed in the individual volumes, as well as to the quality of the contributions. The result is a series of books that are sufficiently short to appeal to the curious reader, but that also offer ample depth of analysis to appeal to the more specialist reader, with contributions from leading academics.

A Sociology of Knowledge of European Integration
The social sciences in the making of Europe
Edited by Rebecca Adler-Nissen and Kristoffer Kropp

Responses to the 'Arabellions'
The EU in Comparative Perspective
Edited by Tanja Börzel,
Assem Dandashly and Thomas Risse

Representation and Democracy in the EU
Does one come at the expense of the other?
Edited by Richard Bellamy and Sandra Kröger

Coping with Crisis: Europe's Challenges and Strategies
Edited by Jale Tosun, Anne Wetzel and Galina Zapyanova

Globalization and EU Competition Policy
Edited by Umut Aydin and Kenneth Thomas

Redefining European Economic Governance
Edited by Michele Chang, Georg Menz and Mitchell P. Smith

PREVIOUSLY PUBLISHED BOOKS FROM THE JOURNAL

The Maastricht Treaty: Second Thoughts after 20 Years
Edited by Thomas Christiansen and Simon Duke

Europe after Enlargement
Edited by Yannis Stivachtis and Mark Webber

A Sociology of Knowledge of European Integration

The social sciences in the making
of Europe

Edited by
Rebecca Adler-Nissen and Kristoffer Kropp

Routledge
Taylor & Francis Group

LONDON AND NEW YORK

First published 2016
by Routledge
2 Park Square, Milton Park, Abingdon, Oxon, OX14 4RN, UK

and by Routledge
711 Third Avenue, New York, NY 10017, USA

First issued in papperback 2017

Routledge is an imprint of the Taylor & Francis Group, an informa business

British Library Cataloguing in Publication Data
A catalogue record for this book is available from the British Library

ISBN 13: 978-1-138-29561-2 (pbk)
ISBN 13: 978-1-138-95847-0 (hbk)

Typeset in Sabon
by RefineCatch Limited, Bungay, Suffolk

Publisher's Note
The publisher accepts responsibility for any inconsistencies that may have
arisen during the conversion of this book from journal articles to book chapters,
namely the possible inclusion of journal terminology.

Disclaimer
Every effort has been made to contact copyright holders for their permission to
reprint material in this book. The publishers would be grateful to hear from any
copyright holder who is not here acknowledged and will undertake to rectify
any errors or omissions in future editions of this book.

Contents

CONTENTS

Citation Information

The chapters in this book were originally published in the *Journal of European Integration*, volume 37, issue 2 (February 2015). When citing this material, please use the original page numbering for each article, as follows:

Chapter 1
A Sociology of Knowledge Approach to European Integration: Four Analytical Principles
Rebecca Adler-Nissen and Kristoffer Kropp
Journal of European Integration, volume 37, issue 2 (February 2015)
pp. 155–174

Chapter 2
Performing Theory/Theorizing Performance in Emergent Supranational Governance: The 'Live' Knowledge Archive of European Integration and the Early European Commission
Ben Rosamond
Journal of European Integration, volume 37, issue 2 (February 2015)
pp. 175–192

Chapter 3
Methodological Europeanism at the Cradle: Eur-lex, the Acquis and the Making of Europe's Cognitive Equipment
Antoine Vauchez
Journal of European Integration, volume 37, issue 2 (February 2015)
pp. 193–210

Chapter 4
In the Eye of the Beholder: A Sociology of Knowledge Perspective on Norm Transfer
Antje Wiener
Journal of European Integration, volume 37, issue 2 (February 2015)
pp. 211–228

CITATION INFORMATION

Chapter 5

The Euro Crisis' Theory Effect: Northern Saints, Southern Sinners, and the Demise of the Eurobond
Matthias Matthijs and Kathleen McNamara
Journal of European Integration, volume 37, issue 2 (February 2015)
pp. 229–246

Chapter 6

Reforming the Bulgarian State of Knowledge: Legal Expertise as a Resource in Modelling States
Ole Hammerslev
Journal of European Integration, volume 37, issue 2 (February 2015)
pp. 247–262

Chapter 7

What is the Nature of the Relationship between Changes in European Higher Education and Social Science Research on Higher Education and (Why) Does It Matter?
Rosemary Deem
Journal of European Integration, volume 37, issue 2 (February 2015)
pp. 263–280

Chapter 8

The Creation of a European Socio-economic Classification: Limits of Expert-driven Statistical Integration
Etienne Penissat and Jay Rowell
Journal of European Integration, volume 37, issue 2 (February 2015)
pp. 281–298

Chapter 9

Sociology of Knowledge and Production of Normative Power in the European Union's External Actions
Ian Manners
Journal of European Integration, volume 37, issue 2 (February 2015)
pp. 299–318

For any permission-related enquiries please visit:
http://www.tandfonline.com/page/help/permissions

Notes on Contributors

Rebecca Adler-Nissen is Associate Professor in the Department of Political Science at the University of Copenhagen, Denmark. Her research focuses on international political sociology, diplomacy, sovereignty, security, and European integration. She is the author of *Opting Out of the European Union: Diplomacy, Sovereignty and European Integration* (2014) and editor of *Bourdieu in International Relations* (2012).

Rosemary Deem is Professor, Vice-Principal (Education), and Dean of the Doctoral School, at Royal Holloway, University of London, UK. Her research interests focus on policy, leadership, governance and management of higher education, the consequences of university league tables, doctoral students, the changing purposes and roles of universities, public service organizations, leadership and change agency and equality in educational settings.

Ole Hammerslev is Professor in the Department of Law at the University of Southern Denmark, Odense, Denmark. He is the editor of *Legal Education and Judicial Training in Europe: The Menu for Justice Project Report* (2013, with Daniela Piana, Philip Langbroek, Tomas Berkmanas and Otilia Pacurari).

Kristoffer Kropp is Associate Professor in the Department of Society and Globalisation at Roskilde University, Denmark. He is interested in the relations between political institutions and social scientific knowledge production. He is the author of *A Historical Account of Danish Sociology* (2015, forthcoming).

Ian Manners is Professor at the Centre for European Politics at the University of Copenhagen, Denmark. He studies the importance of myth and symbols in four main areas: green Europe, social Europe, economic Europe and global Europe. The research focuses on comparing different political agents' use of symbols and myths in these four areas. He is the co-editor of *Foreign Policies of EU Member States* (forthcoming 2015, with Amelia Hadfield and Richard G. Whitman).

Matthias Matthijs is Assistant Professor of International Political Economy at Johns Hopkins University's School of Advanced International Studies (SAIS) in Washington, DC. His research focuses on the politics of economic crises, the role of economic ideas in economic policymaking, the politics of inequality, and the erosion of democratic legitimacy in advanced industrial states. He is co-editor of *The Future of the Euro* (2015, with Mark Blyth), and author of *Ideas and Economic Crises in Britain from Attlee to Blair (1945–2005)* (2011).

Kathleen McNamara is Associate Professor of Government and Foreign Service and Director of the Mortara Center for International Studies at Georgetown University, Washington DC, USA. Her work focuses on the evolution of the European Union, the politics of the Euro and the European Central Bank, and international political economy issues. She is the author of *The Politics of Everyday Europe: Constructing Authority in the European Union* (2015) as well as *The Currency of Ideas: Monetary Politics in the European Union* (1998), and co-editor of *Making History: European Integration and Institution Change at Fifty* (2007).

Etienne Penissat is Research Fellow in the Centre National de la Recherche Scientifique (CNRS), and is based at the Centre for Study and Research in Administration, Politics and Society (CERAPS) at the University of Lille, France. He teaches sociology and political sociology, the social history of the state and quantitative methods in social sciences.

Ben Rosamond is Professor of Political Science at the University of Copenhagen, Denmark. He studies the role of ideas, discourses and knowledge in national and EU-level political economy. He is the co-editor of the *Handbook of European Union Politics* (2007, with Knud Erik Jørgensen and Mark A. Pollack) and currently directs the interdisciplinary EuroChallenge research project at the University of Copenhagen.

Jay Rowell is full-time researcher in sociology at the National Centre for Scientific Research (CNRS), and Director of the Centre for European Political Sociology at the University of Strasbourg, France. His research focuses in particular on disability policy and the uses of statistical instruments in the European polity. He has recently published *La construction des problèmes publics en Europe* (2007, with A. Campana and E. Henry), and *A political sociology of Europe: Reassessing Constructivism* (2010, with M. Mangenot).

Antoine Vauchez is Research Professor at the Centre National de la Recherche Scientifique (CNRS), and is based at Université Paris 1-Sorbonne, France. He has published extensively on the political sociology of law and courts, and his most recent work focuses on the interplay between the European Legal Field and EU polity. He has recently published *Brokering Europe. Euro-lawyers and the making of a transnational polity* (2015) and *Democratizing Europe* (2015, forthcoming).

Antje Wiener is Professor of Political Science at the University of Hamburg, Germany. Her research and teaching expertise are in international relations theories, global governance and global constitutionalism. Specifically, she is interested in the role of 'contestation as a norm generative practice' that is practiced under the condition of internationality in global governance. She is the author of *A Theory of Contestation* (2014).

A Sociology of Knowledge Approach to European Integration: Four Analytical Principles

REBECCA ADLER-NISSEN* & KRISTOFFER KROPP**

*Department of Political Science, University of Copenhagen, Copenhagen, Denmark;
**Department of Society and Globalisation, Roskilde University, Denmark

ABSTRACT Scholars are deeply involved in the process of European integration, but we lack systematic understanding of this involvement. On the one hand, scholars, academic ideas and ideologies shape European integration and policies (e.g. the Economic and Monetary Union and the free movement of people). On the other hand, EU institutions, policies and practitioners produce particular forms of knowledge (e.g. the Eurobarometer and benchmarking of national performances) that inform social scientific choices of theories, methods and research topics. Drawing on the new sociology of knowledge as well as Science and Technology Studies (STS) and political sociology, this introductory article develops a framework for studying the entanglement of EU studies with the EU around four analytical principles: (1) the principle of symmetry, (2) the principle of rejecting the internal/external division, (3) the principle of situatedness and (4) the principle of contextualism. A sociology of knowledge approach provides alternative explanations of the EU's development and of our scholarly attempts to make sense of it.

Introduction

In terms of normative power, I broadly agree: we are one of the most important, if not the most important, normative powers in the world. (José Manuel Barroso quoted in Peterson 2008, 69)

This was the response from President of the European Commission, José Manuel Barroso, in 2007 when he was interviewed by Professor in International Politics, John Peterson, about Europe's role in the world. Few citizens probably understood what this 'normative power' was supposed to mean. Still fewer were aware that Barroso was paraphrasing one of the most quoted articles on EU foreign policy, entitled 'Normative Power Europe' (Manners 2002).[1] Manners argued that the EU had created a peculiar context in which nationalism was seen as a failure, and in which the Union stood as a particular and promising organization. In a later revision of his argument, Manners wrote: 'As José Manuel Barroso argued when asked to comment on my normative power approach, the EU might be one of the most important normative powers in the world because of its ability to establish normative principles and apply them to different realities' (Manners 2008, 60).

This direct exchange between Barroso — a European political leader — and Manners — a scholar specialized in EU studies — is not unique. The social sciences and the EU are deeply interwoven. On the one hand, European integration contributes to the production of particular forms of knowledge and specific research questions (e.g. the Eurobarometer, EU framework programmes, cross-national and cross-disciplinary mega-projects and various kinds of statistics used in benchmarking national performance). On the other hand, social science knowledge shapes European practices and institutions (e.g. the Economic and Monetary Union (EMU), the free movement of people and counter-terrorism).[2]

Different academic disciplines have helped produce the EU. Economics is perhaps the most striking example; a discipline that not only developed economic theories promoting harmonization of the single market and the establishment of the EMU, but also participated in their legitimation and sometimes gained from their establishment in practice (Barry 1993; Hay and Rosamond 2002; Mudge and Vauchez 2012; Ryner 2012). The single market and the EMU point us to the entanglement between the political, economic and cultural processes of European integration on the one hand and developments in the social sciences on the other. In short, it directs our attention to the co-production of theories and practices of European integration.

Notwithstanding the general agreement that the social sciences play an important role in shaping ideas and practices of European integration, the process remains understudied. Rosamond concludes his textbook on European integration theories by stating that 'a full treatment of theories of European integration [...] has to be attentive to "sociology of knowledge" issues' (Rosamond 2000, 196). Similarly, Saurugger insists on understanding the 'social, political or academic context' of European integration theories (Saurugger 2014, 3). Yet, so far, few scholars have picked up on these suggestions. Fifteen years after a path-breaking special issue promoted a constructivist (but not explicitly sociology of knowledge) approach to European integration (Christiansen, Jorgensen, and Wiener 1999), we still lack a systematic understanding of how academic ideas and social knowledge shape European governance and the other way around.

However, the last decade has seen the rise of various forms of critique and reflexivity, not only within European populations, reflected for instance in euro-scepticism, but also among scholars studying European integration. Following the 'normative turn' of EU studies in the 1990s, and the debate on the so-called democratic deficit, there has been a boom in critical and reflectivist works on European integration. Ranging from political theoretical analyses (e.g. Føllesdal 2006), legal critiques (e.g. Walker 1998; Vauchez 2008), political sociological accounts (e.g. Adler-Nissen 2008, 2014; Bernhard 2011; Favell and Guiraudon 2009; Kauppi 2003; Saurugger and Mérand 2010) to anthropological work (e.g. Abélès 1992; Shore 2000) and re-examinations of the integration process (and its aim of 'an ever closer Union'), EU scholars are beginning to reflect more systematically about their own role in the production of knowledge about the EU. In this respect, Radaelli's (1995, 1999) use of concepts such as 'policy paradigms' to understand the diffusion of economic ideas, agenda-setting and policy learning as well as Verdun's (1999) work on how the Delors committee transmitted beliefs of central bankers into the project for a single European currency were pioneering. Both focus on the relationship between knowledge, power and policy, but their use of sociology of knowledge insights is often latent.

This article — and the special issue as a whole — seeks to introduce a sociology of knowledge approach to European integration. Building on reflectivist work in EU studies, the aim is to promote theoretical, methodological and empirical insights on the nature of EU studies and its theory effects. We seek to provide a first step towards an analysis of the co-production of social science research and European integration, understood broadly as a political, legal, economic, social, cultural and philosophical phenomenon. One caveat before we begin: as this introduction is intended as an accessible and brief introduction to a range of concepts and ideas from sociology of knowledge and science, we inevitably engage in a simplifying and reductionist exercise, grossly overlooking important works and ideas. For those interested in continuing the debate, we can only recommend revisiting the original works.

This introductory article is organized as follows. First, we account for some key insights from the new sociology of science and knowledge. We develop four inter-related and overlapping analytical arguments or principles that can be used in the analysis of European integration and EU studies: (1) the principle of symmetry, (2) the principle of rejecting the internal/external division, (3) the principle of situatedness and (4) the principle of contextualism. We do not claim that the four analytical moves are exhaustive or representative of all sociology of knowledge and science. However, we find they are particularly useful for analyzing the co-production of knowledge in settings where academic and politico-bureaucratic knowledge is closely interwoven as is the case with the EU. Below, we briefly illustrate how these analytical principles give rise to new questions and alternative explanations of both current and historical debates on the EU and show how the principles have guided the empirical analysis in the special issue. We conclude by providing an overview of the rest of the special issue.

Introducing Insights from Sociology of Knowledge

There are many ways to present the disciplinary history of EU studies. One of the most common is to tell it as a chronological story of successive schools of thought. EU studies then appears as a progressive development of integration theories (for a discussion of 'progressivism' in EU studies, see Rosamond 2007). With each new approach, a problem encountered by a previous theory could be solved (see also Waever 1998, 690). For example, intergovernmentalism was presented as an improvement to neo-functionalism because it could explain both periods of radical change in the EU (due to converging governmental preferences) and periods of inertia (due to diverging national interests). However, many textbook introductions to European integration do not make as much of out the theories or ideas that failed or were marginalized as the ones that survived. Moreover, they usually pay little attention to the academic, political and social context and situational conditions within which the theories and debates emerged (for important exemptions, see Calhoun 2003; Rosamond 2000; Saurugger 2014; Wiener and Diez 2009; Smith 2011). As such, the established story (or myth) about the development of EU studies as a progressive academic field resembles the story told in most scientific fields about accumulation of knowledge and sophistication of theories through corrections and empirical falsification. But could we tell another story? How do other interests than the 'pure' interest in knowledge influence the production of social scientific knowledge about European integration? In the following sections, we indicate where such questions lead to a rather different understanding of EU studies.

From Classical Sociology to the New Sociology of Knowledge

While a distinct field of sociology of knowledge and science emerged rather late in the history of sociological specialization, questions of sociology of knowledge were also raised by classical sociological theorists such as Marx, Durkheim and Mannheim. With varying degrees, their assumption can be characterized as social determinism of knowledge. This position is perhaps best exemplified by Marx' analysis of ideologies as determined by the basis or substructure. Marx argued that ideas and knowledge are linked to specific material interests, class positions and the general mode of production (Marx and Engels 1970). Marx thus saw knowledge and ideas as inherently different from the real world, and the main function of ideologies and knowledge was to mystify or mask the real world and contribute to the exploitation and accumulation of capital.

In a different vein, Durkheim acknowledged the importance of common symbolic representations, collective identities and social categories for society (Durkheim 1982, 238). Durkheim stressed that collective ideas, including notions of time, space and causality, were products of the social organization and division of labour in society. However, he maintained that the symbolic systems of society are not just mere reflections of economic and material forces, but they are also means through which society becomes conscious of itself. Despite granting symbolic forms an important place in understanding modern societies, Durkheim stayed within the dogma of social determinants of knowledge, stressing the difference between the real and ideational or symbolic forms. As Gieryn notes, neither the classical sociological thinkers nor the second generation, including Mannheim and Scheler, questioned the distinction between formal scientific knowledge and cultural and social phenomena (Gieryn 2001). This distinction was prominently challenged with Merton's work in the 1950s and 1960s. Merton's functionalist sociological approach examined the academic institutions within which scientific knowledge was formed, analysing stratification, meritocracy, growth in scientific production, productivity and specialization and not least analysing the norms and standards of sciences and norm conformity (Merton 1968, 1973; Zuckerman 1988). But Merton did not examine the production of scientific knowledge itself.

Kuhn's (1962) *The Structure of Scientific Revolutions* began to question the nature of scientific knowledge more fundamentally. Kuhn's book swept through the social sciences, riding on the wave of student rebellion. Ever since, his concepts of 'paradigm' and 'incommensurability' have promoted the understanding that social scientific knowledge evolves not just through rational, logical exchanges of ideas, but in particular instances through scientific revolutions where entire worldviews change through intellectual battles between scholars that defend the old paradigm and those that promote a new one.

Within the broader constructivist-realist debate in the social sciences, scholars from what later became known as Science and Technology Studies (STS) and the new sociology of knowledge began to scrutinize everyday scientific knowledge production. The intellectual roots of this development were the so-called strong programme, in explicit opposition to Merton's functionalism (or 'weak programme'). This strong programme was developed in the 1970s at the Science Study Unit in Edinburgh by sociologists such as Bloor and Barnes (Bloor 1991). It also drew on Berger and Luckmann's *The Social Construction of Reality* (1966) that argued that all knowledge, including the most basic, taken-for-granted common-sense knowledge of everyday reality, is derived from and maintained by social interactions. What makes the new sociology of knowledge 'new' is not only that it covers micro-sociological observations of individuals and groups working with particular interests and norms, but also that it includes more complex process-oriented questions of 'how kinds of social organization make whole orderings of knowledge possible' (Swidler and Arditi 1994).

Today, the new sociology of knowledge and STS serve as a reservoir for analysing social scientific knowledge practices. These fields of study recognize that scientific knowledge is neither a mere reflection of society nor the product of a detached and disinterested accumulative development (Camic and Gross 2001; Camic, Gross, and Lamont 2011; Ruppert, Law, and Savage 2013).[3] The subsequent sections develop four analytical principles from the sociology of knowledge and science, and STS illustrated with examples. Of course, other ways of presenting the new sociology of knowledge and science could have been chosen (see e.g. Callon 1995; Camic and Gross 2001; Lynch 1993). The four analytical principles do not amount to a theory as such, but they help us question and examine the relationship between the European integration and what is now known as EU studies.

The Principle of Symmetry

One of the most important propositions in the new sociology of knowledge and science has been a call for *symmetry* in the analysis of scientific knowledge production. In short, the principle of symmetry prescribes approaching all scientific knowledge claims (both the ones we still hold as true and the ones that we now consider false) similarly to avoid writing off marginalized or unsuccessful approaches as examples of pathological or 'failed' science (Bloor 1991; Lynch 1993). This is in contrast to the traditional philosophy of sciences were scientific originality was conceived as an intrinsic evaluation of theoretical and empirical contributions. This first principle evokes an ambition of levelling the playing field so that what are (or were) considered as facts are taken as beliefs to be explained socially (see also Latour 2005). This does not imply that all cases should be explained the same way, but the analytical move seeks to avoid teleology.

One example is McLaughlin's analysis of the rise and fall of Neo-Freudianism and its main proponent Erich Fromm (McLaughlin 1998). McLaughlin asks why some theoretical traditions and schools of thought fail or vanish after a period of relative success. He examines the intellectual trajectory of Neo-Freudianism and psychoanalyst and German *émigré* Erich Fromm. Throughout the 1930s and 1940s, Neo-Freudian theory and psychoanalysis were influential in both academic and public circles in the US, but failed to establish themselves as an independent and institutionalized school of thought. Rather than arguing that Neo-Freudianism provided poor scientific results or explanations, McLaughlin shows that the failure was an effect of complex processes within the Neo-Freudian tradition, changing institutional conditions in the post-war US university system, the specialization of psychology and social sciences, and the development of a mass market for intellectual products. In other words, the 'failure' of Neo-Freudianism was not just a consequence of its cognitive limits and problems. This example highlights the symmetry principle, underlining that the sociology of knowledge should avoid teleological explanations that take scientific knowledge and facts as mere products of a rational accumulative development, and that, rather, it should understand them as the outcome of complex historical and social processes.

In their contribution to this special issue, Matthijs and McNamara draw on the principle of analytical symmetry to analyse responses to the euro crisis. They show why alternatives to ordo-liberalism such as Eurobonds failed to take hold as the euro crisis evolved. In a similar vein, Penissat and Rowell's contribution analyses why the EU's attempts to create harmonized socio-economic statistics, as a way to measure 'social Europe', has so far not succeeded. They show that this is not just a question of lack of political will, but also the effects of conflicting legitimacies within expert networks, the experts' lack of resources and contacts as well as an EU bureaucracy that is more oriented towards economic than sociological methodologies.

Turning to European integration theory with the principle of symmetry forces us to rethink the social and intellectual history of the field. Most obvious could be reconsidering the 'cyclical challenges' to neofunctionalism in the light of the principle of symmetry. Ernst B. Haas' neofunctionalism (1958) was a dominant theory from the late 1950s to late 1960s, how did neofunctionalism fall and later rise again in the 1990s? The textbook explanation is that it overestimated the spillover effect and political tensions leading to the Empty Chair crisis in 1965–1966 (Jensen 2013, 61; Saurugger 2014), but as Ben Rosamond discusses in his contribution and elsewhere (2005), neo-functionalist ideas were also part of the Commission's strategic narrative. Such processes of entanglement contributed to its initial success and its later falling out of academic fashion.

Rejecting the Internal/External Division

The analytical strategy of rejecting the *internal/external division* implies acknowledging that scholarly production is entangled with broader social developments. Traditionally, the sociology of science recognized the importance of material and institutional factors for the growth and production of scientific knowledge, but this restricted the sociology of science from explaining scientific knowledge as such, partly by viewing science an autonomous social institution guided by a set of norms ensuring a rational scientific development (Gieryn 1999; Lamont and Molnár 2002; Shapin 1992, 1995; Shapin and Schaffer 1985). As we noted earlier, classical sociology of knowledge largely focused on the social determinants of knowledge. For Mannheim, for instance, the main task was to distinguish 'socially determined' elements from 'immanent' elements (Mannheim 1985). Since the 1970s attention has shifted, and today focus is predominantly on how scientists, politicians and the public fight over the boundaries of science, how to distinguish experts from layman, science from non-science and one scientific discipline from another. By rejecting the internal/external dimension, the distinction between science and the broader society is turned into an empirical question: how do 'non-academic' resources, materials, viewpoints and ideas help transform and become transformed by scientific products and processes?

Pierre Bourdieu's analysis of German philosopher Martin Heidegger is an example of the rejection of the external/internal divide (Bourdieu 1991). In this book (that serves as a model for analysis of scientific or intellectual social 'fields'), Bourdieu shows how the philosophy of Heidegger was not only produced by dynamics within German philosophy in the first part of the twentieth century. Heidegger's philosophy was also influenced by the political and cultural context of the Weimar Republic through what Bourdieu designates as a 'homologous position', referring to a similar position in different social fields. Heidegger's work was shaped by his particular social trajectories, which were different from the established philosophers, as well as his usages of everyday words, concepts and dichotomies in the otherwise technical philosophical discourse. Bourdieu concludes that one can neither understand Heidegger's philosophy as merely formed by dynamics in German philosophy in the early twentieth century nor as mere reflection of the socio-economic and political environment of the Weimar Republic — Heidegger's thinking was both.

To overcome the external/internal distinction, we can ask how the relationship between different academic fields and specialties and European political and bureaucratic institutions have been established and developed. [4]How have resources in the form of finance, people and institutional recognition connected specific ideas, people and institutions? How has the boundary between sciences and politics been negotiated, policed and crossed and with what consequences?

Turning to EU studies, a number of cases illustrate the value of this analytical perspective. Most obvious is the development of economic ideas and theories that have informed (and have been produced by) the European Commission, as Rosamond shows in his contribution. Another example is the emergence of a distinct European legal order and *acquis communautaire,* as Vauchez shows in his article. In both cases, academic ideas have been closely linked with political ambitions and practical problems. A third example is educational student exchanges, sponsored by the EU, which have been a means to produce a European identity and strengthen personal and cultural bonds between peoples of the different Member States (see also Shore 2000). With the Bologna Process and Lisbon Strategy in the 2000s, education and research became increasingly important parts of the European economic growth strategy. As Deem shows in her contribution and alludes to elsewhere (2006), the rise of research in higher education, also sponsored by the EU, has not only produced new insights on the actual workings of higher education, it has also been shaped by the EU's particular growth ideas. The analytical principle of rejecting the internal/external divide can also be found in some more recent work on policy paradigms, policy transfer and epistemic communities that focus on resources, networks and processes of intellectual socialization of elites (e.g. Cross 2013; Mügge 2011). However, this analytical principle takes such projects one step further in insisting on including questions of data access, scholarly traditions and the broader social field of academic knowledge production in the analysis.

This approach is also relevant when examining general theoretical trends within EU studies. As the EU developed towards a more integrated polity, comparative politics, public administration and governance scholars entered the field with different ways of approaching European integration (Aspinwall and Schneider 2000; Jönsson and Tallberg 2008; Bickerton 2012). The usual (internal) explanation is that the 'governance turn' was a reaction to the 'sterile' debate between intergovernmentalism and neo-functionalism (Hooghe and Marks 2003). However, seen from the perspective of rejecting the external/internal divide, one of the particularities of much of the governance literature is that it often depends on material and data (quantitative and qualitative) that only the European Commission or national bureaucracies produce and possess. This raises interesting questions about boundaries: for instance, how have these studies and scholars contributed to constructing what is now known as the European Administrative Space (Olsen 2003)? How have the European Commission and other bureaucracies produced 'benchmarks' and 'best practices' and how have these notions become popular in European public governance studies?

Such questions highlight the importance of analysing processes of co-production and entanglement.

The Principle of Situatedness

The production of scientific knowledge is often (re)presented as universal and accumulative activities, practised in global, or at least national, scientific disciplines (Camic 1991; Patel 2010; Platt 2010). EU studies, as mentioned above, also tells a progressive story about itself, where the different approaches and perspectives advance though universal theoretical innovations and empirical breakthroughs. Against this, the new sociology of sciences stresses that scientific knowledge is often shaped by local conditions in which it is practised and institutionalized — it emphasizes a *localism* or *situatedness* in knowledge production (Abbott 1999; Knorr Cetina 1999; Lynch 1993). The production of specific kinds of scientific knowledge, and their content and relation to other kinds of scientific knowledge production and institutionalization, is heavily related to situated factors that we need to reconstruct, often through the micro-history of scholars, conferences, meetings, departments and academic schools, to understand how social scientific knowledge was produced (Camic 1995). At the heart of argument for situatedness lies an ethnographic method deriving largely from an anthropological approach to science and knowledge. The argument is that even the most abstract and universally formulated ideas and knowledge claims are inescapably situated. Furthermore, it is argued that scientific knowledge is produced in rather small communities and that understanding the specific organization of and interaction within these small communities are crucial in understanding the social contours of specific knowledge-producing communities. In other words, scientific knowledge claims and facts are judged in the situation, and scientific credibility is thus largely locally produced (Shapin and Schaffer 1985). This directs the focus of research towards the local, often micro-scale, interactions between scholars and their within and between departments, at conferences and meetings. It also focuses on scholars' intellectual interactions though texts.

A programmatic example of this kind of historiography and sociology of social science can be found in Charles Camic's (1995) article about the early institutionalization of US sociology. Camic asks why sociology was conceived and institutionalized in the US in three very distinct ways in the early twentieth century. He shows that the three different approaches to sociology developed from different local circumstances in which scientific judgments were made differently. Thus, both choice of methods and research objects were highly influenced by relations to other disciplines and departments at specific universities as well as the sequence within which the social science disciplines were established at the different US universities. Consequently, US sociologists *in spe* had to relate and legitimate their own knowledge production against different epistemological cultures and disciplines.

Such micro-interactions and relations between scholars as well as non-academics have also played an important role in the development of EU studies. Theories and approaches to European integration have been influenced by scholars from other disciplines — physically or institutionally located close to the offices of EU scholars. Moreover, concrete meetings between academics and agents outside academia (NGOs, bureaucrats, political parties and companies) have shaped both academic thinking and practical politics (for an interesting study of the role of experts in EU research policy, see Tamtik and Creso 2012). Moving to other issues, we could ask how different knowledge producers enter into close relations with policy-makers and bureaucrats and how first-hand experience and personal relations influence knowledge production. Furthermore, how do local epistemological landscapes, personal relations and organizational settings shape theory development in EU studies?

Such processes are described in a fascinating, but rarely quoted article about the interaction between neofunctionalists and the pioneering Hallstein Commission. Jonathan P.J. White shows how specific concepts such as 'spillover' and 'the logic of integration' were conveyed through personal meetings between central agents in the Hallstein Commission and neofunctionalists in Brussels (White 2003). Neofunctionalist theory played an important role, as a live 'knowledge archive', for how the Hallstein Commission made sense of the world and designed policies as Rosamond shows in his contribution. In Ole Hammerslev's contribution, which provides an alternative analysis of the enlargement process, situatedness also takes centre stage. He shows how leading American and European lawyers competed locally in the emerging market of legal expertise in Bulgaria after the fall of the Communist regimes.

The Principle of Contextualism

The fourth and last analytical principle we present here is the claim that scientific knowledge is *contextual*. Similar to the principle of situatedness, this principle emphasizes the historical, geographical and social specificity of scientific knowledge and insists that the meanings of knowledge and ideas are not immediately or universally understandable or transparent (Camic and Gross 2001). The new sociology of science and knowledge stresses that all knowledge is produced in relation to other knowledge claims and in specific knowledge cultures or civic epistemologies (Jasanoff 2005). Scientific knowledge products acquire meaning in relation to other scientific statements and knowledge claims. We therefore need to analyze social scientific knowledge as historical products in relation to their symbolic, linguistic and social context. We have to consider the discussions, debates and world views that researchers subscribe to and are located within. In practice, this often implies accounting for less-known researchers, non-canonized, marginal positions and long forgotten points of view to understand the meaning, intention and success of some scholars.

Michele Lamont's (1987) analysis of the reception of French philosopher Jacques Derrida in France and the US shows the importance of taking the context of production, perception and evaluation of scientific knowledge products into account. Lamont shows how Derrida's work was received and gained prominence in the humanities, mainly philosophy and literary criticism, during the 1960s and 1970s. This took place through different channels of communication, in different academic fields and on different grounds in France and the US. In France, Derrida's work first gained its academic reputation through its connection to the prestigious phenomeno-logical and German philosophical tradition in France, where Derrida's work was defused through cultural journals along with other prominent post-war intellectuals. In the US, Derrida's deconstruction was taken up by literary critics using its critic of logocentrism in western thought in a defence of interpretive humanistic sciences. Here, it gained legitimacy through professional literary criticism, journals and institutions. However, it did not find fertile ground in analytical and language-centred Anglo-American philosophy. Lamont analyses the difference between the two national academic contexts, both in regards to accepted epistemological styles, modes of knowledge circulation and institutional organization (Guetzkow, Lamont, and Mallard 2004; Knorr Cetina 1999).

The 1990s 'normative turn' in EU studies serves as a case for the impor-tance of the context of knowledge production and the kind of questions and explanations it helps produce. What context in different national aca-demic fields led to the surge of interest in legitimacy, democracy and the question of a European public (e.g. Bellamy and Castiglione 2003; Follesdal and Hix 2006; Habermas 2004; Lord and Beetham 2001; Lord and Magnette 2004)? Is this normative focus reflected in the relative decline of EU studies in the US (Andrews 2012)? Some argue that the growing interest in the relationship between democracy and European inte-gration was primarily due to theoretical innovations (i.e. Warleigh 2006, 17). Others claim that the increasing interest in democracy and legitimacy among EU scholars was directly linked to the perception of a lack of popu-lar support for the EU (Bickerton 2012). As Chris Lord writes, 'More than any other single event, it was the crisis in 1992–1993, provoked by the rati-fication of the Maastricht Treaty on European Union (TEU), which shat-tered any illusion that the legitimation of EU power was a 'non-problem'' (Lord 2000, 4). The turn to political theory in the EU made a huge impact, generating a whole new way of doing EU research, but its origins and con-text of development remain unclear.

Table 1 provides an overview of our four sociology of knowledge arguments or analytical principles.

Structure of the Special Issue

The articles in this special issue approach the entanglement of EU and social scientific knowledge from the perspective of the new sociology of knowledge and sciences. While the contributors each have their distinct empirical focus, they all draw on one or several of the four analytical principles.

Ben Rosamond considers the entanglement of theories of international relations and international economics on the one hand and an emergent supranational policy actor on the other. The formation of the European Communities in the late 1950s and early 1960s is well known as a moment of radical supranational institutional creation. This is a period in which

Table 1. Four analytical principles of sociology of knowledge

	(1) Symmetry	(2) Rejection of internal/external divide	(3) Situatedness	(4) Contextualism
Focus	Ensuring impartiality and avoiding teleology in explaining success and failure of scientific knowledge	Socio-economic and political environment	Situatedness, local processes and micro-interactions	Interaction and relation between different forms of knowledge situated in particular spaces
Example	McLaughlin's work on the rise and fall of Fromm's Neo-Freudianism	Bourdieu's work on Heidegger's thinking as both reflecting German philosophy and the society of the Weimer Republic	Camic's work on the institutionalization of US sociology in three schools	Lamont's work on the reception of Derrida in the US vs. in France
Key questions	Why do we conceive certain scientific contributions as more true or original than others?	How do 'non-academic' resources, materials, viewpoints and ideas help transform and become transformed by scientific products and processes?	Where is knowledge produced — by whom and in what institution?	What is the academic environment in which scientific products are being produced and how do they relate to other academic products?
	Why are some theoretical and empirical contributions forgotten after periods of academic recognition while others only gain recognition later?		How do local epistemological settings, coalitions and conflicts, teacher-student ties, career strategies and so on influence knowledge products?	What are perceived as possible, legitimate and interesting research questions and/or conclusions in the specific epistemological community?

both economists and political scientists sought to theorize the processes of regional integration as it was happening. Guided by the principle of understanding science as inherently situated in political and social processes, the article shows that the newly formed European Commission, in both its communicative and coordinative discourse, drew selectively on the 'live' knowledge archive of both international economics and international relations to generate a strategic narrative about what European economic integration entailed, how it would be accomplished, and (crucially) what kind of actor it was. At the same time, the semi-inductive quality of academic knowledge production meant that the Commission's activities were simultaneously being theorized into the live archive from which it was drawing. The article examines the influence of two bodies of theory that led surprisingly parallel lives, but which both influenced the Commission: Balassa's theory of international economic integration and neofunctionalism. Rosamond concludes that the authority of social scientific knowledge is shaped by specific institutional situations and that it is not Economics per se, but rather the metaphors that it generates, that shaped the Commission's strategies.

Antoine Vauchez asks how EU law became widely acknowledged as a specific and self-standing 'body of law'. He tracks the origins of one of Europe's most ubiquitous knowledge instruments: the *acquis*. Instead of considering the *acquis* as a self-explanatory and transparent notion, Vauchez employs the principles of contextualism to understand the rich political meaning of the acquis, pointing at its instrumental role in shaping a law-centred and supranational definition of Europe. Rejecting the internal/external divide and digging deep into individual and institutional genealogies, the article follows the methodological entrepreneurs who crafted new knowledge instruments for calculating Europe's state of affairs (the Celex database) and analyses the process through which they have progressively acquired a monopoly in the calculation of 'the state of the Union', thereby encapsulating within the very rules of the European game itself a form of 'methodological Europeanism'.

Drawing on all the four principles sketched out in this introduction, Antje Wiener develops the concept of 'strategic blueprinting' as a distinct practice of norm transfer, thereby turning the 'normative power approach' on its head. Rather than transferring norms from the inside of liberal communities out, outsiders choose to copy parts of the *acquis communautaire*. The article compares this process with other types of norm transfer such as transplantation and diffusion. She shows that EU norm transfer is a much more contested and complicated form of knowledge co-production, where bits and pieces of the *acquis communautaire* are more or less strategically selected, copied and adapted within the constitutional or proto-constitutional framework of regions outside the EU. This underlines the importance in understanding how knowledge travels across national and regional borders and changes when used in new local and contextual settings.

Matthias M. Matthijs and Kathleen R. McNamara analyse the responses to the euro crisis and asks why austerity and structural reform won out over other plausible, and more 'systemic' solutions, like a pooling of sovereign debt or the formation of an economic government? To under-stand this puzzle, their article draws on the principle of symmetry to argue that the response to the euro crisis was heavily informed by broader social logics. Mapping the fate of the Eurobond proposals in Germany allows them to trace the complex entanglement of economic policy-making and parse out the ways in which social realities are shaped to make particular policy choices seem inevitable when they in fact were the product of social processes. Looking at how the boundaries between economic and politics are negotiated and how economic knowledge was used politically, the arti-cle shows how the 'solution' came to draw heavily on ordoliberal (austerity and the adherence to strict fiscal rules) and neoliberal (importance of struc-tural reform) ideas.

Ole Hammerslev provides an alternative analysis of the enlargement pro-cess. Against the backdrop of an empirical study about how leading Ameri-can and European lawyers competed in Bulgaria after the fall of the Communist regimes, Hammerslev's article builds on the principles of situ-atedness and contextualism to explore how western lawyers were involved in the reorganization of the fields of power in Eastern Europe. The trans-formation of the Eastern European countries from communist states to EU members was supported by massive investments in western discourses and social science knowledge, and export programmes for these from the west to the east. The article thus situates both the production and usage of the 'model of the state'. In the west, and specifically in the US, a market for discourses and knowledge production professionalized and intertwined with institutions that exported specific forms of policy visions of US modes of the State. In the east, the importation of discourses and knowledge became pivotal in the struggles for power of modelling the state and its institutions, and thus as knowledge tools to guide and legitimize the path towards democracy and later towards membership of the EU.

Rosemary Deem examines the relationship between changes in European higher education (HE) and social science research on higher education arguing that studies of higher education in Europe are closely related to policy agendas of the EU. HE research is a new field that has been signifi-cantly assisted by European funding, the Bologna process and the massifi-cation of HE. The field is characterized by many doctoral researchers but fewer established researchers. Deem examines three recent major Euro-pean-funded HE research projects as examples of co-production, specifi-cally looking at the kinds of knowledge produced and the strategies adopted to ensure that research outcomes permeate the policy process. Deem's articles thus draw on the principle of rejecting the internal/external division and show how the relation between studies of HE and the EU is not just a matter of economic and institutional support, but also shapes the research questions asked and type knowledge produced in HE studies.

The principle of symmetry underscores Etienne Penissat and Jay Rowell's contribution. They analyse how, since the 1990s, the EU has sought to cre-ate a harmonized socio-economic classification scheme, which symbolically unifies the social structures of the 28 Member States in a common tool of description. Relying heavily on expert networks, this project, with numerous potential policy applications, has so far failed to come to fruition. After examining the scientific networks and institutional resources of an initial model, which was at the centre of discussions for nearly ten years, the article explores the reason for its ultimate failure. Combining science studies and a political sociology approach, and focusing in particular on the rejection of the internal/external divide, the article highlights the effects of conflicting legitimacies within expert networks, the lack of diversified institutional resources and contacts of the dominant experts, the poor fit of sociologically based methods to an EU administrative culture more focused on knowledge based on economic methodologies, and the lack of a wider European debate and mobilization on inequalities which, in national histories, were key to the creation of national socio-economic classification schemes.

In the last article, Ian Manners analyses the entanglement between the EU's attempts to construct its external actions in global politics and research on the EU as a global actor. Manners traces the spread and use of his own concept of 'normative power' Drawing on the four principles from this introduction, Manners shows the diffusion of the concept between different localities and between scholarly and political contexts. The article argues that both the development of EU external actions and research on EU's external actions suffer from unnecessary dichotomization. Advocates and analysts of the EU's normative power have argued that the separation of norms and interests, both in terms of policy-making and policy analysis, is impossible. In contrast, advocates and analysts of the EU as a 'normal power', a great power pole in the coming multipolar world, have dichotomized the advocacy of policy-making and the analysis of knowledge production of EU external actions. The article shows through an examination of the interlinking of policy-making and policy analysis, how such false dichotomies can weaken both the (sociology of) knowledge about the EU and the production of the EU's external actions.

Acknowledgement

We wish to thank all the presenters, discussants and participants at the workshop held at the University of Copenhagen on 4–5 February 2013, especially Niilo Kauppi, Ole Wæver and Majka Holm. Moreover, we are grateful to Christian Büger, Felix Bethke, the editors and the two anonymous referees for their helpful comments.

Funding

This project was funded by the European Science Foundation [Grant Number EW12–064]; and the Faculty of Social Sciences, University of Copenhagen.

Notes

1. The article had received 1758 quotes according to Google Scholar (accessed 15 September 2015).
2. See Favell for an exemplary critical review of research on migration and European integration (Favell 2011).

3. In this introduction, we can only mention a very small selection of the literature. For important contributions, see the introduction in Camic, Gross, and Lamont (2011) and Callon (1998), Collins (1998), Desrosières (1998), Frickel and Moore (2006), Guilhot (2011), Igo (2009), Lamont (2009), MacKenzie (2006); Mirowski (2002), Porter (1995), Porter and Ross (2003), Rueschemeyer and Skocpol (1996), Steinmetz (2005), Wagner (2001), Whitley (1984), and Wittrock, Wagner, and Wollmann (1991) just to mention a few of the most well-known.
4. For an application of this principle to International Relations, see Büger and Gadinger 2007.

References

Abbott, A. 1999. *Department & discipline, Chicago sociology at one hundred*. Chicago: University of Chicago Press.

Abélès, M. 1992. *La vie quotidienne au Parlement européen*. Paris: Hachette.

Adler-Nissen, R. 2008. Organized duplicity? When states opt out of the European union. In *Sovereignty Games: Instrumentalizing State Sovereignty in Europe and Beyond*, eds. R. Adler-Nissen and T. Gammeltoft-Hansen, 81–103. New York: Palgrave Macmillan.

Adler-Nissen, R. 2014. *Opting out of the European Union: diplomacy, sovereignty and European integration*. Cambridge: Cambridge University Press.

Andrews, D.M. 2012. The rise and fall of EU Studies in the USA. *Journal of European Public Policy* 19, no. 5: 755–75.

Aspinwall, M.D., and G. Schneider. 2000. Same menu, seperate tables: The institutionalist turn in political science and the study of European integration. *European Journal of Political Research* 38, no. 1: 1–36.

Barry, A. 1993. The European Community and European government harmonization, mobility and Eyropean Community and European government. *Economy and Society* 22, no. 3: 314–26.

Bellamy, R., and D. Castiglione. 2003. Legitimizing the Euro-'polity' and its 'Regime': the normative turn in EU studies. *European Journal of Political Theory* 2, no. 1: 7–34.

Berger, P.L., and T. Luckmann. 1966. *The social construction of reality*. Garden City, NY: Anchor.

Bernhard, S. 2011. Beyond constructivism: the political sociology of an EU policy field. *International Political Sociology* 5, no. 4: 426–45.

Bickerton, C.J. 2012. *European integration: From nation-states to member states*. Oxford: OUP.

Bloor, D. 1991. *Knowledge and social imagery*, 2nd edn. Chicago, IL: University of Chicago Press.

Bourdieu, P. 1991. *The political ontology of Martin Heidegger*. Stanford, CA: Stanford University Press.

Büger, C., and F. Gadinger. 2007. Reassembling and dissecting: international relations practice from a science studies perspective. *International Studies Perspectives* 8, no. 1: 90–110.

Callon, M. 1995. Four models for the dynamics in science. In *Handbook of science and technology studies*, Vol. 2, eds. S. Jasanoff, G.E. Markle, J.C. Petersen, and T. Pinch, 29–63. London: Sage.

Callon, M. 1998. *The laws of the markets*. Oxford: Blackwell.

Calhoun, C. 2003. European studies: always already there and still in formation. *Comparative European Politics* 1, no. 1: 5–20.

Camic, C. 1991. Book review: The Impossoble Science: An institutional analysis of American sociology by S.P. Turner and J.H. Turner. *American Journal of Sociology* 96, no. 6: 1542–4.

Camic, C. 1995. Three departments in search of a discipline: localism and interdisciplinary interaction in American sociology, 1890–1940. *Social Research* 62, no. 4: 1003–33.

Camic, C., and N. Gross. 2001. The new sociology of ideas. In *The Blackwell companion to sociology*, ed. J.R. Blau, 236–50. Oxford: Blackwell Publishing.

Camic, C., N. Gross, and M. Lamont, eds. 2011. *Social knowledge in the making*. Chicago, IL: The University of Chicago Press.

Christiansen, T., K.E. Jorgensen, and A. Wiener. 1999. The social construction of Europe. *Journal of European Public Policy* 6, no. 4: 528–44.

Collins, R. 1998. *The sociology of philosophy: a global theory of intellectual change*. Cambridge, MA: The Belknap Press.

Cross, M.A.K.D. 2013. Rethinking epistemic communities twenty years later. *Review of International Studies* 39, no. 01: 137–60.

Deem, R. 2006. Conceptions of contemporary European universities: to do research or not to do research? *European Journal of Education* 41, no. 2: 281–304.

Desrosières, A. 1998. *The politics of large numbers*. Cambridge, MA: Harvard University Press.

Durkheim, E. 1982. *The rules of sociologial method*. Free Press.

Favell, A. 2011. Integration policy and integration research in Europe: a review and critique. In *Citizenship today: global perspectives and practices*, eds. T.A. Aleinikoff and D.B. Klusmeyer, 371–404. Washington, DC: Brookings Institutions Press.

Favell, A., and V. Guiraudon. 2009. The sociology of the European Union: an agenda. *European Union Politics* 10, no. 4: 550–76.

Føllesdal, A. 2006. Survey article: the legitimacy deficits of the European Union. *Journal of Political Philosophy* 14, no. 4: 441–68.

Føllesdal, A., and S. Hix. 2006. Why there is a democratic deficit in the EU: a response to Majone and Moravcsik. *JCMS: Journal of Common Market Studies* 44, no. 3: 533–62.

Frickel, S., and K. Moore. 2006. *The new political sociology of science: institutions, networks, and power*. Madison, WI: University of Wisconsin Press.

Gieryn, T.F. 1999. *Cultural boundaries of science*. Chicago, IL: The University of Chicago Press.

Gieryn, T.F. 2001. "Science, sociology of." In *International encyclopedia of the social & behavioral sciences*, eds. N.J. Smelser and P.B. Baltes, 13692–8. Oxford: Pergamon.

Guetzkow, J., M. Lamont, and G. Mallard. 2004. What is originality in the humanities and the social sciences? *American Sociological Review* 69, no. 2: 190–212.

Guilhot, N. (ed.). 2011. *The invention of international relations theory: realism, the Rockefeller Foundation, and the 1954 conference on theory*. New York: Columbia University Press.

Haas, E.B. 1958. *The uniting of Europe*. Notre Dame, IN: University of Notre Dame Press.

Habermas, J. 2004. Why Europe needs a constitution. In *Developing a constitution for Europe*, eds. E.O. Eriksen, J.E. Fossum and A.J. Menéndez, 17–32. London: Routledge.

Hay, C., and B. Rosamond. 2002. Globalization, European integration and the discursive construction of economic imperatives. *Journal of European Public Policy* 9, no. 2: 147–67.

Hooghe, L., and G. Marks. 2003. *Unraveling the central state, but how?: Types of multi-level governance*. Cambridge: Cambridge University Press.

Igo, S.E. 2009. *The average American: surveys, citizens, and the making of a mass public*. Cambridge, MA: Harvard University Press.

Jasanoff, S. 2005. *Designs on nature, science and democracy in Europe and the United States*. Princeton, NJ: Princeton University Press.

Jensen, C.S. 2013. Neo-functionalism. In *European Union politics*, eds. M. Cini and N.P.S. Borragán, 59–70. Oxford: Oxford University Press.

Jönsson, C., and J. Tallberg. 2008. Institutional theory in international relations. In *Debating institutionalism*, eds. J. Pierre, G. Peters and G. Stoker, 1–30. Manchester, NH: Manchester University Press.

Kauppi, N. 2003. Bourdieu's political sociology and the politics of European integration. *Theory and Society* 32, no. 5/6: 775–89.

Knorr Cetina, K. 1999. *Epistemic cultures: how the sciences make knowledge*. Cambridge: Harvard University Press.

Kuhn, T.S. 1962. *The structure of scientific revolutions*. Chicago, IL: The University of Chicago Press.

Lamont, M. 1987. How to become a dominant French philosopher: the case of Jacques Derrida. *American Journal of Sociology* 93, no. 3: 584–622.

Lamont, M. 2009. *How professors think*. Cambridge, MA: Haverd University Press.

Lamont, M., and V. Molnár. 2002. The study of boundaries in the social sciences. *Annual Review of Sociology* 28, no. 1: 167–95.

Latour, B. 2005. *Reassembling the social: an introduction to actor-network-theory*. Oxford: Oxford University Press.

Lord, C. 2000. Legitimacy, democracy and the EU: when abstract questions become practical policy problems. *Policy Paper* 3: 1–25.

Lord, C., and D. Beetham. 2001. Legitimizing the EU: is there a 'post-parliamentary basis' for its legitimation? *JCMS: Journal of Common Market Studies* 39, no. 3: 443–62.

Lord, C., and P. Magnette. 2004. E pluribus unum? Creative disagreement about legitimacy in the EU. *JCMS. Journal of Common Market Studies* 42, no. 1: 183–202.

Lynch, M. 1993. *Scientific practice and ordinary action, ethnomethodology and social studies of science*. Cambridge: Cambridge University Press.

MacKenzie, D.A. 2006. *An engine, not a camera, how financial models shape markets*. Cambridge, MA: MIT Press.

Manners, I. 2002. Normative power Europe: a contradiction in terms? *JCMS. Journal of Common Market Studies* 40, no. 2: 235–58.

Manners, I. 2008. The normative ethics of the European Union. *International Affairs* 84, no. 1: 45–60.

Mannheim, K. 1985. *Ideology and Utopia: an introduction to the sociology of knowledge*. San Diego, CA: Harcourt Brace Jovanovich.

Marx, K., and F. Engels. 1970. *The German Ideology, Part One, with selections from Parts Two and Three with Supplementary Texts*. Edited and with Introd., by C.J. Arthur. New York: International Publishers.

McLaughlin, N. 1998. How to become a forgotten intellectual: intellectual movements and the rise and fall of Erich Fromm. *Sociological Forum* 13, no. 2: 215–46.

Merton, R.K. 1968. *Social theory and social structure*, Enlarged edn. New York: Free Press.

Merton, R.K. 1973. *The sociology of science, theoretical and empirical investigations*. Edited by Norman W. Storer. The University of Chicago Press.

Mirowski, P. 2002. *Machine Dreams, economics becomes a Cyborg science*. Cambridge: Cambridge University Press.

Mudge, S.L., and A. Vauchez. 2012. Building Europe on a weak field: law, economics, and scholarly avatars in transnational politics. *American Journal of Sociology* 118, no. 2: 449–92.

Mügge, D. 2011. From pragmatism to dogmatism: European Union governance, policy paradigms and financial meltdown. *New Political Economy* 16, no. 2: 185–206.

Olsen, J. 2003. Towards a European administrative space? *Journal of European Public Policy* 10, no. 4: 506–31.

Patel, S., ed. 2010. *The ISA handbook of diverse sociological traditions*. London: Sage.

Peterson, J. 2008. José Manuel Barroso: political scientist, ECPR member. *European Political Science* 7, no. 1, 64–77.

Platt, J. 2010. Sociology. In *The history of the social sciences since 1945*, eds. Roger E. Backhouse and Philippe Fontaine, 102–35. Cambridge: Cambridge University Press.

Porter, T.M. 1995. *Trust in numbers, the pursuit of objectivity in science and public life*. Princeton, NJ: Princeton University Press.

Porter, T.M., and D. Ross. 2003. *The modern social sciences*. Cambridge University Press.

Radaelli, C.M. 1995. The role of knowledge in the policy process. *Journal of European Public Policy* 2, no. 2: 159–83.

Radaelli, C.M. 1999. The public policy of the European Union: whither politics of expertise? *Journal of European Public Policy* 6, no. 5: 757–74.

Rosamond, B. 2000. *Theories of European Integration, the European Union series*. Houndmills: Palgrave.

Rosamond, B. 2005. The uniting of Europe and the foundation of EU studies: Revisiting the neofunctionalism of Ernst B. Haas. *Journal of European Public Policy* 12, no. 2: 237–54.

Rosamond, B. 2007. The political sciences of European integration: disciplinary history and EU studies. *The SAGE handbook of European Union politics*, 7–30. London: Sage.

Rueschemeyer, D., and T. Skocpol, eds. 1996. *States, social knowledge, and the origins of modern social policies*. Princeton, NJ: Princeton University Press.

Ruppert, E., J. Law, and M. Savage. 2013. Reassembling social science methods: the challenge of digital devices. *Theory, Culture & Society* 30, no. 4: 22–46.

Ryner, M. 2012. Financial crisis, orthodoxy and heterodoxy in the production of knowledge about the EU. *Millennium-Journal of International Studies* 40, no. 3: 647–73.

Saurugger, S. 2014. *Theoretical approaches to European integration*. Houndmills: Palgrave.

Saurugger, S., and F. Mérand. 2010. Does European integration theory need sociology? *Comparative European Politics* 8, no. 1: 1–18.

Shapin, S. 1992. Discipline and bounding: the history and sociology of science as seen through the externalism-internalism debate. *History of Science* 30, no. 4: 333–69.

Shapin, S. 1995. Here and everywhere: sociology of scientific knowledge. *Annual Review of Sociology* 21: 289–321.

Shapin, S., and S. Schaffer. 1985. *Leviathan and the air-pump, Hobbes, Boyle, and the experimental life, including a translation of Thomas Hobbes*. Dialogus Physicus de Natura Aeris, by Simon Schaffer. 1. Princeton pbk. print. with corrections. Princeton, NJ: Princeton University Press.

Shore, C. 2000. *Building Europe: the cultural politics of European integration*. London: Routledge.

Smith, A. 2011. French Political Science and European Integration. *Journal of European Public Policy* 7, no. 4: 663–9.

Steinmetz, G. 2005. *The politics of method in the human sciences*. Durham: Duke University Press.

Swidler, A., and J. Arditi. 1994. The new sociology of knowledge. *Annual Review of Sociology*, 20: 305–29.

Tamtik, M., and M.S. Creso. 2012. The role of experts in the European Union's research policy. *Review of Policy Research* 29, no. 4: 449–66.

Vauchez, A. 2008. The force of a weak field: law and lawyers in the government of the European Union (for a renewed research agenda). *International Political Sociology* 20, no. 2: 128–44.

Verdun, A. 1999. The role of the Delors Committee in the creation of EMU: an epistemic community? *Journal of European Public Policy* 6, no. 2: 308–28.

Walker, N. 1998. Sovereignty and differentiated integration in the European Union. *European Law Journal* 4, no. 4: 355–88.

Wæver, O. 1998. The sociology of a not so international discipline: American and European developments in international relations. *International Organization* 52, no. 4: 687–727.

Wagner, P. 2001. *A history and theory of the social sciences*. London: Sage.

Warleigh, A. 2006. Learning from Europe? EU studies and the re-thinking of 'international relations'. *European Journal of International Relations* 12, no. 1: 31–51.

White, J.P. 2003. Theory guiding practice: the neofunctionalists and the Hallstein EEC Commission. *Journal of European Integration History* 9, no. 1: 111–32.

Whitley, R. 1984. *The intellectual and social organization of the sciences*. Oxford: Clarendon Press.

Wiener, A., and T. Diez, eds. 2009. *European integration theory*. Oxford: Oxford University Oress.

Wittrock, B., P. Wagner, and H. Wollmann. 1991. Social science and the modern state: policy knowledge and political institutions in Western Europe and the United States. In *Social sciences and modern states, national experiences and theoretical crossroads*, eds. B. Wittrock, P. Wagner, H. Wollmann, and C.H. Weiss, 28–85. Cambridge: Cambridge University Press.

Zuckerman, H. 1988. The sociology of science. In *Handbook of sociology*, ed. N.J. Smelser, 511–74. Newbury Park: Sage.

Performing Theory/Theorizing Performance in Emergent Supranational Governance: The 'Live' Knowledge Archive of European Integration and the Early European Commission

BEN ROSAMOND

Department of Political Science, University of Copenhagen, Copenhagen, Denmark

ABSTRACT This article considers the entanglement of theories of international politics and international economics on the one hand and an emergent supranational policy actor on the other. The formation of the European Communities in the late 1950s and early 1960s is well known as a moment of radical supranational institutional creation. This is a period in which both economists and political scientists sought to theorize the processes of regional integration as it was happening. The article shows that the newly-formed European Commission, in both its communicative and coordinative discourse, drew selectively on the 'live' knowledge archive of both international economics and international relations to generate a strategic narrative about what European economic integration entailed, how it would be accomplished and (crucially) what kind of actor *it* was. At the same time, the semi-inductive quality of academic knowledge production meant that the Commission's activities were simultaneously being theorized into the live archive from which it was drawing. The paper examines the influence of two bodies of theory: one from economics (Balassa's theory of international economic integration), and the other from political science (neofunctionalism). The former is a striking influence on early discussions, initiated by the Commission, on monetary union, but its finger prints are rather more enduring — being visible in Commission communicative discourse well into the 1970s.

Economics is not unlike the alphabet: it forms a coherent whole, it possesses an inner logic, which is stronger than the capricious dictates of politics. Without this inner logic, there would be no economic science; and one of its results is that action in one field of economic policy has repercussions in all the rest.

Walter Hallstein, President of the European Commission, 1958–1967. (Hallstein 1972, 24)

Introduction

The field of EU studies has a proud tradition of generating theoretically informed knowledge about European integration and European supranational governance. EU studies researchers are not necessarily disinterested in influencing policy-makers, but the primary purpose of their collective endeavour is routinely advertised in terms of the development of robust explanation or deeper understanding. Like most social scientific work, the field of EU studies is premised upon the tenet that the objects it studies are largely separable from the subjects (researchers) who generate knowledge about those objects. It follows that the generation of truths about the world should occur without undue interference from that world. However, once formulated, social scientific knowledge — in the form of data, ideas, concepts and arguments — can be put to use in the world. Indeed, the entire sociology of knowledge/science project upon which this special issue draws constitutes an emphatic rebuttal of the simple and ordered separation of subject and object. This contribution offers further ammunition in support of this general critique of the supposed internal/external division in social science, and in so doing directly questions the degree to which theories of integration have been exterior to the processes that they describe (see also Vauchez 2010). It does so via the use of an especially interesting case: the interplay between the communicative and coordinative policy discourses of the early European Commission, on the one hand, and contemporaneous social scientific theories of the processes over which that very emergent supranational policy actor was presiding, on the other.

The argument of this article is that, during the 1960s, the newly-formed European Commission drew extensively on the 'live' knowledge archive of both international economics and political science to generate a strategic narrative about not only what European economic integration entailed and how it would be accomplished, but also (crucially) about what kind of actor it (the Commission) was. At the same time, the semi-inductive quality of academic knowledge production meant that the Commission's activities were being theorized simultaneously into the live archive from which it was drawing. It is important to emphasize that the focus here is quite specifically on the work done by both general understandings of the nature of integrating (European) economic space and narratives of how integration proceeds. As such the article pays less attention to the ways in which particular schools of economic analysis have informed and influenced the

Commission in particular and the European supranational policy process more generally. The literature here is substantial (see, *inter alia*, Colliat 2012; Dullien and Guérot 2012; Gerber 1998; Jabko 2006; Maes 1998, 2004a, 2004b; McNamara 1999; Snaith 2014) and its insights are not unimportant to the discussion here. The following should thus be read as supplementary to the extant research rather than as a substitute for it.

The article proceeds in the following steps. It begins with a classification of types of economic ideas that might secure traction or influence within the policy world. Whereas much of the discussion of the influence of economic ideas on policy tends to focus on broad systems of economic thought (such as 'neoliberalism'), this piece draws attention to two other sub-types of economic idea, labelled here 'bodies of economic thought' and 'generalizable claims about macroeconomic truth' that seem to be especially important in story of European integration. The article then examines relevant examples of each genre that emerged in Economics in advance of or concurrently with the emergence of the European Communities. The relationship between these and neofunctionalist theories of integration is discussed. The main empirical section of the paper considers how metaphors of the quality and dynamics of integrating European economic space were central to Commission discourse through the 1960s and into the 1970s. The article concludes with some reflections on how this case contributes to more general considerations in the sociology of knowledge.

Economic Ideas and the Policy Process

Of all social scientific fields, Economics is often said to occupy the most privileged position in the policy world. There is a long-standing appreciation (often from economists themselves) that the field of Economics is not a singular-scientific field endowed with objective technical-scientific superiority (Goodwin 1988; Hodgson 2013; McCloskey 1998). What matters is not just the numerical superiority of economists within national and international knowledge regimes (Campbell and Pedersen 2014) or even that such contexts tend to favour certain types of economic knowledge over others (Chwieroth 2010; Fourcade 2009). In various ways, and particularly since the onset of the global financial crisis in 2008, knowledge production in the field of Economics has been held to be deeply complicit in the constitution of the crisis itself as well as in the narrow range of 'orthodox' policy solutions that gather under the label of 'austerity' (Blyth 2013a; Quiggin 2012; Watson 2014) and in ensuring why 'neoliberalism' has proved to be so resilient in the aftermath of the crisis (Blyth 2013b; Crouch 2011; Mirowski 2013; Schmidt and Thatcher 2013).

Following Hall (1993), the literature on economic ideas has tended to focus on the influence, reproduction and transition between paradigms of economic thought, of which 'neoliberalism' seems to be the latest and most robust example. While broad economic paradigms are of obvious important, this contribution focuses instead on two other ways of thinking about economic ideas and their sense-making qualities.

The first variety might be labelled *generalizable claims about macroeconomic truth*. Perhaps the best-known example is the 'impossible trinity theorem', which purports to show that the policy combination of domestic monetary autonomy, fixed exchange rates and capital mobility is impossible (Mundell 1963; Fleming 1962). Such generalizable claims may hold for decades. Alternatively, they may be accepted in policy circles for only a limited period. The 'impossible trinity' theorem seems to have become a background assumption in policy circles since its formulation in the 1960s. Indeed, it is often read retrospectively to explain aspects of the institutional design of the post-war Bretton Woods international economic order. Policy actors work with the assumption that the theoretical claim in question describes economic reality, and consequentially that their actions need to take account of that social fact (Chwieroth and Sinclair 2013; Widmaier 2004). The so-called 'Nixon shock' of 1971 when the US suspended the convertibility of the dollar to gold (thereby ending the Bretton Woods regime) is a prime example of 'impossible trinity' logic at work. The US government destroyed a fixed exchange rate regime in order to secure greater domestic policy autonomy in the face of rising international capital mobility.

The second ideational type consists of *bodies of economic thought that provide templates for the development of policies and for their evaluation.* A prime example is 'Optimum Currency Area' (OCA) theory. The difference between these bodies of economic thought and the generalizable claims about economic truth is that they are more case-specific. The question is less about whether policy possibilities are constrained by an ineluctable quasi-scientific truth, and more about (a) whether the economic space in question is an appropriate or viable case of the category of economic knowledge and (b) whether, once appropriate policy action has been taken, the economic area in question conforms more to the economic knowledge claim. Snaith's discussion of OCA in the context of Eurozone governance provides a vivid illustration (Snaith 2014) of how internal divisions within OCA theory have provided the basis for alternative policy narratives about its application in the EU context.

Bodies of economic thought provide evaluative frames through which policy actors conceive of the economic space (or some key aspect of it) over which they exercise authority. In contrast, generalizable claims about macroeconomic truth present policy actors with a 'scientific' account of how the economy (or some key aspect of it) works in terms of 'if x … then y' type reasoning. To think about the Eurozone in terms of OCA theory not only provides a mental template for what EMU might be *ceteris paribus*. It also sets parameters for the discussion of monetary union in ways that are consistent with the theoretical literature. As Snaith (2014) shows, this need not imply consensus among policy actors, but the use of OCA as their principal referent will nevertheless circumscribe the boundaries of policy deliberation. Meanwhile, a government that accepts the logic of the 'impossible trinity' theorem will 'know' that its domestic macroeconomic policy autonomy is constrained under conditions of fixed exchange rates and an open capital account. Widmaier (2004) suggests that the irreconcilability of the impossible trinity has been hardened into a social fact by the ascendancy of neoclassical understandings of markets in both academic Economics and the policy world (see also Best and Widmaier 2006). This is a useful reminder that claims about economic truth and bodies of economic knowledge are themselves embedded within broader systems of economic analysis.

These ideational types can be investigated in terms of performativity — the observation that social actors, behaving in accordance with the precepts of a claim about the world, bring about and reproduce a world that is consistent with the content of that claim. Both OCA theory and the impossible trinity are aspects of the knowledge archive of Economics that have achieved some sort of traction in the policy world. More precisely, actors have visibly drawn upon these propositions to inform their communicative and coordinative discourses (Schmidt 2008) of the economy and their governing practices in relation to the economy. To label these economic ideas, 'performative' is not to suggest that their enactment necessarily shapes reality in ways that are perfectly consistent with the underlying theory. MacKenzie (2006b) (labels this process 'Barnesian performativity' (after the sociologist Barry Barnes [1988]), a term that captures the particular way in which actors in the real economy perform according to the precepts of abstract models in ways that make reality better conform to the precepts of the model. Indeed that perfect 'Barnesian' loop may only apply to a very special set of cases in the history of economics (MacKenzie 2006a; Watson 2007). It is rather to emphasize that such economic theories are not merely analytic descriptions of the world, but also active forces within it. They do things as well as describe things, and actors find them useful. Theories are carried into the world through the agency of policy actors who — in some way — 'perform' in accordance with their precepts. This might suggest a theory of strategic action where actors look for authoritative knowledge claims that help them to advance their interests in policy-making. It is no doubt true that economic knowledge allows actors to legitimate their choices by underscoring those choices with an air of scientific authenticity (Davies 2011). However, it is not necessary to assume that a simple rational choice logic — where the actor in question uses theory in the service of its pre-formed interests — applies in all such cases. Indeed, the performative use of economic concepts may be part and parcel of the very constitution of an actor's understanding of what its interests are. The use of economic concepts may be 'strategic' in that a policy actor uses narrative projection to shape and order both the world in which it acts and itself as an actor in that world (Miskimmon, O'Loughlin, and Roselle 2013).

The remainder of this article examines the case of the early European Commission in relation to social scientific work, primarily (but not exclusively) from Economics, on European integration. The suggestion here is that two related bodies of work exercised a significant influence over the Commission from the beginning of the 1960s. The first is the literature from International Economics on customs unions and the place of customs unions within wider schemes of economic integration. This literature is illustrative of both types of economic idea (bodies of economic thought and generalizable macroeconomic truth) and their use by the early Commission is extensive. The second body of work — from neofunctionalist political science — is perhaps less obvious in terms of overt citation, but its influence does seem to account for how the Commission in the 1960s thought about the movement through various stages of integration. The political science of integration provided a helpful supplement to economic theories that allowed them to be *read* in a particular way.

Economic Theory, Macroeconomic Truth and the Politics of European Integration in the 1960s

Timing is everything. Historical institutionalist studies of European integration (such as Pierson 1996) righty remind us that the EU's institutional design is a path-dependent legacy of particular choices made by a particular set of actors faced with particular set of dilemmas in the particular historical context of post-war Europe. Likewise, the communities emerged at a particular point in social scientific time. Naturally, a key premise of the sociology of knowledge approach is that intellectual context matters (Adler-Nissen and Kropp 2015). Intellectual context appears to matter in at least two ways in the case of the early communities. First, European integration stimulated social scientific work that developed theories and analytical narratives in response. The American scholars who developed what came to be known as neofunctionalist integration theory alighted upon the new European communities of the 1950s as interesting empirical objects, but they did so via the norms and preoccupations of political science that prevailed in the US context at the time (Haas 2004; Kaiser 1965; Rosamond 2005, 2007). While other national intellectual communities had quickly produced distinct and largely self-referential literatures on European integration by the mid-1960s (Kaiser 1965), it is striking how quickly the 'American' approach to integration theory became accepted as the authentic intellectual response to the construction of Europe (see e.g. Kaiser 1971).

Second, ready-made bodies of (primarily) economic theory offered general accounts into which the specific case of European integration could be read. Again, timing seems to be crucial. Viner's pioneering work on customs union theory (Viner 1950) had prompted a significant debate throughout the 1950s and beyond, primarily about the welfare effects of customs unions (Lipsey 1960). Customs unions are characterized by tariff-free trade amongst participating countries together with a common external tariff levied on imports from outside the union. Common external tariffs imply that customs unions should operate with a single commercial (trade) policy. Viner's principal and lasting contribution was to pose the main animating question of the theory: were customs unions trade creating (potentially open) or trade diverting (potentially protectionist)?

The idea of a creating a customs union was central to the Spaak Report of 1956 (High Authority of the ECSC 1956), which in turn fed into the EEC Treaty (the Treaty of Rome) a year later (EEC 1957). The key innovation of the report and the treaty was to link the aspiration of a European common market — an area of free factor movement — to the accomplishment of the customs union. As Pelkmans noted of the Spaak Report, 'the case for the customs union and the common market is based on assertions and expectations that cannot be verified in available customs union theory' (Pelkmans 1980, 336). Other commentators are even starker in their judgement: 'the building of a European common market progressed in spite of economic orthodoxy rather than because of it' (Mudge and Vauchez 2012, 473; see also Scitovsky 1962; Taugourdeau and Vincensini 2008). The inclusion by policy actors of a dynamic element into a process that had hitherto been theorised as static prompted a form of intellectual catch-up that was realized most emphatically in the work of Balassa (1961). Balassa used the EEC an empirical referent, but his book sought to develop a general theoretical argument about the integration of *national* economies. This last point is important, because it represented the intellectual endorsement of the strategy of the Six from the mid-1950s: a preference for *regional* international integration over sectoral integration. Although unacknowledged, as noted below, this focus rendered Balassian economic theory compatible with neofunctionalist theories of political integration whose regional emphasis distinguished them from earlier functionalist accounts of post-national governance (see Mitrany 1965).

Balassa's theory is best known for positing five sequential stages (or 'forms' to use his preferred term) of economic integration: free trade area, customs union, common market, economic union and complete economic integration (1961, 2–3). The last two stages are characterized by, respectively, a degree of harmonization of national economic policies and the 'unification of monetary, fiscal, social, and countercyclical policies' (1961, 2). The latter would require the establishment of a binding form of supranational public authority. Once again, there are parallels with neofunctionalism's ideas about political spillover — the process by which central pan-regional governing institutions emerge as a logical corollary of deeper economic integration. The idea of spillover was particularly important in Lindberg's version of neofunctionalism. He became interested in how supranational agents might be able engineer progress towards a defined goal (such as the achievement of a common market) in cases where the integration project had stilled. As such spillover

> refers to a situation in which a given action, related to a specific goal, creates a situation in which the original goal can only be assured by taking further actions, which in turn create a further condition and a need for more action and so forth. (Lindberg 1963, 10)

While economic theorists such as Balassa were concerned with thinking through logics of transition from one form of economic integration to another, the neofunctionalists focused on the political systemic consequences of key producer groups orienting their interest-driven activity to the emergent supranational institutional order (Haas 1958, 297; Lindberg 1963, 10). But it is hard not to recognize these two approaches as perfectly complementary and part of a wider intellectual discourse about evolutionary change from national to post-national forms of order.

The intellectual and stylistic resemblance between neofunctionalist political science and Balassa's staged model of integration seems obvious in retrospect to a historian of social science (see Harrison 1974, 15, 190; Webb 1983, 19), but there is very little evidence of communication and exchange between the two communities of scholars at the time. Balassa (1961) cites none of the early neofunctionalist work, notably *The Uniting of Europe*. Equally, neither Haas's stocktake of the first decade or so of integration theory (Haas 1970) nor his retrospective overview of neofunctionalism (Haas 2004) mentions Balassa's work on economic integration. Likewise, Economics literature of any kind does not rate a mention from Haas in a wide-ranging interview on his life's work (Kreisler 2000). It is also worth noting that the Haas's first political science treatment of European integration appeared (in 1958) more or less simultaneously with that of economist Tibor Scitovsky (1962) — a colleague at Berkeley. Neither cites the other, suggesting the already extant force of disciplinary boundaries. There is an allusion to the work of economists of European integration at the end of Lindberg and Scheingold's *Europe's Would-Be Polity*, a key work in the neofunctionalist tradition (Lindberg and Scheingold 1970, 306–307), but only as a way of pointing out that the reality of European economic integration is likely to fall short of economists' criteria for an ideal-type economic union (thereby echoing Balassa's own pragmatic conclusion about the unlikelihood of overarching supranational authority in the context of a monetary union — 1961, 272–273).

The European Commission and the Performance of Theory in the 1960s

The previous section implies that the professional academic literatures on European economic integration from, respectively, political science and Economics, while working within similar mode of reasoning, evolved more or less in parallel and without any significant exchange and communication. The evidence presented in this section suggests that, in contrast to social scientists working in the two distinct fields, the Commission did link (at least implicitly) the two bodies of theory. In short, Balassa's staged model of integration provided a key organizing metaphor in the Commission's communicative and coordinative discourse from the early 1960s. What also emerges from this analysis is a strong sense of the Commission arguing for policy initiatives that contain strong traces of neofunctionalist reasoning. The argument is not simply that the Commission found a useful rhetorical device consisting of both a metaphor for the reorganization of European economic space (economic theories of integration) and an account of why integration would deepen and develop necessary institutional corollaries (political science theories of integration). Rather, the point is also to show that the Commission actively *performed* this permutation of (bowdlerized) theories in the form of a strategic narrative. This strategic narrative was as much about what kind of actor it (the Commission) was and what kind of project European integration would be, as it was about seeking to define the boundaries of policy possibility through rhetorical closure. Others have pointed to the Commission's strategic use of ideational matter, particularly since the 1980s (Fligstein and Mara-Drita 1996; Jabko 2006; Rhinard 2010). The evidence here suggests that this tendency is rather older and was developed as an institutional pathology in the 1960s.

At the turn of the 1960s, as political science and economic theories of integration were beginning to develop, the Commission was still a juvenile bureaucratic actor. It was also working in largely uncharted terrain — a supranational integration project. Its mandate, in terms of its institutional mission and the collective goals for which it had responsibility, was defined by the EEC Treaty, but in ways that were far from precise (Maes 1996). That mandate would in time emerge through the cumulative jurisprudence of the European Court of Justice (Weiler 1999), but in the early phases of the Hallstein Commissions (1958–1967), the Commission was required to clarify its institutional mission while simultaneously enacting it (see Hallstein 1972, 57–63). Moreover, while the Treaty seemed to express a broadly liberal/neoclassical economic worldview (Scharpf 2010), as the exhaustive work of Maes (1996, 1998, 2004a, 2006) has demonstrated, there was significant variation between member-states and within the Commission in terms of underlying economic philosophies. In other words, it would have been difficult to forge a precise policy consensus about the scope and nature of economic integration that could then articulate with a strategic narrative about institutional purpose amongst the mixture of ordoliberals, Colbertists, Keyensians and neoclassical adherents that made up the first Commission. These tensions have remained significant and arguably sit at the heart of the difference between French and German approaches to monetary union (Maes 2004a; Hooghe 2002). Better then to forge a strategic narrative for the 1960s out of 'second level' bodies of economic thought (customs union theory) and generalizable claims about macroeconomic truth (the staged model of integration). Indeed, it mattered little that customs union theory was already being exposed to sustained criticism within Economics by the early 1960s (Lipsey 1960; Tsoukalis 1997, 18–20) or that the Balassian model assumed that the later stages of integration would involve the coordination and harmonization of policies that were assumed unnecessary in the earlier stages (Pelkmans 1980, 334–335). The refutation, qualification and questioning of the theory in the academic world, as is often the case, did little the prick the useful metaphor that emerged. This point might be pushed a step further. The record of EU/EU policy initiatives in relation to extant economic theory is, at best, patchy. For example, it had been well established by the 1990s that the strict application of OCA theory produced negative results in terms of the EU's suitability as a space of monetary integration (Dyson 1994). As such OCA theory could not be used as an official justification of EMU, which in turn led to a search for alternatives to underwrite the treaty commitments made at Maastricht (Taugourdeau and Vincensini 2008, 9–17). What Balassa's model provided instead was a meta-justification for progressing to monetary union under supranational authority. The model carried the implicit imprimatur of professional Economics while remaining more or less immune from refutation through testing against the empirics of European integration.

As the first President of the EEC Commission, Walter Hallstein was a central figure in the development of this strategic office. His memoirs, published shortly after he stood down from the Presidency, frequently articulate an understanding of European economic space that echoes a Balassian approach. For example, he quotes approvingly an old League of Nations pamphlet that was reissued by the United Nations in 1947:

> For a customs union to exist, it is necessary to allow free movement of goods within the union. For a customs union to be a reality, it is necessary to allow free movement of persons. For a customs union to be stable, it is necessary to maintain free exchangeability of currency and stable exchange rates within the union. This implies, *inter alia*, free movement of capital within the union. When there is free movement of goods, persons and capital in any area, diverse economic policies concerned with maintaining economic activity cannot be assumed. (Hallstein 1972, 23)

In the passage that immediately follows, Hallstein writes about a logic of integration that requires (ultimately) political centralization at the supranational level (1972, 24–28). This was not a matter of a retiring official engaging in retrospective construction. As early as the beginning of the 1960s, Hallstein's speeches are characterized by an interpretation of the EEC treaty that reads the common market as the logical outgrowth of the formation of a customs union and which connects matters of technical regulatory harmonization to deeper political integration (see e.g. Hallstein 1961, 1964, 8–9).

In an important paper, White (2003) describes the micro-sociological interaction between a small group of American political science scholars working in Brussels in the early 1960s and officials in the Hallstein Commission. His point, as with the argument presented here, is not to suggest that the early neofunctionalists were the sole or primary influence upon Hallstein and his colleagues, but rather that they played a part — a crucial part as it turns out — in helping this early version of the Commission to understand itself and the process that it was orchestrating. Of particular interest is the idea derived from neofunctionalists about the logic of integration and the methods by which different interests might be brokered in order to secure that logic. Political will and vested interests are seen as intervening variables that block integrative progress. The logic of integration, in other words, is more or less external to politics. White concludes strikingly that the neofunctionalist-style reasoning was fundamental to the strategic and tactical errors that the Commission made in the context of the 1965–1966 'empty chair crisis'. To borrow MacKenzie's (2006b) term, the episode described by White appears to be a textbook case of 'counter-performativity', where an actor's insistence on adhering to a particular theoretical narrative actually renders the world less like the world described in the theory.

As Maes notes, the Commission's 1962 Action Programme (Commission of the European Economic Community 1962) advocated a maximalist and expansive interpretation of the Treaty (Maes 2004b, 14). The Action Programme assumes that European integration is set on a path that culminates in a form of economic union involving, *inter alia*, the irrevocable fixing of exchange rates (monetary union) among member states (Maes 2004b, 17). Within two years, Robert Marjolin, the French Commissioner for Economic and Financial Affairs in the Hallstein Commission, had promised the Community's central bank governors that proposals for monetary union would be forthcoming (Maes 2004b, 19). Two important factors appear to be at work in this period. First, the premise of stimulating progress towards deeper forms of integration (including monetary union) was precisely that this was a higher stage of the integration process, which was needed to protect the (yet unrealized) achievement of the common market. Second, the EEC Treaty contained financial clauses, but left little room for supranational initiative in monetary policy. If it could be argued that (a) monetary union was the logical and inevitable next stage after a common market and (b) supranational initiative in monetary policy was essential to secure the customs union and stimulate progress towards the treaty goal of the common market, then was also obvious that the Commission should be empowered in this area. This represented almost precisely the same logic as outlined by Lindberg (1963) in his definition of 'spillover' cited above. Robert Triffin, the Belgian-American economist best known for showing the fundamental unsustainability of the Bretton Woods international monetary regime, was a known confidante of Marjolin and had been advocating European monetary union since the ratification of the Treaty of Rome (Maes 2004b, 9). Triffin, it has become clear, was also a major influence on the thinking of Pierre Werner (Danescu 2013), who chaired the committee that produced the first blueprint for economic and monetary union in 1970 (Council/Commission of the European Communities 1970). The epistemic power that followed from Triffin's endorsement surely helps to explain the Commission's decision to kick-start the move to monetary union as far back at the early 1960s. However, the suggestion here is that the metaphor provided by Balassa's staged model in combination with the neofunctionalist conception of spillover was also crucial to creating legitimate discursive space for the move to monetary integration.

Thus, relevant policy documentation from the 1960s and 1970s reveals a rather distinct mode of discourse. In essence, the public outputs of the Commission (and too some extent the Council) tend to express a concern with progress towards integration, or more precisely an anxiety (indeed increasing anxiety from the early 1970s) that the programme embodied by the Treaty of Rome was not being achieved. Take, for example, the deliberations of the (all-European) working group set up by the Commission to investigate the failure hitherto to make progress on the financial clauses of the Treaty (Commission of the European Communities 1966). The absence of a European capital market is described as a hindrance to the proper functioning of the Community's common policies, but is also seen as a vital prerequisite for the achievement of further integration in the form of monetary union (1966, 15). In other words, the integration of European economies is imagined once again in terms of its placement within the progressive, teleological and staged process described in the contemporaneous literature on economic integration. The idea of *progression* and *advancement* — or more precisely the lack of it — is integral to the deliberative documents produced by the Commission and its associated agencies in the 1960s and 1970s. The Commission's (again all-European) study group on monetary union that reported in 1975 (Commission of the European Communities 1975 — the 'Marjolin Report') frames its analysis of the inability of the Community to realize the aspirations of the 'Werner Report' (Council/Commission of the European Communities 1970) by posing the question 'where have we got to?' (Commission of the European Communities 1975, 1). The 'Werner Report' itself mobilized a justification for monetary union based upon the disequilibria that would follow from progress in integration without harmonization of economic policy (Council/Commission of the European Communities 1970, 8). This argument reproduces precisely that of the Commission, which in its annual report to the European Parliament of 1967, maintained that

> In the years to follow, the main objective should be to achieve economic union ... if the common market is to function properly. And this is a matter of urgency, because the intermediate phase in which the Community is situated — a complete customs union but only a partial economic union — involves a definite risk of imbalance, perhaps even of disintegration. (Commission of the European Economic Community 1967, 13)

The 1969 *communiqué* issued by the Heads of State or Government meeting that provoked the Werner Report speaks of the need to 'reinforce the Community and its development into an economic union' (Annex 1 of the Werner Report) (Council/Commission of the European Communities 1970, 32). It is perhaps worth noting that the staged progress to monetary union, found in both the Delors Report and the 1992 Treaty on European Union reflected the approach invented by the Werner Report. The 'spillover' logic of economic integration, culminating in monetary unification, is rehearsed in these documents (especially Commission of the European Communities 1973, 10–12), thereby suggesting not only that EMU is an inevitable rather than a contingent outcome, but also drawing upon, authorizing and reproducing the logics inscribed in extant economic knowledge. This form of communicative discourse is visible well into the 1970s (Commission of the European Communities 1976, 1978).

Conclusions

The intention in this article has not been to establish which economic ideas had the greatest leverage over the Commission in the period studied. Rather the point has been to show how the Commission, in its formative years, developed a strategic narrative about itself and the nature of its project that drew upon the live knowledge archive of social science at the time. This process was obviously not one-way traffic. The generation of the knowledge archive in the relevant branches of Economics and political science was occurring at the same time as the Commission was performing aspects of that archive. The precise nature of this reciprocal relationship between subject and object would require micro-sociological study. The textual evidence from patterns of communicative and coordinative discourse does indeed suggest that Balassian understandings of economic integration, themselves resting upon the longer-running literature on customs union theory, combined with something analogous to the neofunctionalist concept of 'spillover' to create a particular conception of European economic space that sits as an ancestor to the more recent idea of the 'European economy' (Rosamond 2012a, 2012b). The Commission's key working groups in the period under review here almost always consisted of Europe-based bankers and academics rather than drawing on the expertise of US-based scholars such as Balassa (a Hungarian émigré who taught at Yale, Berkeley, Columbia and Johns Hopkins — Navarez 1991).

This analysis speaks in interesting ways to the four principles of the sociology of knowledge laid out by Adler-Nissen and Kropp (2015 — in this issue). The principle of symmetry cautions us against the wholesale rejection of past scholarly work simply because the fields from which work emerged have moved on. The story of the Commission's use of theories of economic and political integration in the 1960s is a salutary reminder of why such work matters. It has almost nothing to do with whether customs union theory, Balassa's staged model or neofunctionalism are actually verifiable as explanatory theories through hypothesis testing or empirical analysis. Even if every proposition of each of these bodies of work is refuted, that cannot take away the complex influence that such work has on the emergence of the Commission as an actor and in the formulation of its strategic narratives in the 1960s. The principle of rejecting the internal/external division is the very premise of the paper. Put another way, the article has been interested in how the emergence of the European Communities and the development of theories about it were part of the same epistemic moment. The argument presented here took things further by exploring the performative interplay of those being theorized and the theorist. The principle of situatedness asks us to address the extent to which individual scholars matter. That they do should be obvious from the foregoing, although the precise extent to which they matter would only be possible to establish via the retrospective development of a sociological network analysis that showed the relevant interactions. Finally, the principle of contextualism asks us to be attentive to particular scholarly cultures. What is interesting about the scholarly ideas discussed in this paper — customs union theory, the staged model of economic integration and political science work that gave rise to the dynamic concept of spillover– is their strongly *American* quality. White writes about the influence of the neofunctionalists on the first EEC Commission: 'Hallstein valued the work of [Leon] Lindberg not just because he saw it as accurate, but because he felt it had impartiality and was protected from the concerns of those directly involved in the integration process' (2003, 129). What this suggests, of course, is that certain parts of the knowledge archive have privileged claims to be authoritative.

Much of the contemporary literature on the influence and impact of Economics has been concerned with this question. What this article suggests is that such authority can be contextual in quite specific institutional situations, and that it is not Economics per se, but rather the useful metaphors that it generates, that can have significant influence in the policy world.

Acknowledgements

The research for this article was conducted as part of the 'EuroChallenge' project, funded by the University of Copenhagen's Excellence Programme for Interdisciplinary Research. The author is grateful for comments on earlier drafts of the paper from Rebecca Adler-Nissen, Kristoffer Kropp, Antoine Vauchez and two anonymous referees.

References

Adler-Nissen, R., and K. Kropp. 2015. A sociology of knowledge approach to European Integration. *Journal of European Integration* 37, no. 2: 155–73.

Balassa, B. 1961. *The theory of economic integration.* Homewood, IL: Richard D. Irwin.

Barnes, B. 1988. *The nature of power.* Cambridge: Polity Press.

Best, J., and W. Widmaier. 2006. Micro- or macro- moralities? international economic discourses and policy possibilities. *Review of International Political Economy* 13, no. 4: 609–33.

Blyth, M. 2013a. *Austerity: the history of a dangerous idea.* Oxford: Oxford University Press.

Blyth, M. 2013b. Paradigms and paradox: the politics of economic ideas in two moments of crisis. *Governance* 26, no. 2: 197–215.

Campbell, J.C., and O.K. Pedersen. 2014. *The national origins of policy ideas: knowledge regimes in the United States, France, Germany, and Denmark.* Princeton, NJ: Princeton University Press.

Chwieroth, J.C. 2010. *Capital ideas: the IMF and the rise of financial liberalization.* Princeton, NJ: Princeton University Press.

Chwieroth, J.C., and T.J. Sinclair. 2013. How you stand depends on how we see: international capital mobility as social fact. *Review of International Political Economy* 20, no. 3: 457–85.

Colliat, R. 2012. A critical genealogy of European macroeconomic governance. *European Law Journal* 18, no. 1: 6–23.

Commission of the European Communities. 1966. *The development of a European capital market: report of a group of experts appointed by the EEC commission.* Brussels: Commission of the European Communities.

Commission of the European Communities. 1973. *European economic integration and monetary unification.* Brussels: Commission of the European Communities.

Commission of the European Communities. 1975. *Report of the study group 'economic and monetary union 1980'.* Brussels: Commission of the European Communities.

Commission of the European Communities. 1976. *Optica report '75: towards economic equilibrium and monetary unification in Europe.* Brussels: Commission of the European Communities. COM 11/909/75-E final.

Commission of the European Communities. 1978. *The customs union: today and tomorrow.* Record of the Conference held in Brussels on 6,7 and 8 December 1977. Luxembourg: Office for Official Publications of the European Communities.

Commission of the European Economic Community. 1962. *Mémorandum de la Commission sur le Programme d'Action de la Communauté pendant la 2e Etape.* COM (62) 3000. Bruxelles: Service des publications des Communautés européennes.

Commission of the European Economic Community. 1967. *Tenth general report on the activities of the community* (1 April 1966–31 March 1967). Brussels: Commission of the European Economic Community.

Council/Commission of the European Communities. 1970. *Report of the council and commission on the realisation by stages of economic and monetary union in the community: 'Werner Report'.* Luxembourg: Office for Official Publications of the European Communities.

Crouch, C. 2011. *The strange non-death of neoliberalism.* Cambridge: Polity Press.

Danescu, E.R. 2013. *A rereading of the Werner Report of 8 October 1970 in the light of the Pierre Werner family archives — a detailed study (full version).* Centre Virtuel de la Connaissance sur l'Europe (CVCE). http://www.cvce.eu/en/recherche/unit-content/-/unit/ba6ac883-7a80-470c-9baa-8f95b8372811/ba6ac883-7a80-470c-9baa-8f95b8372811/Resources#fa9f4dda-beb6-4caa-8095-29cfe4e451bc_en&overlay (accessed 29 September 2014).

Davies, W. 2011. Economic advice as a vocation: symbioses of scientific and political authority. *The British Journal of Sociology* 62, no. 2: 304–23.

Dullien, S., and U. Guérot. 2012. The long shadow of ordoliberalism: Germany's approach to the Euro crisis. *European Council on Foreign Relations Policy Brief* 49: 1–16.

Dyson, K. 1994. *Elusive union. The process of economic and monetary union in Europe.* London: Longman.

EEC. 1957. *Treaty Establishing the European Economic Community.* http://aei.pitt.edu/37139/1/EEC_Treaty_1957.pdf (accessed 12 June 2014).

Fleming, J.M. 1962. Domestic financial policies under fixed and floating exchange rates. *IMF Staff Papers* 9: 369–79.

Fligstein, N., and I. Mara-Drita. 1996. How to make a market: reflections on the attempt to create a single market in the European Union. *American Journal of Sociology* 102, no. 1: 1–33.

Fourcade, M. 2009. *Economists and societies. Discipline and profession in the United States, Britain and France, 1890s–1990s.* Princeton, NJ: Princeton University Press.

Gerber, D. 1998. *Law and competition in twentieth century Europe: protecting prometheus.* Oxford: Oxford University Press.

Goodwin, C.D. 1988. The heterogeneity of the economists' discourse: philosopher, priest and hired gun. In *The consequences of economic rhetoric,* eds. A. Kramer, D.N. McCloskey, and R.M. Solow, 207–20. Cambridge: Cambridge University Press.

Haas, E.B. 1958. *The uniting of Europe: political, social and economic forces, 1950–1957.* Stanford, CA: Stanford University Press.

Haas, E.B. 1970. The study of regional integration: reflections on the Joy and Anguish of Pretheorizing. *International Organization* 24, no. 4: 607–46.

Haas, E.B. 2004. Introduction: institutionalism or constructivism? In *The uniting of Europe: political, social and economic forces, 1950–1957,* 3rd ed, xiii–. Notre Dame, IN: University of Notre Dame Press.

Hall, P.A. 1993. Policy paradigms, social learning, and the state: the case of economic policymaking in Britain. *Comparative Politics* 25, no. 3: 275–96.

Hallstein, W. 1961. Speech by Professor Walter Hallstein, President of the Commission of the European Economic Community, at a dinner given by Mr. Robert Lovett at New York on May 24, 1961. http://aei.pitt.edu/14770/1/528.pdf (accessed 12 June 2014).

Hallstein, W. 1964. *Where the common market stands today community topics 13.* Luxembourg: European Community Information Service. http://aei.pitt.edu/14241/1/554.pdf (accessed 12 June 2014).

Hallstein, W. 1972. *Europe in the making.* New York: W.W. Norton & Company.

Harrison, R.J. 1974. *Europe in question: theories of regional international integration.* London: George Allen & Unwin.

High Authority of the ECSC. 1956. *The Brussels report on the general common market (the Spaak Report).* Luxembourg: Information Service of the European Community for Coal and Steel. http://aei.pitt.edu/995/1/Spaak_report.pdf (accessed 12 June 2014).

Hodgson, G. 2013. *From pleasure machines to moral communities: toward an evolutionary economics without homo economicus.* Chicago, IL: University of Chicago Press.

Hooghe, L. 2002. *The European Commission and the Integration of Europe: Images of Governance.* Cambridge: Cambridge University Press.

Jabko, N. 2006. *Playing the market: a political strategy for uniting Europe, 1985–2005.* Ithaca, NY: Cornell University Press.

Kaiser, K. 1965. L'Europe des savants: european integration and the social sciences. *Journal of Common Market Studies* 4, no. 1: 36–46.

Kaiser, R.D. 1971. Toward the Copernican phase of regional integration theory. *Journal of Common Market Studies* 10, no. 3: 207–32.

Kreisler, H.D. 2000. Science and progress in international relations: conversation with Ernst B Haas. http://globetrotter.berkeley.edu/people/Haas/haas-con0.html (accessed 29 September 2014).

Lindberg, L.N. 1963. *The political dynamics of european economic integration.* Stanford, CA: Stanford University Press.

Lindberg, L.N., and S.A. Scheingold. 1970. *Europe's would-be polity: patterns of change in the European community.* Englewood Cliffs, NJ: Prentice-Hall.

Lipsey, R.G. 1960. The theory of customs unions: a general survey. *The Economic Journal* 70, no. 279: 496–513.

Mackenzie, D. 2006a. Is economics performative? Option theory and the construction of derivatives markets. *Journal of the History of Economic Thought* 28, no. 1: 29–55.

Mackenzie, D. 2006b. *An engine, not a camera: how financial models shape markets.* Cambridge, MA: MIT Press.

Maes, I. 1996. The development of economic thought at the European Community institutions. *History of Political Economy* 28, no. supplement: 245–76.

Maes, I. 1998. Macroeconomic thought at the European Commission in the 1970s: the first decade of the annual economic reports. *BNL Quarterly Review* 207: 387–412.

Maes, I. 2004a. On the origins of the Franco-German EMU controversies. *European Journal of Law and Economics* 17, no. 1: 21–39.

Maes, I. 2004b. Macroeconomic and monetary policy-making at the European Commission, from the Rome Treaties to the Hague Summit. National Bank of Belgium Working Paper No. 58.

Maes, I. 2006. The ascent of the European Commission as an actor in the monetary integration process in the 1960s. *Scottish Journal of Political Economy* 53, no. 2: 222–41.

McCloskey, D.N. 1998. *The rhetoric of economics,* 2nd edn. Madison, WI: University of Wisconsin Press.

McNamara, K. 1999. *The currency of ideas: monetary politics in the European Union.* Ithaca, NY: Cornell University Press.

Mirowski, P. 2013. *Never let a serious crisis go to waste: how neoliberalism survived the financial meltdown.* London: Verso.

Miskimmon, A., B. O'Loughlin, and L. Roselle. 2013. *Strategic narratives: communication power in the new world order.* London: Routledge.

Mitrany, D. 1965. The prospect of integration: federal or functional? *Journal of Common Market Studies* 4, no. 2: 123–34.

Mudge, S.L., and A. Vauchez. 2012. State-building on a weak field. Law, economics and the scholarly production of Europe. *American Journal of Sociology* 118, no. 2: 449–92.

Mundell, R.A. 1963. Capital mobility and stabilization policy under fixed and flexible exchange rates. *The Canadian Journal of Economics and Political Science* 29, no. 4: 475–85.

Navarez, A.A. 1991. Bela A. Balassa, 63, Economics professor who fled Hungary. *New York Times,* May 11.

Pelkmans, J. 1980. Economic theories of integration revisited. *Journal of Common Market Studies* 18, no. 4: 333–54.

Pierson, P. 1996. The path to European integration: a historical institutionalist analysis. *Comparative Political Studies* 29, no. 2: 123–63.

Quiggin, J. 2012. *Zombie economics: how dead ideas still walk among us.* Princeton, NJ: Princeton University Press.

Rhinard, M. 2010. *Framing Europe: the policy-shaping strategies of the European Commission.* Dordrecht: Republic of Letters Publishing.

Rosamond, B. 2005. The uniting of Europe and the foundation of EU studies: revisiting the neofunctionalism of Ernst B. Haas. *Journal of European Public Policy* 12, no. 2: 237–54.

Rosamond, B. 2007. European integration and the social science of EU studies: the disciplinary politics of a subfield. *International Affairs* 83, no. 2: 231–52.

Rosamond, B. 2012a. Supranational governance as economic patriotism? The European Union, legitimacy and the reconstruction of state space. *Journal of European Public Policy* 19, no. 3: 324–41.

Rosamond, B. 2012b. The discursive construction of neoliberalism: the EU and the contested Substance of European economic space. In *European regionalism and the left,* eds. G. Strange and O. Worth, 39–61. Manchester, NH: Manchester University Press.

Scharpf, F. 2010. The asymmetry of European integration, or why the EU cannot be a 'social market economy. *Socio-Economic Review* 8, no. 2: 211–50.

Schmidt, V.A. 2008. Discursive institutionalism: the explanatory power of ideas and discourse. *Annual Review of Political Science* 11: 303–26.

Schmidt, V.A., and M. Thatcher. (eds.). 2013. *Resilient liberalism in Europe's political economy.* Cambridge: Cambridge University Press.

Scitovsky, T. 1962. *Economic theory and west European integration, reprint with a new introduction.* London: Unwin University Books.

Snaith, H. 2014. Narratives of Optimum Currency Area Theory and Eurozone Governance. *New Political Economy* 19, no. 2: 183–200.

Taugourdeau, E., and C. Vincensini. 2008. The economic justification of European integration: *ex ante, ex post* or not at all? EAEPE 2008 Conference, Rome, November 6–8.

Tsoukalis, L. 1997. *The new European economy revisited.* Oxford: Oxford University Press.

Vauchez, A. 2010. The transnational politics of judicialization. Van Gend en Loos and the making of EU polity. *European Law Journal* 16, no. 1: 1–28.

Viner, J. 1950. *The customs union issue.* London: Stevens & Sons Limited.

Watson, M. 2007. Searching for the Kuhnian moment: the Black-Scholes-Merton formula and the evolution of modern finance theory. *Economy and Society* 36, no. 2: 326–38.

Watson, M. 2014. *Uneconomic economics and the crisis of the model world.* London: Palgrave Macmillan.

Webb, C. 1983. Theoretical prospects and problems. In *policy-making in the European community*, eds. H. Wallace and W. Wallace, 2nd ed, 1–41. Chichester: Wiley.

Weiler, J.H.H. 1999. *The constitutionalization of Europe.* Cambridge: Cambridge University Press.

White, J.P.J. 2003. Theory guiding practice: the neofunctionalists and the Hallstein EEC commission. *Journal of European Integration History* 9, no. 1: 111–31.

Widmaier, W.W. 2004. The social construction of the 'impossible trinity': the intersubjective bases of monetary cooperation. *International Studies Quarterly* 48, no. 2: 433–53.

Methodological Europeanism at the Cradle: Eur-lex, the *Acquis* and the Making of Europe's Cognitive Equipment

ANTOINE VAUCHEZ

Centre européen de sociologie et science politique, Université Paris 1-Sorbonne/CNRS, Paris, France

ABSTRACT   This article tracks the origins of one of Europe's most ubiquitous instrument: the *acquis*. Thereby, it aims at initiating a new research program on the genealogy of Europe's cognitive and technique equipment. Instead of considering the *acquis* as a self-explanatory and transparent notion, the article unearths its rich political meaning, pointing at its instrumental role in shaping a law-centered, and supranational definition of Europe. Digging deep into individual and institutional genealogies, the article follows the methodological entrepreneurs who crafted new knowledge instruments for calculating Europe's State of affairs (the Celex database) and analyzes the process through which they have progressively acquired a monopoly in the calculation of 'the State of the Union,' thereby encapsulating within the very rules of the European game itself a form of 'methodological Europeanism'.

Even more so than in art, architecture, and engineering, science offers the most extreme cases of complete *artificiality* and complete *objectivity* moving in parallel. (Latour 2005, 89)

Introduction

Ever since Jacques Delors prophesized in 1988 that within one decade 80 percent of national legislation would be of EC/EU origin, the figure has crystallized a passionate debate over issues as different as the loss of national sovereignty, the regulatory burden for business, the risks for national culture, identity, etc.[1] While political, bureaucratic, and academic actors take a great variety of standpoints in these controversies, from welcoming this alleged trend to elaborating strategies to stop this seemingly inexorable increase, all eventually draw from the same toolbox. When it comes to calculating the actual (legal) 'state of the Union,' these actors inescapably rely on the notion of *acquis communautaire* (a concept so naturalized that it has become impossible to translate: Peyro 1999) and its related online database, Eur-lex (*the* official and legally binding source of EU law).[2] Nowadays, this cognitive and technical equipment is not just the instrument that *officially* defines and authenticates that 'Europe' to which the candidates are applying in phases of enlargement;[3] it equally inserts itself into the most routine operations of the EU, turning into Europe's 'constitutional operating system [...], axiomatic, beyond discussion, above the debate, like the rules of democratic discourse, or even the very rules of rationality themselves, which seemed to condition debate but not to be part of it' (Weiler 1997).

Although all textbooks, multiple-choice questionnaires, and European glossaries routinely refer to this toolbox as 'the total sum of obligations that have accumulated since the founding of the European Coal and Steel Community,' it would be misleading to refer to it as a transparent technical device merely 'calculating' a pre-existing body of 'rights and duties' that lie 'out there' in wait to be weighed up. In fact, there is much more to the *acquis* and its related Eur-lex database than just an amount of texts. As a variety of strands in the sociology of scientific knowledge have repeatedly established (Breslau 1997; Callon 1986; Latour 2005), techniques and methods involve a number of operations and procedures that determine at one and the same time units of data aggregation (here: the EU institutions), a logic in ordering them (a supranational constitutional order), and relatedly relevant levels of public policy to act thereupon (the European level). As it formalizes a stable figure of Europe (its foundations, its missions) and of its value objects (its body of law), the *acquis* implicitly *locates* the ability and the responsibility for the 'rational guidance' of European affairs, in particular institutions (here: the Commission and the Court) and professional groups (Euro-lawyers and EU civil servants), while dispossessing others (here: Member States, constitutional courts, national diplomats, bureaucrats, etc.).[4] As such, the instrument therefore encapsulates a form of 'methodological Europeanism' that frames our perception of Europe's polity, defining it as a law-abiding (a 'Union of law'), and supranational entity. Famously, the concept of 'methodological nationalism' has been used extensively by German sociologist Ulrich Beck (Beck 2005). Yet, while the notion proved integral in his critique of Nation-States' iron cage and in his search for transnational ways to overcome these intellectual blinkers, Beck never actually turned the notion into an overall sociological *research* program (Chernilo 2006). Likewise, the notion of 'methodological Europe-anism,' a notion he actually only mentions en passant, is essentially thought of as bearing the same noxious effects as its national counterpart ('methodological nationalism'). However, this article stands on the premise that the notion of 'methodological Europeanism' can actually prove to be a heuristic historical analyzer for how specific knowledge instruments and analytical concepts have been historically 'caged' EU polity, in a way that is analogous to how notions of class, family, society, law, etc. have histori-cally been 'caged' in the framework of Nation-States, thereby molding our understanding of the space of political *possibles* in modernity (Mann 1993). Through the genealogy of one of the Europe's most diffuse building blocks, this article suggests opening a broader research program on the his-torical and contested process of 'assemblage' (Latour 2005) of a variety of theories, methods, and instruments into a form of 'methodological Europeanism' on which Europe's supranational pole of government rests an essential part of its authority.[5]

Tracking this historical process (this genealogy) requires a methodology that seizes the *doctrinal* but also *methodological* entrepreneurs that have contributed to establishing Europe's cognitive and technical equipment. While a new strand of scholarship has recently unearthed the importance of doctrinal entrepreneurs in shaping Europe's foundational pillars such as 'functionalism' (Rosamond 2015; White 2003), 'constitution' (Cohen 2010; Vauchez 2010), 'governance' (Georgakakis and de Lassalle 2012) or 'single market' (Mudge and Vauchez 2012), the role of methodological entrepreneurs shaping the related techniques of data production and collec-tion (historical archives, economic statistics, legal compendia, diplomatic customaries, etc.) has still been given very little attention.[6] Yet, the State-building literature has actually long suggested that knowledge techniques have been an essential lever for modern States to establish their jurisdiction over competing forms of authority (church, feuds, charted cities, etc.).[7] The monopolization of the 'informational capital' allows for a 'theoretical unifi-cation' of the territory and of the corresponding population under the con-trol of the emerging State bureaucratic apparatus: 'taking the vantage point of the whole, of society in its totality, the State claims responsibility for all operations of totalization (especially thanks to census-taking and statistics or national accounting) and of objectivation' (Bourdieu 1994, 3 and 7). In other words, the informational prerogative progressively acquired by State bureaucracies (and the related capacity to assess, compare, predict) paved the way and legitimized State intervention and policies.

Strangely enough, while many scholars of EU studies have usefully drawn from the State-building analogy (Marks 1997), very few have pointed at the role of knowledge instruments in the shaping of Europe's polity[8]. Yet, the operation through which a chaotic set of political compromises, economic rationales, and legal norms is turned into one unique figure of Europe is far from trivial. In fact, in a context in which the production of data has histori-cally been anchored in national bureaucracies (Derosières 2002), the capac-ity to officially reveal 'the state of the Union' has been an essential battleground for Europe's supranational pole of government — in particular for the duopole formed by the European Court and the European Commission (Mudge and Vauchez 2012; Vauchez 2014). Over the years, both these institutions (followed recently by the European Central Bank) have been active producers and collectors of data: And the cognitive advantage they have secured thanks to this supranational outlook (that no Member State or private party has been able to reach) has been one essential platform for their claim of a 'rational guidance' of Europe.[9] In other words, the *political* capacity of the Court or the Commission to represent Europe's general interest and produce specific truths about its nature and future relates in part to their recognized ability to produce a *technically* robust representation of Europe. And this relation proves particularly true in the case of law, as the recognition of a body's capacity to unearth the *authentic* State of the law of the (Euro-)land entails a related capacity to act as the *official* interpreter (and implementer) of its binding effects.[10]

In engaging with this broad *problématique*, the article suggests embracing a sociogenetic approach, as this has proved to be the more potent denaturalizing device. As the article opens the black box of Europe's most ubiquitous instrument,[11] it delineates the complex historical process through which the *acquis* has been formulated, stretched, criticized, revised, finally naturalized as the most rigorous and objective measure of 'Europe' against other possible methods (political, diplomatic, economic, etc.). As this *problématique* calls for a thick description of the context in which these instruments have been initially crafted,[12] the empirical focus is put on two specific moments, the enlargement to Great Britain (1969–1972) and the *relance* of the Single Market agenda (1988–1992), as they are critical junctures for the definition of the 'European project.' The various political, bureaucratic, and academic debates on the best methods for assessing Europe's past achievements as well as the rich literature of EC documentation's guides and digests make up the variegated empirical material for this research.

The article proceeds as follows. The first section depicts the constellation of knowledge producers on the State of the European Communities in the late 1960s as the Common Market is being fulfilled but no agreement exists among private and public, legal and non-legal, national and European actors as to what is the most accurate procedure to calculate 'Europe.' The second section explains how the specific context of enlargement negotiations with Great Britain (1969–1972) form a turning point: It traces the coalescence of constitutional theories of EC law, technical innovations in information retrieval, and the Commission's institutional strategies into a new set of equipment that equates 'Europe' to one single coherent and non-negotiable *corpus* of legally binding norms. This progressive monopolization and juridification of Europe's nature through the notion of *acquis* endows the duopole constituted by the Court and the Commission with the related power to 'authenticate' what the 'rights and duties' of the States are. In the third and last section of this article, I follow how this singular assemblage progressively solidified as Europe's standard operating procedure.

'Europe' as we know it

Up until when the mid-1960s, when the unexpectedly rapid implementation of the Common Market accelerated the pace of European integration, the assessment of the State of the European Communities did not raise a particular problem. Just like for every other international organization, an official gazette — the *Journal Officiel de la Communauté européenne du charbon et de l'acier* — had been created from the very first days of existence of the ECSC (30 December 1952), bringing together acts, resolutions, and parliamentary debates in four languages (French, Italian, Dutch, and German). While the stock of texts initially amounted to few decisions and resolutions by the Council and the Coal and Steel High Authority, the situation changed dramatically from the mid-1960s onwards as the Common Market unfolded swiftly and Europe's legislation developed exponentially. From 2784 pages in 1958 and 7905 pages in 1960, the Official Journal reached more than 45,000 pages a decade later (Prometti 1999–2000)... In the midst of numerous technical and ephemeral regulations on agriculture, it became difficult to ascertain with precision the *current* State of the Communities. In addition, the *Journal Officiel des Communautés européennes* was poorly accessible (only a couple of hundred libraries and ministries received it for free) and hardly intelligible (it was deprived of any totalizing index that would have allowed assessment of the State of the European affairs in one given policy domain). National bureaucracies, parliamentary committees, and research institutes had often engaged in building their own instrument of supervision of the decisions produced at the European level, but they were most often discontinuous in time (as these institutions lacked the resources for a continuous overview) and limited in scope (Heydt 1977, 59–60). All actually acknowledged the difficulty of navigating in this inchoate and scattered ensemble of texts.

The Political Stakes of Calculating Europe

Europe's lack of intelligibility triggered competing attempts to calculate its body of past decisions and resolutions. In a context in which EC regulations were reaching an ever more diversified group of companies and economic sectors, corporate interests were among the first to raise the issue. Various members of the European Parliament, most often close to the corporate sector, started echoing the difficulties that companies were encountering in assessing the State of European affairs in their own specific sectors. German conservative MEP, Arved Deringer, himself a prominent anti-trust lawyer and president of the Legal Committee of the European Parliament (and later of the Common Market Committee), brought the issue to Strasbourg: 'does the Council or the Commission possess a survey (...) of their own law?,' he asked in a written question to the Commission in 1967. In reply, the German MEP was told that such inventory would be useless ('no more than generally informative') since everything of legal value was already published in the Official Journal, and tedious as 'it would require much time and energy' (Deringer 1967). Later on, Belgian MEP and businessman Baron Paul De Keersmaeker continued on the same vein, noting 'how difficult it is for the administrations, legal authorities, and lawyers of the Member States to keep track of all the provisions of EC law' (de Keersmaeker 1974). Legal documentalists and law professors also sent some desperate calls to the office in charge of the Communities' Official Publications (hereafter: Opoce): 'regarding your legal texts, have you nothing which codifies legislation by subject? For instance, where can we find in one place EC laws and Member States' laws on copyright? Have you anything like a citation system, such as Shepard's in the US? We need common sources to refer to (...) We literally beseech you, in the light of the pollution of Communities' publications, to do something about this aspect! (Heydt 1977),' generating an embarrassed answer from the director of Opoce: 'I fully recognize the problem, I personally cannot solve it' (Fitzgerald 1977).

Competing Apprehensions of Europe's Past Achievements

Unsurprisingly, commercial publishers quickly seized this opportunity by developing a vast array of practice-oriented compendia covering EC decisions in domains as different as agriculture, transport, restrictive trade agreements, etc. In the wake of the Common Market, many new book series and specialized newsletters were launched that provided updated digests of the State of EC affairs in a variety of policy domains. In France, a lawyer and former attaché at UNESCO, William Garcin, started a book series in 1958 entitled *Recueil pratique du droit des affaires dans les pays du Marché commun*, known as the *Collection Jupiter*, that would last for two decades.[13] Designed by and for corporate lawyers, in-house jurists, and company managers, these collections selectively compiled EC documentation, setting aside all non-legal material (EC parliamentary debates, Council's political resolutions, etc.). As they aimed at providing legal tools for companies, these companion volumes were sector-specific digests. Thereby, the 'Europe' these commercial compilations were unearthing was made of slices (policy domains) with very little emphasis, if any, on the political and institutional developments of the European project.

However, with the 'legal revolution' that accompanied 1963–64 landmark decisions by the European Court of Justice (*Van Gend en Loos* and *Costa c. ENEL*), a new understanding of Europe's past had crystallized (Vauchez 2010). The emerging constitutional doctrine of EC Treaties paved the way for a new definition of Europe as a distinct 'Community of law' and a coherent and self-sufficient 'legal order' granted with direct effect and supremacy over national bodies of legislation (Vauchez 2014). With the Court's jurisprudence being more and more firmly set on this constitutional track, the Commission established in 1967 a new classificatory system for the Official Journal of the European Communities that mimicked national legal letter codes: Acts and resolutions taken by EC institutions were not anymore presented by the Community (Euratom, Coal and Steel, Economic Community) as had been the case so far, but they were exclusively distinguished in relation to their legal effects: From then onwards, all legally binding texts would be indexed under the 'L' rubric (emblematically entitled 'Legislatio'), while the heterogeneous set of 'merely' declaratory texts (opinions, resolutions, parliamentary debates, claims before the European Court, etc ...) fell under the 'C' rubric ('Communicatio'). Throughout this new coding scheme, the 'Europe' formatted by the Commission's senior civil servants was *one* consistent ensemble of legally binding texts defined in direct relation to the unfolding of the 'European project' whose responsibility it was for the Court and the Commission to safeguard.

This constitutional representation of Europe ran counter to a third conception of Europe's past as a relatively informal and continuously changing series of *political* compromises (the Council's 'package deals,' political resolutions, consolidated diplomatic customs of EC summitry, etc.). The progressive diffusion of the constitutional understanding of European Treaties actually crystallized the emergence of this competing apprehension of Europe's past commitments. On the occasion of the 'empty chair' crisis, French diplomacy had famously managed to impose upon the other five Member States (January 1966) a 'compromise' that stated that 'a vital interest' could suffice to escape from the Treaties' legal prescriptions and treaty procedures. While pan-European lawyers did try to qualify such *political* interpretation of the founding Treaties by refusing to grant any legal value to the 'Luxembourg compromise' and viewing the protocol as a mere *gentlemen's agreement* without any binding value (Cruz 2006), diplomats and foreign affairs ministers still considered it as a defining element of Europe's diplomatic *acquis*.

The existence of these various possible ways of totalizing Europe's past achievements is indicative of the fact that as the Common Market agenda was being completed, there was still a lot of uncertainty regarding which instrument, procedure, and ultimately, institution was most authoritative in assessing the actual State of European affairs.

A New Arithmetic of Europe's State of Affairs

The enlargement negotiations in view of the accession of Great Britain, Denmark, Ireland, and Norway to the European Communities (1969–1972) created a new context. As they required making explicit that 'Europe' to which the candidate countries were applying, the negotiations formed a critical moment in which new methodologies for calculating Europe's past emerged and consolidated.

Methodological Entrepreneurship

While two previous attempts to enlarge the EC to the United Kingdom had ignited many diplomatic controversies, the third attempt raised little debate (Geary 2013). Early on in the process, the Six had come to an important political agreement on requiring that the incumbents accept *all* the texts and norms enacted ever since the creation of the ECSC, thereby obstructing the repeated claims by the UK for an accession *à géométrie variable* in the name of the special links it maintained with the Commonwealth countries[14]. However, while the four candidates would have to adjust to this body of legislation en bloc, it remained unclear whether they were simultaneously adhering to the constitutional doctrine of the Treaties that had emerged throughout the decade in the Court's jurisprudence as well as in the Commission's policies ever since the mid-1960s. Marked as it was by parliamentary sovereignty, the UK did not appear culturally and politically well-equipped to accept the *Van Gend en Loos* doctrine, not to mention the overall constitutional paradigm, leading ECJ Judge Pierre Pescatore to opine in 1970 that 'the new combination of direct impact with supremacy of EC law—which was accepted, though not without difficulties, on the continent—will require a fundamental revision of some deep-rooted habits of political and legal thinking in Great Britain. (...) I am under the impression that this has not yet been fully realized in the United Kingdom' (Pescatore 1970, 66).

The negotiating phase confirmed this fear. Being the terrain par excellence of State sovereignty, the negotiations for the accession treaty actually provided little room for these legal concerns to be voiced (Geary 2013). Unsurprisingly, the recognition of the *Van Gend en Loos* doctrine was quickly rejected from the Accession Acts in the name of the 'probable political difficulties [such a recognition] it would have posed'[15] and because it was deemed impossible to impose on new Member States more obligations than the ones that the Six had initially agreed to when they had signed the Rome Treaties in 1957.

In this context, it is no wonder that the Legal Service of the European Commission, which had been on the frontline in promoting the constitutional doctrine of EC Treaties (Bailleux 2013; Rasmussen 2012; Vauchez 2010), engaged in providing an alternative view of that 'Europe' to which Denmark, Ireland, and Great Britain were adhering. This took the very singular form of a *methodological* undertaking by which the Legal Service crafted a comprehensive and multi-lingual *database* of EC texts, acts and resolutions, baptized Celex (*Communitatis Europae Lex*). As early as 1967, in a period that constituted the heyday of the belief in computerized tools of legal information (Serverin 1985), Hélène Bernet, a young member of the Legal Service, returning from a training course in legal information technology at the University of Michigan,[16] had developed a database on the 'brand new IBM 360' thanks to its 'document processing system' software. 'The Commission's lawyers themselves,' she recalled recently, 'had begun to encounter 'retrieval' problems, and therefore, some IT assistance in distribution and research of legal information appeared sensible.'[17] The fact is the system actually allowed 'to analyze thousands of acts' at once. Thanks to its keywords search engine, it was possible to calculate the *current* and comprehensive 'state of the law.' In December 1969, on the occasion of a conference on computerized legal tools organized at the initiative of the (Commission's) Legal service, the first results drawn from the tedious work of collecting and transferring data into the system were presented (Bernet 2006, 17). Through this instrument, the ca. 2000 acts that were in force at the time had become one long series of punch cards (1 kg or more).[18]

Assembling the Acquis

These first steps toward the aggregation of all the EC documents produced ever since 1952 were certainly not trivial. In fact, the database became concretely engaged in the transformation of the *maquis* of texts and acts of the EC institutions into a veritable legal *corpus* organized according to Europe's constitutional paradigm. In arranging and ordering the Communities' past documents by type of norms (treaties, secondary legislation, preparatory acts, jurisprudence, national measures implementing directives, and parliamentary questions), year of adoption, duration and legal value, and so on (Nunn-Price 1994), the database effectively aggregated as much as it distinguished, bringing into being classes of equivalence between acts and texts born for reasons and in historical contexts which were profoundly different.

In a context in which different expert groups had been tasked with the preparations for the accession of the four candidates 'in order to provide the new Member States with a list of acts in force that they would have to accept and introduce in their national legislations' (Bernet 2006, 10–11), it was far than trivial that this computer database of EU law was to be hosted and controlled by the Commission.[19] As the director of the Legal Service of the Council of Ministers indicated at the time, the enlargement was 'a prodigious occasion to look over the whole of EC law and to arrive at a sort of radioscopy or spectral analysis of "secondary law"' (Puissochet 1974), the Celex technology provided the Commission with a cognitive advantage as it was far more current and comprehensive than what the Member States could gather.

As Celex was progressively bringing to existence Europe's 'body of law,' the Commission coined a new term, the *acquis communautaire*, to name this new aggregate. To the broad principle of acceptance of the existing EC regulations by the new Member States (opinion addressed to the Council on 1 October 1969), the notion of *acquis* added an essential *constitutional* guideline. In an opinion to the Council issued on the very eve of the signature of the Acts of Accession in Egmont Palace in Brussels on 19 January 1972, the European Commission averted that while negotiators had actually kept 'silent on the issue' (Puissochet 1974, 96) of the doctrine of direct effect and the supremacy of EC law, the 'Europe' to which Great Britain adhered did in fact entail a commitment to:

> the legal order created by the Treaties establishing the Communities [which] is essentially characterized by the direct applicability of certain of their dispositions and of certain acts, the supremacy of EC law over national measures which contradict them, and the existence of procedures for ensuring the uniformity of interpretation of EC law; [...] the binding nature of these rules, the respect of which is indispensable for guaranteeing the effectiveness and unity of EC law. (European Commission 1972, published 1987)

Thereby, the notion of *acquis* promoted by the Commission meant that the new Member States had to accept the underlying *constitutional* logic that

47

ordered Europe's past decisions by legal importance.[20] Combined with its technical equipment (Celex) and its purported rigorous calculus of the content and the contours of what 'Europe' really meant, the *acquis* concretely brought into being the 'Community of law,' thereby substantiating the Court's and the Commission's roles as the best exegetes of Europe's general interest.

Europe's Boundary Object

Having successfully passed the test of the first enlargement negotiations, where its representativeness had been both tested and given the official seal of approval, the *acquis* progressively became the working basis for the European Communities as a whole. By a sort of boomerang effect, the notion, initially aimed outwards, became the essential benchmark of the Communities' *internal* affairs. In this last section, I argue that this singular position as Europe's 'boundary object,' 'both inhabiting several communities of practice and satisfying the information requirements of each of them' (Leigh and Griesemer 1989), is the by-product of a continuous tension and balance between two partly contradicting elements: the first one relates to the increasing variety of *users* (national bureaucracies, interest groups, NGOs, journalists, etc ...), turning the *acquis* into an ubiquitous tool of Europe's polity; the second element is the continued *robustness* of the instrument by which I mean its recognized technical capacity to objectively represent the 'state of the Union.'

A Platform for European Affairs

Just a couple of years after Celex had been crafted, the European Court of Justice embraced it in its standard operating procedures. It proved instrumental in a context in which the generation of judges that had championed the *Van Gend en Loos* doctrine was progressively leaving the Court, putting the continuity of this 'judicial revolution' at risk. This prompted a variety of attempts to solidify ECJ constitutional jurisprudence among the most active pan-European judges and *référendaires*. Chief among these judges was the very influential Judge Pierre Pescatore who had been nominated at the Luxembourgish seat of the Court of Justice (1967–1984) after having contributed to the drafting of the Rome Treaties. Intellectually, he formalized the existence of what he called a 'judicial *acquis*' 'of constitutional rank' that was now an integral part of the Treaties themselves, and which was grounded on 'four decisions: *Commission c. Luxembourg et Belgique* (1962), *Van Gend en Loos* (1963), *Costa* (1964) et *Consten et Grundig* (1966)' (Pescatore 1981, 620 and 648). In the same period, he also forged the methodological device that would secure the consistency of this jurisprudence. As all ECJ Decisions and opinions had now been fully integrated into Celex (1974), Pescatore wrote for his colleagues and their *référendaires* an internal document entitled *Vade-Mecum — Recueil de Formules et de Conseils Pratiques à l'Usage des Rédacteurs d'Arrêts*[21] that called for a rationalization of the Court's judicial writing. The new digital context of Celex served as an essential lever for defining a stable lexicon ('*une bibliothèque de phrases*') for the Court's jurisprudence. But the Judicial Compendium was not just about style, it also insisted on the fact that judges had to frame their decisions within the framework of previous decisions, thereby securing a continuous 'jurisprudential chain' with the constitutional decisions of *Van Gend en Loos* and *Costa*: 'the decisions of the Court are not referable by computer, nor can they achieve their greatest influence as 'precedents' unless they are created in terms which include easily identifiable elements' (Pescatore 2007, 30). The rationalizing effects of the Celex system (and of the standardization of linguistic equivalencies: McAuliffe 2013) proved essential in locking in the Court's constitutional path (Vauchez 2012).

The *acquis* also became an essential instrument for the empowerment of both the European Commission and the European Parliament *vis-à-vis* Member States. In pretty much the same way it had allowed the Commission to involve itself in the diplomatic discussions about enlargement, Celex became one of the essential levers to monitor the implementation of EC directives in each one of the Member States. The late 1970s was marked by a considerable reinforcement of the Legal service's control over EC law implementation (Snyder 1993). To this aim, a new database was crafted on the basis of Celex (Asmodee: Automated System for Monitoring Directives Execution) but extending it to national implementation measures. Although the gathering of this national information was not without creating tensions with national bureaucracies, this new technical equipment made it possible for the first time to follow and compare the pace with which the different Member States were conforming to EC law. As Asmodee provided an essential technical support for reinforcing the *legal* guardianship of Europe's past body of texts, it allowed the Commission to develop an *autonomous* policy for detecting violations (not anymore based exclusively on complaints brought by external actors), bringing more and more cases before the ECJ. This resulted in concrete legal consequences: While only 30 total actions had been filed by the Commission between 1958 and 1977 on this basis, 100 were submitted in the period from 1977 to 1983 alone (Audretsch 1986, 161)!

It did not take long before the European Parliament took advantage of these new data. As they brought to light the extent of States' violations of EC regulations, they provided the statistical material for various reports from 1981 to 1982 in which the Committee of Legal Affairs of the European Parliament became alarmed at States' non-respect of their obligations. Supporting the Commission's new course of action, the Parliament called upon it to report annually on the State of national violations of EC law (Sieglerschmidt 1981). Thanks to the Asmodee database that allowed for a continuous evaluation sector by sector, country by country, and act by act, of the implementation of directives (European Commission 1984), the European Parliament became the arena in which, every year, MEPs and Commissioners, with numbers and data in hand, would point the finger at national pathologies and deficiencies, giving out good and bad points to the Member States (the latter mainly to Mediterranean countries, perceived as being systematically late or at fault ...), thereby substantiating the new political role it claimed for its self in the context of the post-1979 period (Börzel 2001).

Here is not the place to account for all the usages of the *acquis*. Suffice it to say that during the 1970–80s, the network of users actually significantly increased and diversified, making its way into the routine operations of the Communities.

Europe's Official Code

As Celex became increasingly used as the *official* calculation for States and individuals' rights and duties, the expectations toward the database progressively moved toward a more *political* repertoire. It should be said that from the late 1980s onwards, the scope and the reach of EU law evolved dramatically, particularly with the completion of the *paquet Delors* which brought EC legislation to new record highs (more than 500 new regulations per year in the 1986–1991 period) and the entry into force of the Maastricht Treaty's political union. An increasingly diverse set of interest groups, NGOs, firms, and national bureaucracies kept track of European affairs: subscriptions to the Official Journal of the European Communities actually grew exponentially, after stagnating at around 10,000 paying subscriptions (9500 in 1974; 9727 in 1985), the number of subscribers to the Official Journal rose to 12,000 in 1988 and more than 14,000 in 1991 (Official Publications Office, 1974 and following).

With this extension of the scope of EC-implicated policy domains and actors, new political and social expectations progressively emerged which increasingly referred to issues of 'European citizenship,' questioning the database in terms of its representativity, accessibility, and independence. Librarians, scholars, interest groups, NGOs, and others pointed to its various biases and technical flaws. First among the issues was the question of representativity: While the database could claim to be comprehensive in terms of scope, Celex still had a linguistic bias as its French and German versions were far more complete (and therefore accurate) than the other versions (Hanson 1989). How could this official basis that potentially impacted all EU citizens fail to be fully multi-lingual? In a context in which the notion of European citizenship had made its way into the Treaties at Maastricht (1992), the issue of accessibility also came to the forefront. Although in 1981 it opened to users external to the European Commission, the Celex database was still commercialized by a private company (Honeywell Bull) and access remained de facto limited to 'ministers and para-State organs, parliamentary assemblies, law firms, industrial and commercial groups, research centers, and universities' (European Commission 1982) who could afford the cost of the fees. Along the same lines, many criticized the lack of practicability of Celex, which was most often described as 'not (being) a database for novices' because its 'language (was) quite inaccessible' (Jeffries 1991, 241). Last but not least, the issue of the database's independence from specific institutional interests also became salient. As Celex was the undisputed basis for all European negotiations, the fact that it was under the control of the Commission was more and more difficult to swallow inside as well as outside EC institutions. Under pressure from the Secretariat General of the Commission, and then from the 'legal I.T.' working group created within the Council in 1974, the database had already moved away from the Legal Service to DG Administration[22]; but as it was still 'produced' by the Commission, its capacity to be recognized as an objective measure of Europe was undermined.

These challenges to Celex were not trivial as they all questioned its capacity to be *the* official code of Europe and the inescapable working device for all EU-related negotiation tables. In fact, from the aftermaths of the Maastricht Treaty (European Council 1992) to the Commission's *Livre blanc* on European Governance (2001c), 'access, openness, and transparency' of EU law documents had become a defining element of the emerging 'European citizenship' policy. As a result, the *acquis* itself turned into an object of policy in its own right, with a variety of attempts to simplify and codify it (European Commission 2001a; de Witte 2002). The related transformations of the database were crucial, as in less than a decade Celex became accessible via the Web (1997), then free of charge (2004), eventually aggregating with Eur-lex into a unique portal of legal information on the EU as we know it today (Duro 2006). In the meantime, the database had also left the Commission's umbrella to join an inter-institutional organ (Opoce), thereby marking its autonomy from its initial creators. On the whole, the process through which the *acquis* has become Europe's key boundary object profoundly transformed the instrument itself from the Commission's Legal Service, semi-public database to Europe's official code. The 2013 Council Regulation that restricted the authentic (legally binding) version of the Official Journal to its Eur-lex online version is just one additional acknowledgment of the saliency of this cognitive and technical equipment.[23]

Conclusion

This article has traced the genealogy of one of Europe's most ubiquitous instruments: the *acquis*. The notion is so deeply entrenched in Europe's daily practices that it has now become practically invisible. While most scholarship takes it as a self-evident fact, the article has opened this black box and debunked the complex historical process through which this specific model of measuring EU law has been produced and defined as Europe's best proxy. In particular, the article points at the role of methodological entrepreneurs and their many investments in terms of equipment, maintenance, and administration as they craft what has now become the very terrain on which European affairs take place.

This result is not trivial if we consider that knowledge instruments are not just mere *descriptions* of Europe's reality but one essential channel through which it is actually filtered and framed into sets of possible alternatives (*inter alia*: Diez 1999). Interestingly, the *acquis* apprehends 'Europe' as one specific supranational (legal) order; a unitary and closed (*autopoietic*) system that has its own causal mechanism, with internal relations and hierarchies, distinct from Member States. In other words, the European Union has an autonomy of its own and it exists in and out of itself. As the *acquis* delineates the EU as a self-sufficient ecology and the primary unit of analysis, it pinpoints the EU as the relevant level for both negotiations and problem-solving strategies. Thereby, it is an essential brick in the equation between the concept of Europe and that of the European Union, best coined as a 'methodological Europeanism,' on which Europe's supranational pole of government rests an essential part of its authority.

Acknowledgement

This article was written while I was a senior Emile Noël fellow at the New York University's Jean Monnet Center. I am grateful to the participants at the Spring 2014 Jean Monnet Workshop at NYU and EU Law Workshop at Columbia University for helpful comments on earlier versions of the text. Special thanks to Megan Donaldson, Grainne de Burca, Dan Kelemen, Peter Lindseth, and Jonathan Yovel for stimulating exchanges.

Notes

1. While the Commission estimated this amount to 80,000 pages in 2001 (cf. European Commission 2001b), many have discussed the accuracy and the relevance of this figure ever since: see, *inter alia*, Open Europe (2007), and Bertoncini (2009).
2. The Eur-lex website actually claims '468,000 references, about 5.7 million documents in total, an average of 12,000 references are added each year, 23 languages' and an average of 7 million visits every month.
3. On the *acquis* as the inescapable frame of reference in the recent enlargement negotiations to eastern and central European countries, see Robert (2003) and Adler-Nissen (2011).
4. On the 'political potential' of methodologies, see Breslau (1997).
5. While part of the empirical material presented here is brought from my previous research on the genesis of EU law's definitional power (Vauchez 2013), the present article expands it and brings it into a new research program on the genealogy of 'methodological Europeanism.'
6. But see Rowell and Penissat (2014) on Eurostat in this dossier and Philippe Aldrin on the Eurobarometer (2010).
7. In a very rich and diverse literature, see the seminal book by Alain Derosieres (2002), Pierre Bourdieu's Lectures at the Collège de France on the State (2014) and the important project on the genesis of the modern State in Europe led by Wim Blockmans and Jean-Philippe Genet (1993).
8. While the literature on 'policy instruments' bears similarities with our approach, it does not, however, provide a specific statute for *knowledge* instruments and data collection (Lascoumes and Le Galès 2007).
9. On the importance of this cognitive advantage in establishing jurisdiction over a given social problem, see Abbott (2005).
10. For an enlightening parallel, see the historical account of the creation of the Official Journal in France (Gougeon 1995).
11. While there are many interesting studies of the *acquis* that point at its strategic importance in embodying the unity of the European project (Jorgensen 1999; Wiener 1998), none actually questioned its genesis and how this may have concretely *shaped* Europe.
12. On the principle of contextualism as a key empirical strategy for the sociology of knowledge, see the introduction to this dossier by Adler-Nissen and Kropp (2015).
13. Cf. 'Droit des affaires et Marché commun,' *Le Monde*, 9 April 1958. For an English-speaking equivalent, see the *Encyclopedia of European Community Law* published from 1973 onwards by Sweet and Maxwell.

14. The Council's declaration after The Hague conference of heads of States and of government, 1 and 2 December 1969.
15. In the words of the Director of the Council's Legal Service, Puissochet (1974).
16. In 1972, she would actually defend a doctoral thesis in German law at the University of Frankfurt am Main on the logic applied in international multilingual law (Bernet 1983, 2006).
17. Hélène Bernet, Email exchanges with the author, 2008. Our translation.
18. *Ibid.*
19. Strikingly, until 1981, only the Legal Service and a limited network of 'Celex correspondents' in the directorates-general were 'entitled to consult the records and effect retrieval' of EU law on Celex terminals (Gaskell 1977, 79).
20. While the opinion of the Commission would not gain official recognition in the subsequent Acts of Accession, it would continuously recall its importance in opinions copy-pasted from that of January 1972: for example, European Commission (1981, 119).
21. The document was published only 22 years later (Pescatore 2007).
22. On the history of Celex's institutional affiliations (Official Publications Office 2006).
23. Ever since Council Regulation 216/2013, only the electronic editions of the OJ (e-OJ) published after 1 July 2013 are authentic (have legal force).

References

Abbott, A. 2005. Linked ecologies: states and universities as environments for profession. *Sociological Theory* 23, no. 3: 245–74.

Adler-Nissen, R. 2011. Opting out of an ever closer union: the integration doxa and the management of sovereignty. *West European Politics* 34, no. 5: 1095–113.

Adler-Nissen, R., and K. Kropp. 2015. A sociology of knowledge approach to European Integration. *Journal of European Integration* 37, no. 2: 155–73.

Aldrin, P. 2010. L'invention de l'opinion publique européenne. Genèse intellectuelle et politique de l'Eurobaromètre (1950–1973) [The invention of European public opinion. Intellectual and political genesis of the Eurobarometer (1950–1973)]. *Politix - Revue des sciences sociales du politique* 23, no. 89: 79–101.

Audretsch, H.A.H. 1986. *Supervision in European EC law*, 2nd edn. Amsterdam: Elsevier.

Bailleux, J. 2013. Michel Gaudet as a law entrepreneur: the role of the legal service of the European executives in the invention of EC Law. *Common Market Law Review* 50, no. 2: 359–67.

Beck, U. 2005. *Cosmopolitan Europe*. London: Polity.

Bernet, H. 1983. *Droit, informatique et traduction. L'expérience de la Communauté économique européenne. La puce et le dragon à sept langues* [Law, computers and translation. The experience of the European Economic Communities]. Québec: Gouvernement du Québec, Conseil de la langue française.

Bernet, H. 2006. Les racines. Histoire de Celex de 1963 à 1986 [The roots. History of Celex from 1963 to 1985]. In *25 années de droit européen en ligne* [25 years of EU law online]. Luxembourg: Office for Official Publications of the European Communities.

Bertoncini, Y. 2009. La législation nationale d'origine communautaire: Briser le mythe des 80%. *Notre Europe, Les Brefs*, no. 13.

Blockmans, Wim, and J.-P. Genet (eds.). 1993. *Les Origines de l'État moderne en Europe* [Visions on the development of European States]. Paris: Presses Universitaires de France.

Börzel, T. 2001. *Non-compliance in the European Union. Pathology or statistical artefact*. Working Paper RSCAS, 28, European University Institute.

Bourdieu, P. 1994. Rethinking the state. Genesis and structure of the bureaucratic field. *Sociological Theory* 12, no. 1.

Bourdieu, P. 2014. *On the state. Lectures at the Collège de France (1989–1992)*. London: Polity.

Breslau, D. 1997. The political power of research methods: knowledge regimes in US labor-market policy. *Theory and Society* 26: 869–902.

Callon, M. 1986. Some elements for a sociology of translation: domestication of the scallops and the fishermen of St-Brieuc Bay. In *Power, action and belief: a new sociology of knowledge?*, ed. J. Law, 196–223. London: Routledge.

Chernillo, D. 2006. Social theory's methodological nationalism. *European Journal of Social Theory* 9, no. 1: 5–22.

Cohen, A. 2010. Legal professionals or political entrepreneurs? Constitution making as a process of social construction and political mobilization. *International Political Sociology* 4: 107–23.

Cruz, J.B. 2006. The Luxemburg compromise from a legal perspective. In *Visions votes and vetos. The empty chair crises*, eds. J.-M. Palayret and H. Wallace, 251–77. Brussels: P.I.E. Lang.

De Keersmaeker, P. 1974. Written Question n°350/74 by Mr. De Keersmaeker to the Commission of the European Communities, 16 September.

Deringer, A. 1967. Written question no. 155/67 by Arved Deringer to the Commission of the European Communities, 20 September.

Derosieres, A. 2002. *The politics of large numbers. A history of statistical reasoning.* Cambridge, MA: Harvard University Press.

Diez, T. 1999. Speaking 'Europe'. The politics of integration discourse. *Journal of European Public Policy*, 6 no. 4.

Duro, M. 2006. Celex grows up. In *25 years of European law online*. Luxembourg: Office for the Official Publications of the European Communities, EUR Publication Office.

European Commission. 1972. Commission opinion of 19 January 1972 on the application to the European Communities by the Kingdom of Denmark, Ireland, the Kingdom of Norway and the United Kingdom of Great Britain and Northern Ireland, 11972B/AVI/COM, Official Journal L 073, 27/03/1972.

European Commission. 1981. Avis du 27 mai 1979 on Greece [Opinion of 23 May 1979]. In *Actes relatifs à l'adhésion de la Grèce* [The application for accession to the European Communities by the Hellenic Republic]. Luxembourg: EUR Publication Office.

European Commission. 1982. *Seizième Rapport général sur l'activité des Communautés européennes* [Sixteenth General Report on the Activities of the Communities in 1981]. Luxembourg: Office des publications officielles des Communautés.

European Commission. 1984. *Premier rapport annuel au Parlement européen de la commission contrôlant la mise en œuvre du droit communautaire* [First annual report of the national implementation of EC Law – 1983]. COM(84).

European Commission. 2001a. Communication: simplifying and improving the regulatory environment (COM(2001)726), 5 December.

European Commission. 2001b. Communication from the Commission to the European Parliament and Council. Codification of the *Acquis* Communautaire. 21 November, COM(2001)645.

European Commission. 2001c. *European Governance – A While Paper.* COM (2001) 428 final, 25 July.

European Council. 1992. Conclusions of the presidency - Edinburgh, December 12.

Fitzgerald, F. 1977. Publications policy and activities of the OPOCE. *International Journal of Law Library* 5, no. 1: 60–70.

Gaskell, E. 1977. Library and documentation services of the European communities. *International Journal of Law Library* 5, no. 76.

Geary, M. 2013. *Enlarging the European union. The commission seeking influence (1961–1973).* London: Macmillan.

Georgakakis, D., and M. de Lassalle (eds.). 2012. *The political uses of governance studying an EU white paper.* Leverkusen-Opladen: Barbara Budrich.

Gougeon, P. 1995. Nul n'est censé ignoré la loi' [The who-says-what of the acquis]. La publication au Journal Officiel: Genèse d'un mode d'universalisation de la 'puissance publique [Noone is supposed to be unaware of the law. The publication of the official journal. Genesis of a mode of univerlization of the public authority]. *Politix* 8, no. 32: 66–88.

Hanson, T. 1989. An introduction to celex: the database of European EC law. *European Access*, no. 3: 29–32.

Heydt, V. 1977. How to use the primary source material of the European Communities. *International Journal of Law Library* 5, no. 1: 57–95.

Jeffries, J. 1991. Online legal databases. France and the European Communities. *Law Library Journal* 83: 237–51.

Jorgensen, K. 1999. The social construction of the *acquis* communautaire: a cornerstone of the European edifice. *European Integration online Papers (EIoP)* 3, no. 5.

Lascoumes, P., and P. Le Galès. 2007. Understanding public policy through its instruments—From the nature of instruments to the sociology of public policy instrumentation. *Governance* 20, no. 1: 1–21.

Latour, B. 2005. *Reassembling the social – an introduction to actor-network-theory.* Oxford: Oxford University Press.

Leigh, S., and J. Griesemer. 1989. Institutional ecology, 'translations' and boundary objects. Amateurs and professionals in Berkeley's Museum of Vertebrate Zoology (1907–1939). *Social Studies of Science* 19: 387–420.

Mann, M. 1993. *The sources of social power. The rise of classes and nation states 1760–1914.* Cambridge: Cambridge University Press.

Marks, G. 1997. A third lens. Comparing European integration and state building. In *European integration in social historical perspective*, eds. J. Klausen and L.A. Tilly, 23–50. Lanham: Rowman & Littlefield.

McAuliffe, K. 2013. Precedent at the ECJ: the linguistic aspect. Law and language. *Current Legal Issues* 15.

Mudge, S., and A. Vauchez. 2012. Building Europe on a weak field. Law, economics, scholarly avatars in transnational politics. *American Journal of Sociology* 118, no. 2: 449–92.

Nunn-Price, N. 1994. *The CELEX database: a guide to European community law.* London: Context Ltd.

Office for Official Publications of the European Community. 2006. *25 years of European law online.* Luxembourg: EUR Publication Office.

Official Publications Office of the European Communities. 1974. *The celex database: celex 2. User guide.* Luxembourg: EUR Publication Office.

Open Europe. 2007. *Open Europe briefing note: Just how big is the Acquis Communautaire?* Retrived from: http://www.openeurope.org.uk/Page/Research/en/LIVE

Peryo, F. 1999. Le qui-dit-quoi de l'acquis communautaire. *Terminologie et traduction* 2: 52–75.

Pescatore, P. 1970. The common market. *The Scots Law Times* 74: 64–8.

Pescatore, P. 1981. Aspects judiciaires de 'l'acquis communautaire' [Judicial aspects of the acquis]. *Revue trimestrielle de droit européen* 21.

Pescatore, P. 2007. *Vade-mecum. Recueil de formules et de conseils pratiques à l'usage des rédacteurs d'arrêts* [Vade-mecum. Compendium of formula and practical advices for those writing judicial decisions]. Brussels: Bruylant.

Prometti, D. 1999–2000. *Storia dell'ufficio delle pubblicazioni delle Communità europee; trent'anni al servizio delle istituzioni e dei cittadini* [The enlargement of the European Communities. presentation and commentary of the treaty and accession acts of the United Kingdom, Danemarj and Ireland]. Tesi di laurea, Univ. di Firenze.

Puissochet, J.P. 1974. *L'élargissement des Communautés Européennes: Présentation et commentaire du Traité et des Actes relatifs à l'adhésión du Royaume-Uni, du Danemark et de l'Irlande.* Paris: Éditions techniques et économiques.

Rasmussen, M. 2012. Establishing a constitutional practice of European law. The history of the legal service of the European executive (1952–1965). *Contemporary European History* 21, no. 3: 375–97.

Robert, C. 2003. L'Europe sociale face à son élargissement. Les déterminants institutionnels du débat communautaire sur la dimension sociale de l'élargissement à l'Est [Social Europe in the front of the enlargment. Institutional determinants of the Community debate of the social dimension of the enlargement to Eastern countries]. *Annuaire français des relations internationales* 4: 426–37.

Robert, C., and A. Vauchez. 2010. L'académie européenne: Savoirs, savants et experts dans le gouvernement de l'Europe [The Europea Academia. Knowledge, academics and experts in the government of Europe]. *Politix* 89: 9–34.

Rosamond, B. 2015. Performing theory/theorizing performance in emergent supranational governance: the 'Live' knowledge archive of European Integration and the early European Commission. *Journal of European Integration* 37, no. 2: 175–91.

Rowell, J., and E. Penissat. 2014. From an instrument to the instrumentalisation of 'European opinion'. In *What Europe constructs. Reassessing constructivism*, eds. M. Mangenot and J. Rowell. Manchester, NH: Manchester University Press.

Serverin, E. 1985. *De la jurisprudence en droit privé. Théorie d'une pratique* [Jurisprudence in private law. Theory of a practice]. Lyon: Presses universitaires de Lyon.

Sieglerschmidt, H. 1981. *Report on drawn on behalf of the Legal affairs committee of the European Parliament on the responsibility of the European Court of Justice for the uniform application of EC law in the Member States.* Luxembourg: European Parliament Documents 1-414/81.

Snyder, F. 1993. The effectiveness of European community law: institutions, processes, tools and techniques. *Modern Law Review* 56: 19–54.

Vauchez, A. 2010. The transnational politics of judicialization: van Gend en Loos and the making of EU polity. *European Law Journal* 16: 1–28.

Vauchez, A. 2012. Keeping the dream alive: the European Court of Justice and the transnational fabric of integrationist jurisprudence. *European Political Science Review* 4, no. 1: 51–71.

Vauchez, A. 2013. *Brokering Europe. Euro-lawyers and the making of a transnational polity.* Cambridge: Cambridge University Press.

Vauchez, A. 2014. *Démocratiser l'Europe* [Democratizing Europe]. Paris: Seuil.

Weiler, J. 1997. The reformation of European constitutionalism. *Journal of Common Market Studies* 35, no. 1: 97–131.

White, J. 2003. Theory guiding practice: the neo-functionalists and the Hallstein EEC commission. *Journal of European Integration History* 9, no. 1: 111–31.

Wiener, A. 1998. The embedded *Acquis Communautaire*: transmission belt and prism of governance. *European Law Journal* 4, no. 3: 294–315.

de Witte, B. 2002. Simplification and reorganization of the European treaties. *Common Market Law Review* 6, no. 39: 1255–87.

In the Eye of the Beholder: A Sociology of Knowledge Perspective on Norm Transfer

ANTJE WIENER

Chair of Political Science, especially Global Governance, University of Hamburg and EURIAS Senior Fellow, Netherlands Institute for Advanced Studies (NIAS), Wassenaar

ABSTRACT   The article introduces the concept of 'strategic blueprinting' as a distinct practice of norm transfer, thereby turning the 'normative-power approach' on its head. Rather than transferring norms from the inside of liberal communities out, outsiders choose to copy parts of the *acquis communautaire*. European integration is thus perceived through the eye of the beholder. To elaborate on this strategy, the article compares it with other types of norm transfer such as transplantation and diffusion. The intention is to establish parameters for further research on norm transfer along the four principled dimensions of the new sociology of knowledge: (1) identify and define the practice (internal/external division); (2) situate the practice within the broader field of integration theories and the parallel development of integration policy and politics (symmetry principle); (3) reconstruct the practice (situatedness principle); and (4) establish its potential with regard to governance and constitutionalism in the global realm (contextualism).

Introduction

This article sheds light on Europe as a normative power that is attractive to others. In doing so, it effectively turns the normative power Europe approach, which was originally advanced by Manners (2002, 2006) on its head. Rather than taking a view from the inside out, with the intention to diffuse norms from the centre towards the periphery of liberal communities, it suggests the reverse perspective from the outside into these communities. While the former works according to the logic of appropriateness, the latter is guided by the principle of contestedness. This attraction is indicated by outsiders from other regions who choose to copy 'bits and pieces' (Curtin 1993) of the EU's *acquis communautaire*. The beauty of European integration is thus perceived as lying in the eye of the beholder, so to speak. To my knowledge, this article is the first to take up this particular strategy. It is defined as the practice of *strategic blueprinting*. Drawing on an increasing number of references to the European Union (EU) that take the body of the *acquis communautaire* as a sort of pool containing hard and soft institutions which has been established over time and which bears the socio-cultural imprint of the specific experience of European integration (Michalski and Wallace 1992; Gialdino 1995; Jørgensen 1998; Wiener 1998; Merlingen *et al.* 2000; Vauchez 2015) it is suggested that picking and choosing institutions (norms, principles, rules and routinised procedures) from this pool has consequences. In other words, although it seems promising with a view to advancing integration in their respective regional contexts, norm transfer from the EU context to other areas is expected to generate unexpected outcomes elsewhere.

This article seeks to elaborate on this expectation. To that end, it assesses the potential for socio-cultural detail that is provided by distinct approaches to norm transfer. The discussion is structured by leading insights from the (new) sociology-of-knowledge approach, including the four principles of symmetry, internal/external division, situatedness and contextualism.[1] Given the scope and limited space provided by this special issue, the intention is to establish parameters to organise more specific and detailed empirical research on norm transfer along for the four principled dimensions of the new sociology of knowledge: first, to identify and define the practice (internal/external division); second, to situate the practice within the broader field of integration theories and the parallel development of integration policy and politics (symmetry principle); third, to reconstruct some cases in which the practice is applied (situatedness principle); and fourth, to offer a conclusion about the potential of this practice with regard to future development of global governance and global constitutionalism (contextualism).

While the transfer of norms between established and emerging regional orders or organisations is not new, the proposed concept of strategic blueprinting includes two innovative moves. The first regards the phenomenological dimension, i.e. the decision to engage in blueprinting is taken outside rather than inside the EU context of policy-making and politics. This includes a shift of perspective, which is conceptualised as a distinct new dynamic of engagement with the *acquis communautaire*. Relatedly, the second innovation regards the theoretical dimension, i.e. the reference to the EU's set of formal and informal institutions and the decision to apply a selection (bits and pieces) of this *acquis* in another context, and it brings new — situated — cultural experiences to bear on these very bits and pieces of the *acquis*. It is argued that in order to understand the impact of this process, research needs to be sensitive to the cultural roots of hard and soft institutions, both in the context of the EU, and in the other, regional context. These cultural roots matter at both ends of the exchange, i.e. the receiving and the providing contexts. A reflexive approach allows for incorporating the interactive practices that contribute to norm generation (or institution building) in each context.

The conceptual challenge lies in bringing the sum of cultural experiences, including interactive norm generation in each context, to bear for the analysis of blueprinting. The stakes of this project are raised by variations of neo-institutionalism that have focused predominantly on formal institutions and their functional logics (Jenson and Merand 2010) and thus effectively contributed to almost editing out the complex interplay between contextualised and therefore regionally and locally distinct normative structures of meaning-in-use as carriers of socio-cultural experiences. To elaborate on this process, the following draws on reflexive approaches advanced by earlier research on European integration which has advanced the concept of the 'embedded *acquis communautaire*' (Wiener 1998; Merlingen *et al.* 2000). This reflexive perspective had been enabled by the constructivist turn in the 1990s. Recent calls for a more consistent focus on the political sociology of integration as opposed to studying 'formal organisations and a social norms' (Jenson and Merand 2010, 74) have picked up on the loose ends of this reflexive approach to European integration. This is in tune with the broader contextual approach that understands (1) norms as embedded in social and cultural contexts (Finnemore and Toope 2001); and (2) social interaction as norm-generative practices. The following understands institutions as bearing culturally distinct meaning. Accordingly, it is argued that in addition to the dimensions of formal validity and social recognition, the inter-national inter-active work of norms requires the additional focus on cultural validation (Wiener 2014). In sum, it is held that norm-diffusion research generally suffers from two central oversights. *First*, social constructivist approaches that consider norms as having a structuring impact on the behaviour of states miss out on the reflexive dimension of norms. This leads to a bracketing of negotiated normativity, and consequently, the normative quality of norms based on distinct degrees of moral reach that is ascribed to different 'types of norms' (Wiener 2008, 66; Bernstein and Coleman 2009; Park and Vetterlein 2010). Accordingly, the norm-generative focus on contestation is neglected. *Second*, work on norm diffusion tends to prioritise the spread of norms from the EU towards other areas over interactive negotiations involving the EU and other regions. In doing so, it is likely to reify the EU's set of values. Scrutinising these shortcomings offers the opportunity to reconstruct the normative change that actually does take place through interaction among a multiplicity of regional actors.

To that end, the following proceeds in three further sections. The *first* section lists a number of regional integration contexts in which norm transfer is observed. It points to selected cases of such norm transfer in order to demonstrate that global processes of regional integration do share references to norms, principles and institutional design. In some cases more than in others, a specific interest in learning from European experience is notable. This article's interest lies in raising a question about whether, and if so how, such learning has taken place at a region's own initiative, or whether normative adaptation was conducted in compliance with EU demands. While this article does not intend to provide an answer to this query, it takes the invitation to revive integration theories with recourse to the new sociology of knowledge as a starting point to explore two distinct research perspectives with a view to further empirical inquiry on the matter. A caveat applies with regard to the following, for, due to limited space in the context of this special issue, the following is restricted to the decidedly theoretical exploration of how to account for blueprinting. Section *two* then proceeds to critically review the approaches to norm transfer in the wake of the normative power Europe discussion, thereby paying particular notice to the focus of these approaches on processes and effects of inter-contextual reflection and inter-cultural learning. Based on this critical review, section *three* introduces the concept of strategic blueprinting as a reflexive alternative to prevailing approaches of norm diffusion. In the concluding section, the concept of blueprinting is recalled as a practice-based alternative to political and legal norm-diffusion of global governance theories on the one hand, and the normative-power approach, on the other.

Norm Transfer and Regional Integration

The two conceptually quite distinct perspectives on norm transfer which will be introduced in the following two sections (i.e. norm diffusion and strategic blueprinting) share an interest in developing a concise understanding of norm transfer from one polity to another. Thus, the literature on norm diffusion defines this process as *transplanting* norms by diffusion from the European inside towards other regions (i.e. following an EU-based strategy). In turn, the proposed alternative defines strategic *blueprinting* as fetching bits and pieces of the *acquis communautaire* in order to establish them within the constitutional or proto-constitutional framework of one's home region (i.e. following the strategic interests of regional politicians and policy-makers outside the EU). According to the new sociology-of-knowledge approach and its four leading principles, the distinct normative purpose and expectation, which need to be reconstructed in order to assess the potential impact of the respective norm transfer, stand to be identified by the following research questions that are to guide empirical research: Where is the norm transfer initiated (symmetry; inside/outside)? Who triggers the process (situatedness)? How is the transfer perceived within the receiving context — including both the immediate situation for example a specific organisational committee, and the wider societal context for example the national or regional context (contextualism; inside)?

Like transplanting, blueprinting begins by observing that reference to the EU's institutional and/or constitutional settings is made in contexts outside Europe. However, in contrast to the functional or utilitarian approaches of transplanting or diffusing norms, blueprinting involves a multiplicity of different actor constellations and therefore equally multi-directional power vectors. Rather than diffusing ideas — however useful they may seem to the receiver — blueprinting is conceptualised as an interactive practice. This implies that the normative meaning generated by the practice depends on the context in which the meaning-in-use is enacted. The result is to be 'read-off' at the receiving end. By reversing the direction, i.e. rather than assuming an EU interest in diffusing their legal order to others, it focuses on the interest in turning towards the EU for inspiration in the utterances of others. Research on blueprinting is distinct as it is interested in first, identifying the motivation of others to turn to Europe, and second, understanding how social practices that re-enact normative structures of meaning-in-use change the latter through adaptation. For, in the process, normative structures of meaning are both used (i.e. applied, copied, implemented or transferred) and changed (i.e. bestowed with meaning derived from experience and expectation).

The resulting structures of the respective normative orders elsewhere therefore reflect the interaction between the diverse repertoire of cultural experiences in the root contexts in which the EU's norms are embedded and the cultural experiences of the external context to which they have been incorporated. Both consist of complex normative structures of meaning-in-use that derive their meanings through a web of binary oppositions that are brought to bear through the practice of enacting *within* their respective contexts and *across* these contexts. This transfer of normative quality reflects the normative power potential of the EU in a way that remains undiscovered by both the normative-power approach and the norm-diffusion approach, respectively, as these approaches understand norm transfer as something which operates according to a centrifugal logic. Reflexive approaches to global constitutionalism turn this logic on its head by attributing an active part of the interaction to those looking 'in' on the EU's normative order from the outside. Accordingly, the outcome is to be *read off* the practice at the other end, outside the EU. It follows that while the interest in imitating aspects of the European normative order does confirm the appeal of that order to others, the practice of blueprinting reveals its — empowering — effect. To assess the latter, more detailed empirical research is required. It cannot be predicted by normative theory, but should rely on both, normative and empirical research, i.e. applying a *bifocal* approach.

To do this, it is helpful to distinguish two types of interaction as part of the practice of blueprinting. The *first type* includes other regional organisations such as Mercosur, the African Union (AU), the BRICS (Brazil, Russia, India, China, South Africa), ASEAN or NAFTA (North Atlantic Free Trade Area) that seek to establish organisational settings which are similar to the EU. These actors compare their *institutional settings* to the EU's institutions and then decide to copy the EU's formal institutions, such as the political organs i.e. the Parliament, the Council, the Commission or the courts. The *second type* refers to international organisations such as the World Trade Organisation (WTO), the United Nations (UN) or NATO (North Atlantic Treaty Organisation) that have adopted core constitutional principles and norms which are central to the EU's *constitutional setting* or vice versa. This perspective has generated research by scholars, who compared the role *courts* play in the EU with their role in other regional bodies (De Búrca and Weiler 2012) or how the neo-Kantian *regulatory ideal* could be made to work in other organisational contexts (Fossum and Menéndez 2011).

The following illustrates how blueprinting strategies may differ according to either the purpose of adding organisational details to an existing regional organisation, or incorporating constitutional norms in a constitutional context.[2] To that end, the following presents a selection of potential empirical studies of regional organisations to address the research objective of blueprinting and the two questions of *first*, what was the motivation to turn to the EU's normative order?, and *second*, how did the transfer of parts of that order play out with regard to the situated structures of normative meaning-in-use? Given the interest in blueprinting normative order from the perspective of contexts outside of the EU, the following stresses the relevance of processes of constitution building in post-revolutionary settings. In these settings, the main focus is set on fundamental constitutional norms (type 1) such as democracy, the rule of law, human rights and citizenship. The assumption is that the attraction of the EU's constitutional setting stems from its experience with unbound constitutionalism, i.e. the development of constitutional quality that is not state-bound. To indicate the terrain for follow-up research, the selected examples of regional organisations are intended to illustrate the range of different locations from which an interest in the EU's *acquis* has been expressed.

The *first* turns to a range of non-European regional organisations. While there are plenty other regional organisations, the following turns to recent examples where regional actors made explicit reference to bits and pieces of the EU normative order. In all selected cases, a move towards creating a *community* rather than a mere treaty organisation or conference is notable. Among them is the 'Mercado Comun del Sur', the South American union of states which is commonly known as 'Mercosur', and which was founded in 1994 in the city of Asuncion by four countries (Uruguay, Argentina, Brazil and Paraguay) by the Treaty of Asuncion. The main goal of this union was to enhance economic progress and to improve social justice (Tratado, 1994, 1). In 2014, Mercosur established formal political bodies, some of which follow the EU's model, for example, the Parliament, which was inaugurated in 2006. However, in contrast to the EU, in the Mercosur context, the Parliament remained without political power. While the underlying principle does focus on promoting democracy, in the absence of the principle of voting rights for Mercosur citizens (as a community of citizens), rather than for citizens of each member state, the Parliament remains more of an advisory body.[3] Another South American organisation, the Court of Justice of the Andean Community (original Spanish name of the organisation: Tribunal de Justicia de la Comunidad Andina, TJCA) was founded as the 'Court of Justice of the Cartagena Agreement and was then renamed and modified in 1996 by the Protocol of Trujillo to interpret, enforce, and settle disputes arising from Community law.'[4] It has been analysed as being 'explicitly' modelled 'on the ECJ (i.e. the European Court of Justice, AW)' (Alter *et al.* 2012, 631). To assess the underlying strategy from a sociology of knowledge perspective, empirical research would want to reconstruct the Court's set-up on the basis of document research, expert interviews and expressive interviews in order to reconstruct the strategies underlying the founding decisions as well as the long-term effects of the transfer of bits and pieces of the *acquis communautaire* from the EU into the Andean region.

In Asia, in turn, the 'ASEAN Economic Community' (AEC) still stands to be established in 2015. It builds on the ten former ASEAN member states in order to develop an economic community based on the principle of free movement, which represents the founding principle of the European Economic Communities (EEC) as the precursor of the EU. Yet, while the prospect of a common market based on the principle of free movement of labour, goods and capital is the principal first step, in 2012 Najib Razak, the Malaysian Prime Minister, envisions democracy and peace to follow. As he notes,

> (C)ommon markets require common rules and independent decision-making bodies, which contribute to the improvement of governance. Similar to the European project's support for smaller member states' development towards mature democracies, the AEC will be able to strengthen institutions and support good governance in our region.[5]

While referring to the EU's successful common market-building principles, Razak cautions: 'Of course, Asia is not Europe. Our implementation of a single market will necessarily differ. But the fundamental principles behind free trade are the same wherever you are in the world.'[6] At the time of the EU's struggle with countering the financial crisis, the envisioned progressive integration from economic to political union, and the promise of democracy and peace comes with a grain of salt: for while the perception of the sequence of integrative steps persists, the threat of the problems currently experienced in the EU invites to careful re-assessment. In this sense, the prospective AEC will be able to benefit from the EU's experience by making careful choices of which integrative steps to copy and how. It is here that the concept of blueprinting allows for a reflexive approach to norm transfer. The new Asian organisation builds on its forerunner, ASEAN, and 'blueprints' from them to begin with. As the AEC website states:

> The ASEAN leaders adopted the ASEAN Economic Blueprint at the 13th ASEAN Summit on 20 November 2007 in Singapore to serve as a coherent master plan guiding the establishment of the ASEAN Economic Community 2015.[7]

However, the decision in favour of further integration, which led to the founding of the AEC, does build on the European experience and the promise of growth, wealth and democracy that it entails. As Razak notes,

> these may be well-known waters, but ASEAN's members will choose their own course. Based on the right approach, the AEC can build on the successes of the European project and learn from its experiences. My hope is that in the coming decades the people of South Asia be able to enjoy that wealth and peace which comes with closer economic cooperation. (Alter et al. 2012)

To turn to the third geopolitically important process of regional integration, in 1992 the Southern African Development Community (SADC) was founded through the transformation of the Southern African Development Co-ordination Conference (SADCC) as its forerunner. The SADCC was established in April 1980 by Governments of the nine Southern African countries of Angola, Botswana, Lesotho, Malawi, Mozambique, Swaziland, Tanzania, Zambia and Zimbabwe.[8] According to Schöman, regional organisation in South Africa was politically motivated (Schöman, 2001).[9]

> The SADCC or the conference was formed with four principal objectives, namely: (1) to reduce Member States' dependence, particularly, but not only, on apartheid South Africa; (2) to implement programmes and projects with national and regional impact; (3) to mobilise Member States' resources, in the quest for collective self-reliance; and (4) to secure international understanding and support. (Schöman 2001)

SADC and its Member States are expected to act according to the following principles:

- sovereign equality of all Member States;
- solidarity, peace and security;
- human rights, democracy, and the rule of law;
- equity, balance and mutual benefit; and
- peaceful settlement of disputes (Schöman 2001).

Notably, a number of unbound constitutional practices of the EU, such as the practice of regular 'summit' meetings as well as the introduction of the practice of sharing governance responsibility based on a 'troika' (i.e. applying a model that builds on collective experience), reveal a notable similarity with the EU's way of organising policy and politics of regional integration. Thus, the 'principal institutions of SADC' include a 'summit — made up of Heads of State and/or Government; the Summit is the ultimate policy-making institution of SADC'. The Summit is responsible for the overall policy direction and control of functions of the Community. It usually meets once a year around August/September in a Member State at which a new Chairperson and Deputy are elected. Under the new structure, it is recommended that the Summit meet twice a year. The current Chairperson of SADC is President Sam Nujoma of Namibia, and the Deputy Chairperson is President Bakili Muluzi of Malawi. More functions of the Summit are enumerated under Article 10 of the SADC Treaty (Schöman 2001). The 'troika — the extraordinary Summit decided to formalise the practice of a troika system consisting of the chair, incoming chair and the outgoing chair of SADC'. This system was established in August 1999. It includes that

> other Member States may be co-opted into the troika as and when necessary. This system has enabled the organisation to execute tasks and implement decisions expeditiously as well as provide policy direction to SADC institutions in the period between regular SADC

meetings. The troika system will operate at the level of the Summit, the Organ on Politics, Defence and Security, Council and Standing Committee of Senior Officials. (Schöman 2001)

In turn, the BRICS countries, Brazil, Russia, India, China and South Africa, which have become known as new 'emerging powers' (Nabers 2010; Nolte 2010), created an alternative institution to the UN's World Bank in order to rebalance the representation of states and support the creation of global justice. According to South Africa's finance minister, Pravin Gordhan,

(T)he roots of the World Bank and IMF still lie in the post-World-War-Two environment. The reforms that have taken place are still inadequate in terms of addressing the current environment. We still have a situation where certain parts of the world are over-represented.[10]

The World Bank and IMF continue to be dominated by America and Europe. And as Russia's Prime Minister Dmitry Medvedev said, the main point of the meeting was to show that 'the BRICS countries should create conditions for a more just world order'.[11]

Finally, another regional organisation, the African Union (AU), was founded by the *Constitutive Act (CA)* in 2001.[12] It is the follow-up organisation, which replaces the former Union of African States (UAS) and has currently 53 Member States. While European perspectives note that the AU has been conceived with an institutional setting and refers to a 'similar' set of values to the EU (Schmidt 2008, 1), a closer look at the distinctive embeddedness of these values reveals that the AU's normative order leads beyond 'copying' the institutional setting. This is particularly noticeable with regard to the active role that is bestowed on the 'people' as an actor in addition to 'states'. For example, it notes the 'participation of the African peoples in the activities of the Union' as a lead 'principle' (CA Article 4 (c)), and it details fundamental norms of legitimate intervention in its Member States when these are in breach with the African Charter of Human Rights and Peoples' Rights (see CA, Article 3 (h)); as well as the right of the 'Union to intervene in a Member State pursuant to a decision of the Assembly in respect of grave circumstances, namely: war crimes, genocide and crimes against humanity' (CA, Article 4 (h)).

The Normative Turn in European Integration and Its Practice *Lacuna*

Current European integration theories include three theoretical approaches that address normative change. They include, first, the *normative-power approach* that was kicked off by Manners a decade ago and has been thriving since as an alternative soft-power perspective to international relations theories' neo-realist perspectives; and second, the *norm-diffusion approach* that was developed in conjunction with the prospect of massive enlargement to the East. The third is *critical norms research* that was developed with reference to the constitutional debates in the EU and beyond, as one of several precursors — next to democratic theory and international law — to the new interdisciplinary theory of global constitutionalism. To scrutinise these with regard to the observed *lacuna* of 'practice', the following discusses the distinct ways in which these three approaches address normative change according to their respective tools. Given its focus on unbound constitutionalisation, the latter in particular is important for research that seeks to shed light on the choice and process of blueprinting bits and pieces of the EU's normative order. The following recalls reflexive roots that pre-empt the new sociology-of-knowledge approach as the core theoretical framework of the range of constructivist theories of European integration.

Constructivist research on *norms* facilitated a thriving norm-diffusion research culture, interested in compliance with the 1993 Copenhagen criteria that set the standards (i.e. type 3 norms) for massive eastern enlargement in 2004 (Schimmelfennig and Sedelmeier 2005), as well as the critical and/or consistent constructivist norm research agenda, which focused mainly on fundamental norms (i.e. type 1 norms) that were discussed in interdisciplinary research in the fields of international relations theories and international law. This section demonstrates how, despite constructivists' 'seizing the middle-ground' between positivist rational choice approaches and reflexive sociology-of-knowledge approaches (Adler 1997), 'limits of bridging the gap' prevailed (Wiener 2003). In sum, the 1990s' constructivist theories of European integration brought the ontological stress on ideas, identities, norms and language to the, by then, rather stale theoretical repertoire of grand theories to the table. This move followed the key argument of Berger and Luckmann's sociology of knowledge; that all knowledge is socially constructed, and that therefore interactive practices in context mattered for our understanding of European integration (Berger and Luckmann 1967). In the beginning, the key role of constructivist thought lay in providing a meta-theoretical move away from a baseline between realist and poststructuralist perception of the EU who had remained largely incommunicado. Constructivists then had an enabling function with regard to academic exchange about the leading questions, main concepts and methodological approaches that mattered for European integration theories. This communicative turn had a hugely informative impact on the entire discipline of European integration, for it made the discipline attractive to students and serious academic debate. Based on the tool-kit of the middle-ground, focused constructivists soon generated an impressive number of case studies.

Kratochwil's query about the way norms 'work' (Kratochwil 1984) was approached from increasingly different perspectives that resulted in three distinct constructivist strands: conventional constructivists were interested in pursuing the question of how norms influenced state behaviour; consistent constructivists studied the way new rules were set through speech acts, thus concentrating not so much on social practices as on discursive and strategic interventions to change the rules of the — political — game; and critical constructivists questioned the shared meaning of norms that remained invisible to behavioural and strategic studies, and therefore suggested making invisible meanings of norms accountable with reference to enacting normative structures of meaning-in-use and cultural repertoires.

Instead of engaging with the development of these three constructivist strands — that ultimately mattered more for the development of international relations theories than European integration studies — the remainder of this section points to the widening gap between positivist and normative approaches. This is because this quite noticeable gap in the literature matters most for understanding the EU's impact on the global normative order, and hence, the allocation of the practice *lacuna*.

On the one hand, the EU is portrayed as a norm-entrepreneur with long-term experience in diffusing norms to candidate countries, and subsequently, the power to facilitate norm diffusion to post-conflict areas so as to improve 'governance in areas of limited statehood' (Risse and Lehmkuhl 2007). This approach builds on the compliance, cooperation and governance literatures. On the other hand, the EU has been conceptualised as a 'normative power'; a rather more elusive civilisational force of sorts in the global realm (Manners 2002, 2013; Whitman 2013). At first sight, both approaches do have their merits, especially for European foreign offices that demand manuals for operations in post-conflict areas. Thus, the former diffusion approach offers relatively straight-forward fixes that take their central persuasive force from the compliance literature, while the latter normative-power approach paints a picture of the EU's soft-power as a civilised counterpart to the US and other hard powers. In particular, the latter approach has taken pains to develop a more sophisticated critical view of the transfer of norms, ideas and values from the EU to the global realm. Thus, Whitman notes that

(B)y distinguishing the concept of normative power from the previous discussions on military power (Bull 1982) and civilian power (Duchêne 1972), Manners placed the identity and nature of the Union into a different framework in which he aimed at replacing 'the state as the centre of concern' (Manners 2002, 236) and refocusing on the ideations and power of norms as the substantive basics of the EU studies. (Whitman 2013, 172)

While Whitman is right in stressing the importance of the shift of focus, this article contends that the potential of this normative perspective remains unexplored. This is largely due to leaving to one side the sociology-of-knowledge approach that lay at the centre of the erstwhile constructivist turn in European integration theories (Christiansen *et al.* 1999). That is, like the norm-diffusion approach, the normative-power approach ultimately operates according to the neo-Kantian regulative ideal of political organisation that is common to Western European nation-states and which rests on the underlying belief in the universality of Western European norms, ideas and values and their presumptive value-added elsewhere (Habermas 2011). By contrast, this article's shift towards the eyes of the beholder elaborates on the potential of norm-generative interaction as a key empirical indicator for studying the way norms work. For example, Manners describes the normative-power approach thus:

(T)he *contagion diffusion* of norms takes place through the diffusion of ideas between the EU and other global actors. An example of *pouvoir normatif* in action through contagion can be found in the ways in which ideas and means of regional integration have diffused between continents. Hence ideas such as the creation of a "common high authority", "four freedoms" and even "single currency" are seen in other regions of the world as being *worthy of imitation.* (Manners 2013, 315, emphasis added AW)

Just how precisely the process of 'imitation' works remains bracketed, and accordingly it is hard to see how empirical research would proceed in order to establish whether or not, and if so to what effect, 'contagion diffusion' unfolds. It appears that when authors refer — often critically — to Manners' 'normative power' concept, two perceptions dominate the literature. The first refers to 'Normative Power Europe (NPE)' as a concept that conceives the EU as appreciatively referred to from abroad, upon which ground it is considered as constitutive for a perception of the EU as a civilian as opposed to a military power (Manners 2002; Nicolaides and Whitman 2013). The second is Manners' own further development of the concept towards the 'normative-power approach' (NPA), which, in his more recent work, stresses the active role of the EU in the process of spreading European normative values and ideas (Sjursen 2006). The strategic normative-power approach is summarised by an understanding of 'others', such as ASEAN, the AU and MERCOSUR, as behaving like copycats. As Manners writes, '(C)ontagion diffusion relies on a number of mechanisms of imitation, emulation and mimicry/*mimétisme* including the persuasive attraction of ideas, as well as the prestige and status associated with regional integration organisations' (Sjursen 2006). While the NPA therefore does rely on a range of 'mechanisms' facilitating the actual incorporation of normative ideas elsewhere, its power results from a vector that is directed *away* from Europe. Its value added is thus mainly defined as a means towards the end of strategic power, in keeping with E. H. Carr's concept of power over opinion as hence 'power-over' others (Mearsheimer 2005, 139). In turn, the concept of blueprinting sheds light on the EU's normative order as having empowering potential.

Similar to the strategic normative-power approach, Alter holds that European institutions are 'emulated' or 'transplanted' from the EU to other non-European social contexts, which is demonstrated by accounting for 'copies' of the ECJ around the globe (Alter 2012; Alter *et al.* 2012). The rationale underlying this kind of copying is the attraction of the possibility of co-existing supranational institutions and domestic institutions that is demonstrated by the EU's example. As research about 'the consequences of copying a European supranational judicial institution' (Alter *et al.* 2012, 632) reveals, the notion of co-existing institutions — rather than the meanings attached to them — does not reveal the related change of normative meanings attached to these institutions when transferred to a different social environment. This is because this meaning is expected to be enmeshed with situated cultural repertoires, and therefore, it is expected to change as institutions become established and used by other actors elsewhere. This is confirmed by the findings, 'that copying the ECJ is selective rather than wholesale, which suggests that adapting a court to local legal and political contexts may be necessary for successful transplantation', and 'that importing a supranational judicial institution does not necessarily copy the institution's politics' (Alter *et al.* 2012, 633). The normative change of meaning-in-use that is triggered by copying institutions remains to be examined as 'the success of a transplant will depend on its ability to graft onto existing legal norms and practices' (Alter *et al.* 2012, 634, citing Watson 1976). Even though the approach is conscious of and careful with distinguishing the process from colonialist strategies, the approach ultimately advances an interest in transplanting judicial institutions. Its focus on the 'effectiveness of the imported legal order' (Alter et al. 2012, 635) puts its utilitarian motive on a par with Manners' normative-power approach.

To summarise, normative order has predominantly been studied with a focus on changing institutional and/or constitutional settings *inside* the EU or alternatively, change initiated *by* the EU vis-à-vis others so as to make others comply with the EU's normative settings. The latter is well demonstrated by the enlargement literature's focus on accession candidates and the normative foreign-policy literature. Both have laid the grounds for the norm-diffusion approach and the normative-order approach, respectively. In turn, this article's reflexive perspective on interactive contestations about norms and their impact on the global normative order views norm transfer from a different perspective. Following the assumption that norms are socially constructed and the normative theoretical claim that, in principle, norms must always be contestable by their addressees, critical constructivists have raised critical questions about the sustainable effects of norm diffusion. Studies have noted that compliance with norms detailed in the Copenhagen Agreement was not the standard behaviour, instead 'contested compliance' was observed (Wiener 2004; Lerch and Schwellnus 2006; Brosig 2012). And a new range of critical constructivist research, which benefitted from interdisciplinary exchanges with IR theories and international law, linked the way normative meaning-in-use was re-enacted in this process with changes of the global normative order.

Blueprinting Bits and Pieces of the *Acquis Communautaire*

Drawing on the reflexive approaches that benefit from the four principles advanced by the new sociology of knowledge, this final section suggests developing an interactive alternative to norm-diffusion approaches. It points out that, central to understanding its impact is that the practice of blueprinting is an ongoing (i.e. unfinished and ever-changing reference). That is, a norm that has been blueprinted will therefore never be fully adopted elsewhere. As it travels across cultural borders, it remains subject to 'translation' (Walker 2003). Importantly, a number of non-European actors have been engaged in copying some of the EU's political and legal structures. By doing so, they have contributed to bestowing the function of a 'blueprint' to the EU's normative order. As a political practice, blueprinting involves the conscious choice to copy an institutional and/or constitutional detail. As a social interaction, it extends beyond that decision and includes the process of approaching that detail in the European context of origin from the outside, transferring it to another outside destination, and enacting it according to the normative structure of meaning-in-use of that other context. This complex interactive process is analytically distinct from diffusing norms in various ways, for example through contagion by compliance mechanisms or by transplanting the norms. This is therefore advanced as an alternative conceptual approach to the concept of Europe as a 'normative power' that was triggered by Manners' erstwhile argument (Manners 2002, 2006, 2013; Sjursen 2006, 2007; Whitman 2013).

It is argued that the way in which norms, ideas and principles are incorporated from one context (e.g. the *acquis communautaire*) into another (e.g. the African Union's Constitutive Act) matters for the ultimate meaning that is attached to — and can therefore empirically be read off from — the respective norms. As critical norms research indicates, norm interpretation depends critically on the cultural background experience of those who enact a norm. As binary opposition analysis has shown, for example, even long-term EU Member States such as the United Kingdom and Germany reveal different interpretations of fundamental constitutional norms such as democracy, the rule of law and fundamental rights. Given these distinctly different interpretations among EU Member States with shared normative roots, it is expected that norm transfer between contexts in which cultural repertoires differ considerably more, the likelihood is much higher of conflictive norm implementation following the expectation of compliance with norms that are diffused from the EU centre to the periphery.

The concept of strategic blueprinting suggests that the EU's global political attraction stems from its unparalleled experience with building a quasi-constitutional framework of non-state polity. In the process, the EU established an embedded *acquis communautaire* including a considerable wealth of widely accepted constitutional norms, rules and regulations (Weiler 1999; Weiler and Wind 2003; De Búrca and Weiler 2012; compare Figure 1).

These bits and pieces of the *acquis* have proved attractive to others insofar as they carry a promise regarding the construction of their own constitutional blueprint of regional integration. The tool towards this process appears to be the strategic incorporation of bits and pieces of the *acquis* to their own specific contexts. That is, we observe an interactive incorporation of norms from the EU to other regions around the globe. This reference function of the EU's quasi-constitutional order works for two types of actors, including regional actors such as Mercosur, ASEAN, UNASUR or the African Union as well as other international organisations such as the WTO or the UN. Blueprinting comprises the strategic choice of incorporating bits and pieces from institutional and constitutional settings of other normative orders. This is based on the substantial assumption that norms entail a 'dual quality' (Wiener 2007). That is, they are constructed through practice while having a structuring impact on behaviour at the same time (Giddens 1979). Accordingly, no two normative structures are the same (compare the principles of situatedness and contextualism). This

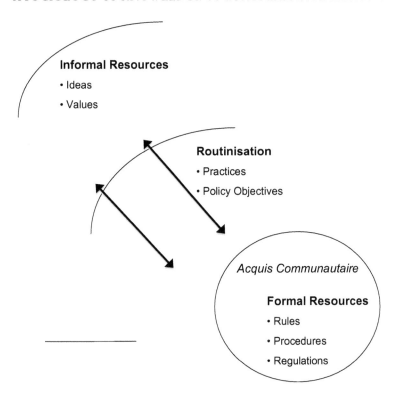

Figure 1. The embedded *acquis communautaire*
Source: Wiener (1998, 302).

insight was most prominently taken forward by Milliken's suggestion to examine inter-national interaction as the practice of re-/enacting 'normative structures of meaning-in-use' (Milliken 1999, 132). With this interactive conceptualisation of normative structures, Milliken recalled Derrida's societal sub-structures, which are used and put to work as inter-national interaction unfolds (Derrida 1976). The concept provides an empirical access point for ethno-methodological research that seeks to account for ways in which normative structures are both used *and* changed at the same time. Blueprinting indicates that by re-enacting normative structure 'A' in a context other than its root context, its substance is brought to interact with existing settings of a normative structure 'B'. It follows that, if others re-enact European normative structures through blueprinting, their own normative substance begins to incorporate a diverse repertoire of cultural experiences. These reflect both the norm-generative practices from the root context (A) and those of the target context (B).

Conclusion

As this article demonstrated, the strategy of blueprinting offers an alternative practice-based perspective on interregional norm transfer. It was argued that first, the socially constructed normative order of the EU entails a quite robust constitutional quality, and more importantly, second, as a normative order that is unbound from the state, the EU offers a reference frame for political re-orientation in post-conflict and/or post-revolutionary contexts. Accordingly, it was noted that the identification of socially recognised and culturally validated ground rules (type 2 norms) that could work as a common reference for political parties that stand to be integrated in post-revolutionary (or post-crisis) contexts, lies in *agreeing* on basic rules of procedure. It was argued that, while formal settings consisting of standardised norms (type 3) may be exported akin to the EU's enlargement *acquis*, the ways in which norms travel are not predictable, for the *acquis* of all polities is embedded within a larger context of ideas and routinised practices.

In other words, norms are always contingent and therefore contested all the way down. It is therefore key for empirical research to take into account that constitutional quality (expressed by the dominant constitutional narrative) develops through the process of re-/enacting normative meaning-in-use. That is, it depends on precisely what the involved constituent power makes of it. This implies establishing constitutional ground rules through contestatory politics all the way up rather than complying with expectations of the normative orders of others all the way down. For appropriateness develops exclusively through direct interaction with norms, even if these were blueprinted from institutional and/or constitutional settings elsewhere. In turn, this implies that blueprinting involves a change of the respective *local* normative structure of meaning as well as of the larger *global* normative order, as both are interrelated and therefore re-/enacted in the same process. It follows that blueprinting matters beyond the strategic interaction between regions elsewhere and Europe. The more interaction between regions, as well as between multiple constituent powers occurs on a global scale, the more change of normative global order can be expected. The normative global order's social recognition and political legitimacy is likely to rise with interactions between a plurality of constitutional orders worldwide.

Notes

1. For the adaptation of the 'new' sociology of knowledge, compare the argument developed by the introduction to this special issue (Adler-Nissen and Kropp 2015); for earlier notions of the sociology of knowledge compare the seminal work by Berger and Luckmann (1967), which has been the starting point for reflectivist approaches to European integration, and more generally, international relations theories (compare for example, Christiansen *et al.* 1999; Fierke and Jørgensen 2001).
2. Please note that more detailed substantiation of these illustrations remains to be facilitated by further empirical research for which this article is intended to set the framework approach, and which, therefore, leads beyond the purpose of this predominantly conceptual piece.
3. Compare, e.g. the assessment of *International Democracy Watch* (for details: http://www.internationaldemocracywatch.org/index.php/mercosur-parliament, accessed on 9 September 2014).
4. Compare IJRC at: http://www.ijrcenter.org/regional-communities/court-of-justice-of-the-andean-community/ (accessed on 9 September 2014).
5. See: 'Europe as an Example for Asia' in: *DIE ZEIT*, 5 November 2012, 258 (all translations from German original texts, AW).

6. See: Huffington Post, 6/11/2012 (http://www.huffingtonpost.co.uk/prime-minister-najib-razak/na jib-razak-learning-from-europe_b_2080744.html, accessed on 9 September 2012).
7. For details, see the AEC's website at: http://www.asean.org/communities/asean-economic-commu nity (accessed 26 August 2013).
8. For details, see AU's website: http://www.africa-union.org/root/au/recs/sadc.htm (accessed 27 August 2013).
9. Compare: http://www.alternative-regionalisms.org/wp-content/uploads/2009/07/schoemar_from sadcctosadc.pdf.
10. *The Guardian*, 28 March 2013.
11. *The Guardian*, 8 May 2013.
12. For details, see the AU's website: http://www.africa-union.org/root/au/aboutau/constitutive_act_en. htm (accessed on 3 July 2013).

References

Adler, E. 1997. Seizing the middle ground: constructivism in world politics. *European Journal of International Relations* 3, no. 3: 319–63.

Alter, K. 2012. The global spread of european style international courts: the experience of the Andean tribunal of justice. *West European Politics* 35, no. 1: 135–54.

Adler-Nissen, R., and K. Kropp. 2015. A sociology of knowledge approach to European Integration. *Journal of European Integration* 37, no. 2: 155–73.

Alter, K., L.A. Helfer, and O. Saldias. 2012. Transplanting the European court of justice: findings from the experience of the Andean tribunal of justice. *American Journal of Comparative Law* 60, no. 3: 629–64.

Berger, P.L., and T. Luckmann. 1967. *The social construction of reality: a treatise in the sociology of knowledge.* Anchor Books.

Bernstein, S., and W.D. Coleman (eds.). 2009. *Unsettled legitimacy: political community, power, and authority in a global era.* Vancouver: University of British Columbia Press.

Brosig, M. 2012. No space for constructivism? A critical appraisal of european compliance research. *Perspectives on European Politics and Society* 13, no. 4: 390–407.

Christiansen, T., K.E. Jørgensen, and A. Wiener. 1999. The social construction of Europe. *Journal of European Public Policy* 6, no. 4: 528–44.

Curtin, D. 1993. The constitutional structure of the union: a Europe of bits and pieces. *Common Market Law Review* 27: 709–39.

De Búrca, G., and J.H.H. Weiler (eds.). 2012. *The worlds of European constitutionalism.* Cambridge: Cambridge University Press.

Derrida, J. 1976. *Of grammatology.* Baltimore, MD: Johns Hopkins University Press.

Fierke, K.M., and K.E. Jørgensen (eds.). 2001. *Constructing international Relations: the next generation.* Armonk, NY: M.E. Sharpe.

Finnemore, M., and S.J. Toope. 2001. Alternatives to 'legalization': richer views of law and politics. *International Organization* 55, no. 3: 743–58.

Fossum, J.E., and A.J. Menéndez. 2011. *The constitution's gift: a constitutional theory for a democratic european union.* Plymouth: Rowman & Littlefield.

Gialdino, C.C. 1995. Some reflections on the acquis communautaire. *Common Market Law Review* 32: 1089–121.

Giddens, A. 1979. *Central problems in social theory.* Berkeley: University of California Press.

Habermas, J. 2011. *Zur Verfassung Europas. Ein Essay.* Frankfurt am Main: Suhrkamp Verlag.

Jenson, J., and F. Merand. 2010. Sociology, institutionalism and the European Union. *Comparative European Politics* 8, no. 1: 74–92.

Jørgensen, K.E. 1998. The social construction of the acquis communautaire. A cornerstone of the European Edifice. Paper read at International Studies Association. Minneapolis, MN. 17–21 March.

Kratochwil, F. 1984. The force of prescriptions. *International Organization* 38, no. 4: 685–708.

Lerch, M., and G. Schwellnus. 2006. Normative by nature? The role of coherence in justifying the EU's external human rights policy. *European Journal of Public Policy* 13, no. 2: 304–21.

Manners, I. 2002. Normative power Europe: a contradiction in terms?. *Journal of Common Market Studies* 40, no. 2: 235–58.

Manners, I. 2006. Normative power europe reconsidered: beyond the crossroads. *Journal of European Public Policy* 13, no. 2: 182–99.

Manners, I. 2013. Assessing the decennial, reassessing the global: understanding European Union normative power in global politics. *Cooperation and Conflict* 48, no. 2: 304–29.

Mearsheimer, J.J. 2005. E H Carr vs idealism: the battle rages on. *International Relations* 19, no. 2: 139–52.

Merlingen, M., C. Mudde, and U. Sedelmeier. 2000. Constitutional politics and the 'Embedded Acquis Communautaire': the case of the EU fourteen against the Austrian Government. *Constitutionalism Web-Papers, ConWEB*, 17 pp. *ConWEB*. http://www.qub.ac.uk/ies/onlinepapers/const.html (accessed April 2000).

Michalski, A., and H. Wallace. 1992. *The European community: the challenge of enlargement.* London: Royal Institute of International Affairs.

Milliken, J. 1999. The study of discourse in international relations: a critique of research and methods. *European Journal of International Relations* 5, no. 2: 225–54.

Nabers, D. 2010. Power, leadership, and hegemony in international politics: the case of East Asia. Review of International Studies 36, no. 4: 931–49.

Nicolaïdis, K., and R.G. Whitman. 2013. Preface, special issue. *Cooperation and Conflict* 48, no. 2: 167–70.

Nolte, D. 2010. How to compare regional powers: analytical concepts and research topics. *Review of International Studies* 36, no. 4: 881–901.

Park, S., and A. Vetterlein. 2010. *Owning development: creating global policy norms in the IMF and the world bank.* Cambridge: CUP.

Risse, T., and U. Lehmkuhl (eds.). 2007. *Regieren ohne Staat? Governance in Raeumen begrenzter Staatlichkeit.* Baden-Baden: Nomos.

Schimmelfennig, F., and U. Sedelmeier (eds.). 2005. *The politics of European Union enlargement: theoretical approaches.* London: Routledge.

Schmidt, S. 2008. *Die EU als Retterin der AU?, Working Paper Series GIGA Focus - Afrika,* 5, http://www.giga-hamburg.de/dl/download.php?d=/content/publikationen/pdf/gf_afrika_0805.pdf.

Schöman, M. 2001. From SADCC to SADC and beyond: the politics of economic integration. Analysis on regional integration - Africa, http://www.alternative-regionalisms.org/wp-content/uploads/2009/07/schoemar_fromsadcctosadc (accessed 13 January 2015).

Sjursen, H. 2006. What kind of power? *Journal of European Public Policy* 13, no. 2: 169–81.

Sjursen, H. 2007. 'Doing good' in the world? Reconsidering the basis of the research agenda on the EU's foreign and security policy. *RECON Online Working Paper 2007/09.*

Tratado. 1994. *Tratado de Asuncion 1991.* http://www.rau.edu.uy/mercosur/tratasp.htm (accessed 5 December 2014).

Vauchez, A. 2015. Methodological europeanism at the cradle: eur-lex, the Acquis and the making of Europe's cognitive equipment. *Journal of European Integration* 37, no. 2: 193–210.

Walker, N. 2003. Postnational constitutionalism and the problem of translation. In *European constitutionalism beyond the state,* eds. J.H.H. Weiler and M. Wind, 27–54. Cambridge: Cambridge University Press.

Weiler, J.H.H. 1999. *The constitution of Europe. 'Do the new clothes have an emperor?' and other essays on European integration.* Cambridge: Cambridge University Press.

Weiler, J.H.H., and M. Wind (eds.). 2003. *European constitutionalism beyond the state.* Cambridge: CUP.

Whitman, R.G. 2013. The neo-normative turn in theorising the EU's international presence. *Cooperation and Conflict* 48, no. 2: 171–93.

Wiener, A. 1998. The embedded acquis communautaire: Transmission belt and prism of new governance. *European Law Journal* 4, no. 3: 294–315.

Wiener, A. 2003. Constructivism: the limits of bridging gaps. *Journal of International Relations and Development* 6, no. 3: 252–75.

Wiener, A. 2004. Contested compliance: interventions on the normative structure of world politics. *European Journal of International Relations* 10, no. 2: 189–234.

Wiener, A. 2007. The dual quality of norms and governance beyond the state: sociological and normative approaches to interaction. *Critical Review of International Social and Political Philosophy* 10, no. 1: 47–69.

Wiener, A. 2008. *The invisible constitution of politics: contested norms and international encounters.* Cambridge: Cambridge University Press.

Wiener, A. 2014. *A theory of contestation.* London: Springer.

The Euro Crisis' Theory Effect: Northern Saints, Southern Sinners, and the Demise of the Eurobond

MATTHIAS MATTHIJS* & KATHLEEN MCNAMARA**

*International Political Economy, Johns Hopkins University – SAIS, Washington, DC, USA;
**Government and Foreign Service, Georgetown University, Mortara Center for International Studies, Washington, DC, USA

ABSTRACT Of the multiple narratives EU policymakers could have chosen at the onset of the euro crisis, why did austerity and structural reform win out over other plausible cures for member states' problems? Arguably, sovereign debt pooling or more federalized economic governance would have been a solution to member states' national deficits and competitiveness woes. To understand this puzzle, we draw on the sociology of knowledge literature. We argue that the response to the euro crisis was heavily informed by broader social logics that constructed the problem and the solution heavily toward ordoliberal and neoliberal ideas. Mapping the fate of the Eurobond proposals allows us to trace the complex entanglement of economic policy-making and parse out the ways in which social realities are shaped to make particular policy choices seem inevitable, even as they are themselves the product of social processes.

Introduction: Northern Saints and Southern Sinners

Of the multiple narratives EU policymakers could have chosen at the onset of the euro crisis, why did austerity and structural reform win out over other plausible cures for member states' problems? Arguably, sovereign debt pooling or more federalized economic governance would have been a solution to member states' national deficits and competitiveness woes. The austerity-cum-reform narrative fueled the insistence by Northern lenders and politicians for policies that overwhelmingly emphasized the slashing of public spending in the periphery, joined with politically tough reforms meant to make markets more efficient for future business and investment. Swift implementation of those policies, the argument went, would produce both fiscal discipline and labor market flexibility, and the crisis would gradually go away (Matthijs 2014a, 211–4).

Yet the winning narrative and subsequent set of policy prescriptions is puzzling since the 'fiscal sin' explanation only really worked in the case of Greece and did not fit the facts on the ground in Ireland, Portugal, or Spain, let alone Italy. Plausible systemic counter-narratives of what went wrong included the Eurozone's lack of supporting economic governance institutions, or the pressures of persistent trade and financial imbalances, yet neither of those would end up driving the debate, nor the solutions offered. Most strikingly, by far, the most potentially efficacious alternative solution to the euro's woes — the introduction and joint issuance of a common debt instrument or 'Eurobond' — received only lukewarm support.

To understand this puzzle, we draw on the emerging literature on the sociology of knowledge to argue that the response to the euro crisis was heavily informed by broader social logics. These social logics constructed the problem, and the solution, toward ordoliberal (austerity combined with the adherence to strict fiscal rules) and neoliberal (emphasis on structural reform) ideas. The dominant analysis of the crisis was shaped by academics, think tanks, private and public sector actors, specifically German economists and powerful business and financial interests, whose ideas had long underwritten the euro's institutional design at Maastricht and Amsterdam during the euro's formative decade. Berlin, Frankfurt, and Brussels early on fashioned the crisis into a 'normative' morality tale of Southern profligacy vs. Northern thrift.

Rather than correct the institutional flaws in the euro's design and build the necessary fiscal, financial, and political unions, leaders doubled down on a story of Northern Saints and Southern Sinners. Political efforts focused on a strengthened Stability and Growth Pact with quasi-constitutional balanced budget rules, a European Central Bank still mainly focused on price stability and only conditionally acting as a lender of last resort, a half-house banking union without common deposit insurance or a Europe-wide fiscal backstop, and a 'tough love' combination of austerity and reform in the Eurozone periphery. These wholesale reforms have not yet succeeded and may never do so given political pushback and institutional stickiness of the varieties of capitalism found across Europe (Hall 2014). Yet, the emphasis on fiscal austerity over economic governance has already been highly consequential for the everyday lives of Southern Europeans. Austerity policies have slowed economic growth and exacerbated unemployment in the wake of the financial crisis and have fueled a host of anti-Europe parties across the European Union (Matthijs 2014b). These effects were put on display during the Eurosceptic assault on Brussels in the May 2014 elections for a new European Parliament. Voters openly questioned the EU's democratic legitimacy and underscored their fundamental lack of trust in EU institutions.

Our argument is that the dominant euro crisis narrative, and its deleterious effects, was not the logical result of inexorable functionalist pressures that dictated austerity as the only answer to the Eurozone's ills. Instead, the putative answers to the crisis arose out of deeply entrenched social structures that informed economic debates, privileging certain definitions and solutions over others. These social structures were generated out of the interaction of academic theorists with a broader world of bankers, investors, government officials, and others with high stakes in the outcome of the euro crisis. As such, the euro crisis narrative both demonstrates the permeability of the internal/external divide between these worlds, and maps the role of power infusing those social structures.

The adoption of the path of austerity, or alternatively the building of a set of European level governance institutions, had major and divergent distributional consequences. As such, the ideas were informed by, but not directly a product of, the various material interests at play. As the editors of this special issue remind us, the field of economics is 'a discipline that helped to develop not only economic theories promoting harmonization of the single market and the establishment of the EMU, but also participating in their legitimation and sometimes gaining from their establishment in practice' (Adler-Nissen and Kropp 2015). When the tsunami of the global financial crisis revealed the shortcomings in Europe's EMU, once again the academic and policy worlds collided to shift the debate in one particular direction.

To make our case, the article proceeds as follows. We first draw on the editors' introduction and the volume's overall themes to frame the entanglement of economic policy-making in theoretical terms and illustrate how academic ideas both serve and structure reality. We then briefly assess how the euro problem was defined early on and how the debate was structured, in both Berlin and Brussels, toward fiscal austerity and domestic reforms. Our empirical evaluation then takes up Adler-Nissen and Kropp's call for analytic symmetry by examining why the alternative solution of a Eurobond failed to take hold, with its advocates unable to change minds in Berlin. Mapping the fate of the Eurobond proposals allows us to trace the entanglement of economic policy-making and parse out the ways in which social realities are shaped to make particular policy choices seem inevitable — when they in fact are the product of social processes. We then conclude with a discussion of what the euro crisis' theory effect portends for the study of European integration.

The Entanglement of Economic Policy-making

As with other policy arenas investigated in this journal's special issue, macroeconomic policy is deeply intertwined with certain academic fields of study, most centrally economics, while surprisingly disconnected from others that may seem intuitively appropriate interlocutors. This entanglement is a mutually constitutive interaction with reciprocal causality between the academy and the policy world. Academic ideas may drive policy developments, but social scientists' ideas are in turn often prompted and conditioned by real-world problems. Policy challenges, political realities, and material interests are present in both diffuse and specific ways, even as academic ideas (misleadingly) appear to be developing in their own sphere.

The concept of entanglement opens up the trajectory of response to the Eurozone crisis to a series of important questions. How did the analyses favored by the most powerful private and public actors — be they financial interests, central bankers, German politicians, or EU policymakers — intersect with academic analyses? Who has been successful in exerting definitional monopoly and conceptual legitimacy over the conversation about how to solve the Eurozone crisis? We answer these questions by mapping a specific policy debate, that over the potential introduction of Eurobonds. Eurobonds were a plausible functional response to the ills that plagued Europe's monetary union, yet they were set aside in favor of policies of austerity and structural reform, even as they arguably made the problem worse. Telling the story of the rise and fall of Eurobonds allows us to understand the entanglement of economic policy-making around the euro, a project at the heart of European integration and critical to its future path. But first, we sketch out more precisely our theoretical framework.

How Academic Ideas Serve and Structure Reality

Our analysis begins with a focus on the social production of knowledge and its impact through actors and shared meanings on EU outcomes. In the introduction to this special issue, the editors emphasize the need to reject the internal/external division of theory vs. practice and to instead locate the study of policy-making in terms of the situatedness and contextualism that exists in any realm of academic inquiry (Adler-Nissen and Kropp 2015). To do this, we first note that the arena of European macroeconomic policy can be characterized in terms of Bourdieu's classic notion of a field (Bourdieu 1993). A field, as Mudge and Vauchez write, is a 'system of relations in which actors struggle over political authority, partly in the form of authority over policy agendas and governing bureaucracies' (Mudge and Vauchez 2012, 455). This view rejects the notion that there is a set of atomistic actors individually discovering the truth regarding the workings of markets in general, or the euro in particular. Instead, the field perspective portrays the arena in which scholarly work is performed and generated regarding knotty problems of monetary, exchange rate, fiscal, and banking policy as a delineated social structure. This social structure is made up of actors whose positions vis-à-vis each other and whose ideas themselves become power resources in the broader world. Lawyers developing international legal norms, environmental scientists working on climate change, or trade economists developing rules around anti-dumping all work in fields intimately connected to the systems of professions in which they are trained and socialized (Abbott 1988).

Such fields will inevitably be structured so that one dominant set of actors will acquire a definitional monopoly over the issue at hand. This monopoly is centered on the ability to construct the problem in a certain way, to define the issues at hand as well as their solutions. In the case of the euro crisis, this power was critical in legitimating social divisions of the Eurozone world into the sober orthodox saints — primarily Germany, but also Finland, Austria, and the Netherlands — and the profligate 'PIIGS' — Portugal, Ireland, Italy, Greece, and Spain. Such segmenting, categorizing, and classifying can then become a potent power resource for actors outside the academy who want to structure the discourse toward a specific outcome and adopt the legitimated tropes from the professional field (Bourdieu 1984, 1993; Foucault 1977).

The monopoly over the construction of the problem arises from 'social movement-like processes in which institutional entrepreneurs mobilize cultural frames — often in response to some real or perceived crisis — in order to initiate, reinvigorate, or redirect Europe building' (Mudge and Vauchez 2012, 454). We will see in examining the Eurozone crisis discourse that these cultural frames tie together the scholarly and the policy world in important ways, as actors undertake the entrepreneurial manipulation of meanings, and the symbolic production and valuation of particular frames over others. For example, concepts that seem self-evident (such as 'the market,' 'financial sobriety,' or 'economic health') are actually not stable and fixed through time, but rather objects of action whose meanings are contingent on the particular cultural frame and social setting (Fourcade 2009; Knorr Cetina and Preda 2005; Zelizer 1994).

The Co-production of Knowledge

A parallel set of investigations in the field of Science and Technology Studies (S&TS) deepens our understanding of social fields by zeroing in on the co-production of knowledge in particular political and cultural formations, as 'the ways we know and represent the world are inseparable from the ways in which we choose to live in it' (Jasanoff 2004, 2). This approach reminds us that 'scientific knowledge is not a transcendent mirror of reality. It both embeds and is embedded in social practices, identities, norms, conventions, discourses, instruments, and institutions — in short, in all the building blocks of what we term the *social*' (Jasanoff 2004, 3). A stylized model of the co-production of knowledge flows forward in four steps: (1) the emergence and stabilization of new objects or phenomena, which involves the recognizing, naming, and marking off from other phenomena; (2) the framing and resolution of controversy; (3) the intelligibility and portability of products of science and technology or knowledge, which implicates the standardization of measures and tools; and finally (4) cultural practices of science and technology that endow their products with legitimacy and meaning in an 'enculturation of scientific practices' (Jasanoff 2004). We will see this process playing out in the debates around the euro crisis, shaping the outcome away from Eurobonds and toward austerity and reform.

Fields and the co-production of knowledge within particular cultural and political settings combine to produce what the editors of this special issue have called the 'theory effect.' With the theory effect, a particular vision of the social world transforms that world, as practices conform to the representation advanced in the theory (MacKenzie 2006; Mudge and Vauchez 2012). Theories get performed by actors and call into being the very thing they seem to merely represent (Butler 1993). Although many political scientists have explored the impact that particular ideas of agents have on outcomes (Berman 1998; Blyth 2002; Matthijs 2011; McNamara 1998; Parsons 2003), here we are arguing something different. Instead of ideas, we focus on more fundamental social structures encompassing agents that define the terms of the debate, legitimate certain frames over others and create 'the given' while defining away the unthinkable.

The literature on the co-production of social knowledge mined in this special issue can help us construct an analytical framework for understanding the path of the Eurozone crisis debate. In particular, it helps explain the social construction of saints and sinners during the crisis and the ways in which the academic analysis was entangled with the very real material and political interests at play. Rather than seeing material logics and social logics as competing explanations, we argue for an interaction of the two logics in the field of economic policy-making. Only then, can we fully explain the Northern saints' insistence on policies of domestic austerity and reform for the Southern sinner states of Europe, instead of policies that would have built a comprehensive system of European governance to frame the single currency, with Eurobonds as its centerpiece.

Below we offer an empirical analysis of the euro crisis debate in Germany and its entanglement between the scholarly and the political worlds, demonstrating how fields and the co-production of knowledge led to the legitimation and the adoption of particular ways of diagnosing the crisis. Those policies have put Europe on a path that pushes the Southern European states toward a German model of economic institutions. This in turn creates a politically combustible set of economic hardships and a contentious rhetoric of saints and sinners, both of which are fraying the European integration project. Rather than seeing this outcome as the inevitable result of the laws of economics, we should more correctly understand it in terms of an actual theory effect: the favoring of the austerity and reform narrative at the national level over one emphasizing the need for Eurobonds, economic governance, and institutional embeddedness at the European level (Matthijs and Blyth 2015a; McNamara 2015).

The Structuring of the Euro Crisis Debate

Why did the chosen strategies for coping with the Eurozone crisis take the shape they did? Why were the national solutions of fiscal austerity and structural reform chosen over the systemic solution of a Eurobond and debt pooling, which could have been the precursor of a more federal economic government for the single currency? In process tracing the narrative that evolved over time during the euro crisis, we focus on the path the debate over Eurobonds took in terms of the model of co-production of knowledge that weaves through the micro histories of individual scholars and policy-makers, as well as the role of Germany's ordoliberal tradition and stability culture in shaping the field of economics and the understanding of monetary unions. Academic economists and think tank public intellectuals established a foundation for the narrative, but there were key points or critical junctures in which the debate could have gone a different way.

The myriad explanatory narratives of the Eurozone debt crisis emerged in a process of recognition, naming, and marking off from other phenomena that split between largely systemic accounts and mainly national accounts. The systemic solutions would have the single currency more fully embedded in common social and political institutions allowing for market stability (Polanyi 2001). National accounts, on the other hand, focused on failings within the individual member states and thereby turned the euro crisis narrative into a 'morality tale' (Fourcade 2013). Hard work, prudent savings, moderate consumption, wage restraint, and fiscal stability in Germany were seen as Northern virtues and were juxtaposed to the Southern vices of low competitiveness, meager savings, undeserved consumption, inflated wages, and fiscal profligacy in the Mediterranean. The solution to the crisis accordingly became one of 'necessary' pain and atonement in the countries of the periphery. This strategy would force the Eurozone as a whole onto a path toward some kind of *Modell Deutschland* writ large, by making wage and price flexibility in the periphery into the main shock absorbers during future crises (Matthijs and Blyth 2015a).

The debate over Eurobonds should be seen within this ideational context: Berlin's rejection of 'systemic' Eurobonds — due to the risk of moral hazard — was framed in such a way as to further strengthen the case for 'national' austerity: you cannot keep throwing more good money after bad (Newman 2015). Early support for austerity and structural reform in Germany as a solution to the Greek crisis, and later to the Eurozone debt crisis overall after contagion set in to the rest of the periphery, spread across the public sphere and the German establishment's steadfast and enduring rejection of Eurobonds as a 'quick fix' to the debt crisis held firm. The legacy of German orthodoxy underlined not only the permeability of the internal/external divide between academia and policy, but also the key role of 'contextualism,' i.e. the German cultural disposition toward a certain way of seeing the crisis and therefore its potential solutions.

The fact that several key actors in favor of Eurobonds were present in Brussels and elsewhere in Europe did not prove to be enough to tilt the debate in the field in favor of the European level solution. The arguments in favor of Eurobonds may have gotten a favorable hearing with the European Commission and, to some extent, the European Council, they would never get the upper hand in Berlin (Matthijs and Blyth 2015b). Instead, German thinkers, opinion writers, and policymakers played a pivotal role in making the diagnosis of the euro's ills as well as in stipulating its cure, framing and ultimately 'resolving' the crisis (Jacoby 2015; Newman 2015).

German power in this process was not simply material but also ideational. German Finance Minister Schäuble put his government's view most rigidly in an opinion piece in the Financial Times with the title 'Why austerity is only cure for the Eurozone.' In it, he wrote: 'it is an indisputable fact that excessive state spending has led to unsustainable levels of debt and deficits that now threaten our economic welfare. Piling on more debt now will stunt rather than stimulate growth in the long run. Governments in and beyond the Eurozone need not just commit to fiscal consolidation and improved competitiveness — they need to start delivering on these now' (Schäuble 2011). By favoring the 'positive' causes of fiscal profligacy and lack of competitiveness over others and by stressing the risk of moral hazard in throwing ever more good money after bad, the narrative was structured in such a way that European or federal level solutions, most notably Eurobonds, were off the table. But, did it have to be that way?

Why No Eurobonds? Defining, Resolving and Legitimating Austerity

While Merkel initially dug in her heels in December 2009 over fiscal austerity and structural reform, affirming in a press conference that 'Greece must accept its responsibility for reform,' and again in February 2010, when she reiterated her government's well-known mantra that the rules must be followed, it soon became clear that reform in Athens alone was not going to make the Greek problem go away (Jones 2010b, 21). Fears of contagion to the rest of the Eurozone periphery — including Ireland and Portugal, but also Spain and Italy — started to haunt sovereign bond traders and financial market participants. A systemic solution to the Greek predicament would be essential if Brussels was to avoid a bond market run and safeguard the overall integrity of the euro. However, the cultural foundations for such a systemic solution were not necessarily in place, as a survey of the key voices in the Eurobond debate makes clear.

Early Proposals for Eurobonds

While the history of European monetary union has been marked by an emphasis on German ordoliberal and Anglo-Saxon neoliberal policy consensus (McNamara 1998), the field that structured the euro crisis debate included some dissenting voices that gained legitimacy from the seemingly endless rounds of financial contagion sweeping over Europe. Over the course of the Greek crisis, between September 2009 and June 2010, there had been a series of independent policy proposals by at least three different think tanks to establish a common debt instrument — a Eurobond — that could strengthen the overall macroeconomic governance framework of the Eurozone. John Springford, a researcher at the British liberal think tank *Centre Forum* trained in international relations and economic history, was the first to launch the idea of a common Eurozone bond as a way to strengthen the flawed Stability and Growth Pact, but the idea was seen as premature at the time and not picked up in policy circles (Springford 2009).

In March 2010, in a policy brief for the Italian think tank ISPI or *Instituto per gli Studi di Politica Internazionale*, the US-born political economist Erik Jones, based at Johns Hopkins University's Bologna Center in Italy, launched another Eurobond proposal 'to promote stability and liquidity while preventing moral hazard' (Jones 2010a). Jones was primarily concerned with the flight to safety out of Greek bond markets into other mainly Northern European bond markets, which only aggravated Athens' liquidity problems. A Eurozone bond would guarantee that investors could swap one set of 'national' Greek obligations for another set of Greek 'Eurobonds' — underwritten by the Eurozone as a whole — thereby keeping capital in Greece and avoiding a liquidity crisis and slow moving bank run in the struggling member state.

The Eurobond proposal that got by far the most attention was the one suggested by two researchers at Bruegel, the influential Brussels-based economics think tank. Bruegel has a broad funding base that includes subscriptions from most of the EU states, major multinational corporations such as Deutsche Bank, Google, and Novartis, and large project-based grants from the EU itself, among others. The researchers' professional pedigrees also reflected a broad intellectual profile, with Jacques Delpla holding a French masters in economics with experience in private banking and the French Finance Ministry and Jakob von Weizsäcker, a former World Banker as well as venture capitalist, who received higher degrees in economics and physics from France. Their outsider views of what to do about the crisis were tempered by the insider position of Bruegel in the field of European economic policy-making.

Bruegel's 'Blue Bond Proposal' addressed the common German concern of moral hazard by making the case for the introduction of two types of sovereign debt in the Eurozone: blue bonds and red bonds. The senior 'blue bonds' of up to 60 percent of GDP for each member state would pool sovereign debt among participating countries and be issued under joint and several liability, while the junior 'red bonds' would keep debt in excess of 60 percent of GDP as a purely national responsibility. Any national red debt beyond a country's blue debt would have clear procedures for default, which would increase the marginal cost of public borrowing. As red debt would remain the sole responsibility of the member state, this would further enhance fiscal discipline, as financial markets would surely want a significant interest premium to buy those riskier bonds (Delpla and von Weizsäcker 2010).

Delpla and von Weizsäcker further suggested the establishment of a so-called 'Independent Stability Council' for the Eurozone with representatives of national parliaments to oversee the annual allocation of blue bonds and to uphold member states' fiscal responsibility. The authors of what became known as the 'Bruegel Proposal' went out of their way to emphasize that this was not meant to be a quick fix. Instead, they saw blue bonds as an incentive-based and sustainable way out of the Eurozone's sovereign debt crisis that would 'prepare the ground for the rise of the euro as an important reserve currency, which could reduce borrowing costs for everybody involved' (Delpla and von Weizsäcker 2010). For them, it was win–win. Smaller Northern member state countries, such as Finland and Austria, would gain from the higher levels of liquidity of the blue bond, while Southern member states with high existing levels of sovereign debt, such as Italy and Greece, would have a strong incentive for fiscal adjustment. Europe as a whole would become a more attractive place to invest, as the blue bonds would be equally attractive safe havens as United States treasury bills.

Both Delpla and von Weiszäcker came from backgrounds not based in the orthodox doctoral study of economics. Having had experience in international organizations, private banking, and both the French and German finance ministries, had socialized them with finding practical solutions to real economic problems. As we will see, while their proposal received substantial attention in the policy debate and had a lot of supporters within the United States economics profession, as well as within EU policy circles, it got nowhere with the German political establishment.

The Commission Gets Involved

In May 2010, the idea of a Eurobond clearly seemed premature. The main objection in Germany remained that of 'moral hazard' and the Bruegel proposal was simply dismissed by German opinion leaders. The policy focus remained on implementing spending cuts and enacting fiscal reform, along with the establishment of a European Financial Stability Facility (EFSF), which combined loans from Eurozone member states, collateral from the European Commission, and funds from the International Monetary Fund to marshal a $1 trillion response. Despite this, and after further bailouts for Ireland in the fall of 2010 and Portugal in the spring of 2011, the crisis spread to Italy and Spain during the summer of 2011, giving the Eurozone crisis truly systemic proportions.

It was therefore no surprise that the idea of a common Eurobond would resurface. This time, however, new proposals would not just be floated in think tanks, university classrooms or the opinion pages of the Financial Times. In November 2011, the European Commission — well aware that the term 'Eurobond' had become toxic in the German popular press — itself presented a Green Paper assessing the feasibility of introducing what they carefully termed 'Stability Bonds' (European Commission 2011). As stability has been a key precept of postwar German economic and political culture, the Commission was attempting to use their prominent position in the debate to reclassify and relabel the solution so as to structure the economic reality differently and legitimate their approach, just as the co-production of knowledge approach would suggest.

The Commission Green Paper set out three broad approaches to the common issuance of Eurobonds, based on the degree of substitution of national issuance — full or partial — and the structure of the underlying guarantee of the bonds — joint and several liability or several (i.e., no joint guarantees). The first option was full Eurobonds with joint and several liability, which would replace each member state's entire national debt with Eurobonds. Clearly, as the Commission itself admitted, this held by far the highest risk of moral hazard and was therefore deemed politically unrealistic at the time. The second option was to have partial Eurobonds with joint and several liability, up to a certain percentage of GDP, which would also need a change to the Lisbon Treaty. This second option echoed a proposal made two weeks earlier by the German Council of Economic Experts, which continued to oppose Eurobonds in principle, but had recommended the establishment of a European Redemption Pact (Franz *et al.* 2011). The third option, partial Eurobonds without joint guarantees, would again cover only parts of the debt and would impose strict entry conditions for a smaller group of countries to pool some of their sovereign debt and allow for the removal of countries that do not meet their fiscal obligations. Unlike the first two approaches, this would involve 'several but not joint' government guarantees and could therefore be implemented relatively quickly and without any treaty change (European Commission 2011).

The European Commission believed the introduction of its proposed Stability Bonds 'could potentially quickly alleviate the current sovereign debt crisis, as the high-yield Member States could benefit from stronger creditworthiness of the low-yield Member States' (European Commission 2011). But therein lay also the rub. While countries in the Eurozone periphery would clearly gain from a Eurobond, the effects of joint debt issuance were not seen to be as benign in the core countries that were not affected by the euro crisis. Not just in Germany, but also in Finland, Austria, and the Netherlands, many people failed to understand why they should help a group of states — which in their minds had borrowed excessively and broken the common rules of the Stability and Growth Pact — borrow even more via jointly guaranteed Eurobonds. Despite the Commission's efforts to restructure the terms of the debate to legitimize a more federal approach, national level solutions of austerity still won out among the Northern states. Germany's growing position of structural power within the Eurozone only further enhanced the power of its orthodox ideas.[1] The debate was now in full swing, and it would be especially heated — and prove crucial for the actual outcome — in Berlin.

The Debate in Germany

The interaction of economic theory, material interest, and political strategizing was evident in the 'contextualism' of German discourse. The debate in the media was highly animated and drove home the saints and sinners dichotomy. Some media — especially Die Welt, Bild Zeitung, and the Frankfurter Allgemeine Zeitung (FAZ) — seized on the controversy over Eurobonds to force politicians from all parties to declare their stance. In a special issue on Eurobonds, a Bild editorial read: 'What are these euro bonds in the first place? Put simply, instead of a single country the entire EU is liable for the debt. There is only one interest rate for all euro area countries. The debt sinners (i.e. Greece) pay MUCH LESS interest — because Germany guarantees everything with its good name. We pay MUCH MORE — because the credit markets across the EU are weaker compared to Germany alone. Experts expect up to 47 billion euro in additional costs for the German taxpayers — every year!' (Bild 2012). In another editorial, the FAZ put its opposition to Eurobonds only slightly less colorful: 'The community does not expect a better future, if the sweet life is continued on credit at the expense of the last solid debtors in Europe, until even those solid debtors collapse. Euro bonds create such perverse incentives' (FAZ 2012).

Other newspapers were more nuanced. For example, the TAZ, a left-leaning newspaper, reported on the distinction between red and blue bonds and used a tone that was a lot more sympathetic toward Eurobonds

(Hermann 2011). Some bloggers and commentators followed this nuanced stance, as summarized by Schuseil in a blog post for Bruegel's website (Schuseil 2012). For example, Claus Hulverscheidt in the Süddeutsche Zeitung approvingly quoted FDP politician Rainer Brüderle saying that 'introducing Eurobonds now' would be the same as 'giving whiskey to an alcoholic' but that their introduction may be possible in the long run, but only as the final step of the European integration process (Hulverscheidt 2012).

Financial Times columnist Münchau supported the introduction of Eurobonds from the beginning and lamented that the SPD did not have the courage to claim 'real' Eurobonds and thereby missed an opportunity to advance the European integration process due to its 'lack of killer instinct' (Münchau 2012). André Kühnlenz agreed that Eurobonds could help the exodus of capital from the European periphery, but agreed with the Bundesbank that a fiscal union was necessary first (Kühnlenz 2012). However, commentators who opposed Eurobonds generally dominated the debate in the German media. In the most important German business daily Handelsblatt, Thomas Hanke and Wolfram Weimer argued that Eurobonds should by no means be introduced. They would not help to achieve growth in Europe and constituted nothing else than the socialization of national debt at the expense of Germany (Weimer 2012).

Most politicians and political party leaders in Germany spoke out against Eurobonds. CDU Chancellor Merkel put it most succinctly in the Bundestag in response to a question of a liberal FDP member in June 2012: 'As long as I live there will be no Eurobonds' (Der Spiegel 2012). Wolfgang Schäuble, her finance minister, warned against setting disincentives in the absence of a common fiscal policy, pointing out that 'a single euro country cannot decide to go into debt and make everyone else pay for the risk' (Schäuble 2012). Alexander Dobrindt, the former secretary general of the CSU, the Bavarian sister party of the CDU, was more blunt by saying that his party

> continues to refuse the adoption of debts from other euro countries ... prior to any further support for Greece or any other Dolce Vita country, which are characterized by exuberant debt, we need to say: you have to pay your debt yourself (Dobrindt 2011)

The FDP, Merkel's pro-market liberal coalition partner between 2009 and 2013, also vigorously opposed Eurobonds and seemed ready to sacrifice the government coalition over the issue. Rainer Brüderle, head of the FDP parliamentary group, called Eurobonds 'interest rate socialism, for which Germany and other successful countries would have to pay a lot' (Die Welt 2012c).

The position of the social democratic SPD and the Greens was more ambiguous. Originally, they had supported the introduction of Eurobonds, but both parties made a U-turn on the issue in May 2012, when Merkel relied on the votes of the SPD to ratify the Fiscal Pact in the *Bundestag*. The Social Democratic Party's speaker in the *Bundestag* Thomas Opperman said that 'we oppose the uncontrolled pooling of debt ... there is absolutely no need for general Eurobonds' (Die Welt 2012b). Instead, the SPD supported the introduction of measures to generate growth and fight youth unemployment in Europe. The Green party followed the stance of the SPD and also rejected Eurobonds in May 2012. Die Welt quotes Jürgen Tritin as saying that while he agreed with the economic principles behind them, they were the wrong solution at the time, not least because it would require changing the EU Treaties (Die Welt 2012a). Die Linke was the only political party in Germany to consistently support the introduction of Eurobonds. A number of popular opinion polls suggested a large majority of Germans in almost hostile opposition to the idea (Hawley 2011).

As for the commercial sector, most German interest groups, business lobby associations, banks, and financial institutions supported Merkel's opposition to Eurobonds. Hans-Peter Keitel, president of the Federation of German Industries (BDI), hoped 'very much that Ms. Merkel will stick to her position and resist demands for Euro bonds' (Rheinische Post 2011). Martin Wansleben, president of the Association of German Chambers of Industry and Commerce pointedly declared: 'Euro bonds are the wrong way. For what kind of signal would this send? Only that one wants to make it easier to take on debt' (Handelsblatt 2012). Others noted that common European debt vehicles blurred the lines between liability and incentives, while Thomas Mayer, chief economist of Deutsche Bank, summed up the debate as follows: 'it's enormously difficult to have common liability without a political union … We could have a European Tea Party that takes up the battle cry: no taxation without representation.' Only the German exporters' association had a different stance in August 2011 when it noted that 'all alternatives to Eurobonds will cost us even more money in the end' (Walker 2011).

What about the academic and think tank world? Most economists and economic think tanks in Germany also came out firmly against the idea of Eurobonds, once again underscoring the porousness of the internal/external divide, whereby ideas in German academia and preferences in Germany's policy community mutually reinforced one another. The most vocal opponent was the Munich-based Center for Economic Studies or Ifo Institute, led by economist Hans-Werner Sinn, who calculated that the introduction of Eurobonds would cost the German taxpayer up to €47 billion per year, due to the higher interest rates Germany would face on its own sovereign debt. Consequently, the report concluded: 'Even in the case of the proportionate liability for the Eurobonds on which we based our calculations, the Ifo institute strongly advises against the introduction of Eurobonds. Even if Europe had the strength to form a federal state, it would make no sense to communitarise the liability for government debt that has been taken on … The principle of liability is the basic principle of any rational economic activity and one of the cornerstones of a market economy. Whoever abandons this places Europe's future in jeopardy' (Ifo Institute 2011).

Many other economists in Germany broadly supported the Ifo's position vis-à-vis Eurobonds. Even the German Institute for Economic Research (DIW), which is often seen as a left-leaning think tank, did not support the introduction of Eurobonds. Ansgar Belke, Professor at the University

Duisburg-Essen and Research Director for International Macroeconomics at the DIW, argued: 'although Euro bonds can provide short-run relief for some countries, in the long-run they will lead to disaster, because they open the door for even more debt.' Consequently, in Belke's opinion, Eurobonds would only be viable if there were a common fiscal policy, but such a common fiscal policy would undermine the democratic sovereignty of each member state (EurActiv.de 2011). There were, however, a few other voices in Germany that saw Eurobonds as a last resort to solve the euro crisis. Thomas Straubhaar, for example, the Director of the Hamburg Institute of International Economics, argued that if individual countries were not able to borrow money on the capital market under 'reasonable conditions,' Eurobonds could help those countries to ease access to credit.

As mentioned earlier, the German Council of Economic Experts in early November 2011 argued in favor of a European Redemption Pact, around the same time of the European Commission proposals for the introduction of stability bonds. In the official German 2012 Annual Economic Report of the economics ministry, however, both the federal government and the Council of Economic Experts continued to outright reject the idea of Eurobonds. Yet, the report left some room for maneuver by mentioning again the possibility of setting up a debt redemption pact if the stabilization measures already agreed at the EU level were to prove inadequate (German Federal Ministry of Economics and Technology 2012). The Bundesbank remained a bastion of opposition to Eurobonds. In an interview with Le Monde in May 2012, Jens Weidman, its president, stated in no unclear terms that 'believing Eurobonds would solve the current crisis is an illusion ... you do not confide your credit card to someone without any possibility to control his expenditures' (Weidman 2012).

In the end, the German national arguments against the introduction of Eurobonds carried the day against the European systemic arguments in favor. While especially the Bruegel proposal benefited from a favorable audience in Brussels, making it into both the European Commission and European Council's blueprints for a 'genuine' Economic and Monetary Union, it faltered in the face of frontal assaults by the German academic, media, and policy establishment. It is striking how Eurobonds play a central role in almost any think tank's blueprint for the future of the euro, including proposals by the British-based Centre for European Reform and the French-based Eiffel Group, but are notably absent in the EMU blueprint of the German-based Glienicker Group, which is made up of eleven German economists, political scientists, and legal scholars (Matthijs and Blyth 2015b). While German journalists played a key role in framing the debate on Eurobonds, Germany's growing power and structural position within the Eurozone decision-making bodies proved decisive in putting all ideas of sovereign debt pooling on the back burner for the foreseeable future.

Conclusion: The Euro crisis' Theory Effect

Merkel's tough stance against Eurobonds as well as her overall economic policy toward the Eurozone crisis would be vindicated during the September 2013 elections, when she won the largest share of the vote for her CDU since the 1950s. The thorny issue of the introduction of a common debt instrument has remained off the table in Germany, and Europe, since then. The whole debate over Eurobonds during the most acute phases of the euro crisis demonstrated the strength of the German economics profession and the dominant view of the euro as an economic problem with mainly national economic solutions. Alternative views of the crisis could paint a functional picture of governance as the major issue, where a single currency disembedded from the standard historical institutions of nation-states would create serious problems no matter what the policies of the individual member states were (McNamara 2015).

The role of European integration studies as a 'weak field' joined the material and political interests opposing a federalized European debt instrument and made it unsurprising that such proposals got such little traction while national level economic prescriptions of austerity were legitimated. European Union studies have been promulgated and funded by the European Commission but the social power of political scientists, sociologists, historians, and anthropologists of the EU is limited compared to the role of economists in the public sphere.

Instead, the theory effect that unfolded in the Eurozone crisis was situated squarely in the vision of ordoliberalism and neoliberalism that has illuminated the German public policy sphere throughout the postwar era. Even the potentially catastrophic stresses of the EU-wide contagion unleashed by Greece's fiscal insolvency and subsequent financial crisis could not dislodge the view that national problems of fiscal profligacy and weak competitiveness were the source of the problem. Eurobonds stood no chance of being adopted, despite their functionality in addressing the euro's woes, given the ways in which the ideas about Northern saints and Southern sinners both served and structured the reality of the euro crisis.

Acknowledgments

The authors thank Björn Bremer and Brian Fox for helpful research assistance, as well as the two anonymous reviewers for their constructive comments.

Note

1. Even Polish Foreign Minister Radoslaw Sikorski, in a speech in 2011, referred to Germany as Europe's 'indispensable nation,' adding that he feared German inaction less than German power (Sikorski 2011).

References

Abbott, A. 1988. *The system of professions: an essay on the division of expert labor*. Chicago, IL: University of Chicago Press.

Adler-Nissen, R., and K. Kropp. 2015. A sociology of knowledge approach to European Integration. *Journal of European Integration* 37, no. 2: 155–73.

Berman, S. 1998. *The social democratic moment: ideas and politics in the making of interwar Europe*. Cambridge: Harvard University Press.

Bild. 2012. Diese Neun Buchstaben Bergen Sprengstoff: Eurobonds. Special. Available online at http://www.bild.de/themen/specials/euro-bonds/politik-nachrichten-news-fotos-videos-19546248.bild. html

Blyth, M. 2002. *Great transformations*. Cambridge: Cambridge University Press.

Bourdieu, P. 1984. *Distinction: a social critique of the judgement of taste*. London: Routledge.

Bourdieu, P. 1993. *The field of cultural production*. Cambridge: Polity Press.

Butler, J. 1993. *Bodies that matter: on the discursive limits of 'sex'*. New York: Routledge.

Der Spiegel. 2012. Merkel zur Schuldenpolitik: "Keine Euro-Bonds, Solange Ich Lebe". June 26. Available online at http://www.spiegel.de/politik/ausland/kanzlerin-merkel-schliesst-euro-bonds-aus-a-841115.html

Delpla, J., and J. von Weizsäcker. 2010. The blue bond proposal. *Bruegel Policy Brief* 2010:03, May 6. http://www.bruegel.org/publications/show/publication/the-blue-bond-proposal.html

Die Welt. 2012a. Rot-Grün distanziert sich von Hollandes Euro-Bonds, May 24. Available online at http://www.welt.de/politik/deutschland/article106372213/Rot-Gruen-distanziert-sich-von-Hollandes-Euro-Bonds.html

Die Welt. 2012b. Merkel sucht den Blockadebrecher, May 25. Available online at http://www.welt.de/print/die_welt/politik/article106369586/Merkel-sucht-den-Blockadebrecher.html

Die Welt. 2012c. Für Brüderle sind Euro-Bonds 'Zinssozialismus', May 28. Available online at http://www.welt.de/wirtschaft/article106383864/Fuer-Bruederle-sind-Euro-Bonds-Zinssozialismus.html

Dobrindt, A. 2011. Interview with *Die Bild*, August 7. Available online at http://www.bild.de/politik/inland/csu/dobrindt-geht-steil-teil-1-19264010.bild.html

EurActiv.de. 2011. Ifo-Institute zu Euro-Bonds: 'Europas Zukunft nicht auf Spiel setzen', August 17. Available online at http://www.euractiv.de/finanzen-und-wachstum/artikel/euro-bonds-ifo-kritisiert-bruegel-modell-005245

European Commission. 2011. *Green Paper on the feasibility of introducing Stability Bonds*. Memo/11/820. Available online at http://europa.eu/rapid/press-release_MEMO-11-820_en.pdf

FAZ. 2012. Mit Eurobonds in die Schuldenunion. Available online at http://www.faz.net/aktuell/wirtschaft/europa-mit-eurobonds-in-die-schuldenunion-11760311.html

Foucault, M. 1977. *Discipline and punish: the birth of the prison*. New York: Pantheon Press.

Fourcade, M. 2009. *Economists and societies*. Princeton: Princeton University Press.

Fourcade, M. 2013. The economy as morality play, and implications for the Eurozone crisis. *Socio-Economic Review* 11: 620–7.

Franz, W., P. Bofinger, L. Feld, C. Schmidt and B. Weber di Mauro. 2011. A European redemption pact. *Vox-EU Online*, November 9. Available online at http://www.sachverstaendigenrat-wirtschaft.de/a-european-redemption-pact.0.html

German Federal Ministry of Economics and Technology. 2012. *Annual economic Growth*. Berlin: BMWi Public Relations. Available online at http://www.bmwi.de/English/Redaktion/Pdf/2012-annual-economic-report-boosting-confidence,property=pdf,bereich=bmwi,sprache=en,rwb=true.pdf

Hall, P. 2014. Varieties of capitalism and the Euro crisis. *West European Politics* 37, no. 6: 1223–43.

Handelsblatt. 2012. Eurobonds sind Zinssozialismus. Available online at http://www.handelsblatt.com/politik/deutschland/fdp-fraktionschef-eurobonds-sind-zinssozialismus/6680888.html

Hawley, C. 2011. The return of 'Madame Non': why Merkel remains opposed to euro bonds. *Spiegel Online*, November 24. Available online at http://www.spiegel.de/international/europe/the-return-of-madame-non-why-merkel-remains-opposed-to-euro-bonds-a-799803.html

Hermann, U. 2011. Und was hätten wir davon? *Die Tageszeitung*, August 16. Available online at http://www.taz.de/!76340/; http://neuewirtschaftswunder.de/2012/05/24/marktwirtschaft-stoppt-den-euro-der-lemminge-wir-brauchen-eurobonds/

Hulverscheidt, C. 2012. Whisky für den Alkoholiker. *Süddeutsche Zeitung*, May 24. Available online at http://www.sueddeutsche.de/wirtschaft/debatte-um-euro-bonds-whisky-fuer-den-alkoholiker-1.1365351

Ifo Institute. 2011. What will Euro-bonds costs? *Press Release*, August 17. Available online at http://www.cesifo-group.de/portal/page/portal/ifoContent/N/pr/pr-PDFs/PM_20110817_Eurobonds_de.pdf

Jacoby, W. 2015. Europe's new German problem: the timing of politics and the politics of timing. Chapter 9, in *The future of the Euro*, eds. M. Matthijs and M. Blyth, 187–209. New York: Oxford University Press.

Jasanoff, S. 2004. The idiom of co-production. In *States of knowledge*, ed. S. Jasanoff, 1–12. London: Routledge.

Jones, E. 2010a. *A Eurobond proposal to promote stability and liquidity while preventing moral hazard*. ISPI Policy Brief. Istituto per gli Studi di Politica Internazionale.

Jones, E. 2010b. Merkel's folly. *Survival* 52, no. 3: 21–38.

Knorr Cetina, K., and A. Preda (eds.). 2005. *The sociology of financial markets*. New York: Oxford University Press.

Kühnlenz, A. 2012. Stoppt den Euro der Lemminge, wir brauchen Eurobonds! *Wirtschafswunder*, May 24. Available online at http://neuewirtschaftswunder.de/2012/05/24/marktwirtschaft-stoppt-den-euro-der-lemminge-wir-brauchen-eurobonds/

Mackenzie, D. 2006. *An engine, not a camera*. Cambridge: MIT Press.

Matthijs, M. 2011. *Ideas and economic crises in Britain from Attlee to Blair (1945–2005)*. London: Routledge.

Matthijs, M. 2014a. The Eurozone crisis: growing pains or doomed from the start? Chapter 14, in *Handbook of global economic governance: players, power, and paradigms*, eds. M. Moschella and C. Weaver, 201–17. Abingdon: Routledge.

Matthijs, M. 2014b. Mediterranean blues: the crisis in Southern Europe. *Journal of Democracy* 25, no. 1: 101–15.

Matthijs, M., and M. Blyth. 2015a. Introduction: the future of the Euro and the politics of embedded currency areas. In *The future of the Euro*, eds. M. Matthijs and M. Blyth, 1–17. New York: Oxford University Press.

Matthijs, M., and M. Blyth. 2015b. Conclusion: the future of the Euro—possible futures, risks, and uncertainties. In *The future of the Euro*, eds. M. Matthijs and M. Blyth, 249–69. New York: Oxford University Press.

McNamara, K. 1998. *The currency of ideas: monetary politics in the European Union*. Ithaca: Cornell University Press.

McNamara, K. 2015. Forgotten embeddedness: history lessons for the Euro. Chapter 2, in *The future of the Euro*, eds. M. Matthijs and M. Blyth, 21–43. New York: Oxford University Press.

Mudge, S., and A. Vauchez. 2012. Building Europe on a weak field: law, economics, and scholarly avatars in transnational politics. *American Journal of Sociology* 118, no. 2: 449–92.

Münchau, W. 2012. S.P.O.N.—Die Spur des Geldes: Der SPD fehlt der Killerinstikt. *Spiegel Online*, May 23. Available online at http://www.spiegel.de/wirtschaft/streit-ueber-euro-bonds-spd-scheut-konflikt-mit-merkel-a-834663.html

Newman, A. 2015. Germany's Euro experience and the long shadow of reunification. Chapter 6, in *The future of the Euro*, eds. M. Matthijs and M. Blyth, 117–35. New York: Oxford University Press.

Parsons, C. 2003. *A certain idea of Europe*. Ithaca: Cornell University Press.

Polanyi, K. 2001. *The great transformation*, 2nd ed. New York: Beacon Press.

Rheinische Post. 2011. Eurobonds-Streit wird schärfer, November 24. Available online at http://www.rp-online.de/politik/eu/eurobonds-streit-wird-schaerfer-aid-1.2614481

Schäuble, W. 2011. Why austerity is only cure for the Eurozone. *Financial Times*, September 5. Available online at http://www.ft.com/intl/cms/s/0/97b826e2-d7ab-11e0-a06b-00144feabdc0.html#axzz355KUI33Z

Schäuble, W. 2012. Interview with *Mannheimer Morgen*, May 24. Available online at http://www.bundesfinanzministerium.de/Content/DE/Interviews/2012/2012-05-24-mannheimer-morgen.html?view=renderPrint

Schuseil, P. 2012. Germany: what about Eurobonds? *Bruegel.Org*, May 31. Available online at http://www.bruegel.org/nc/blog/detail/article/799-germany-what-about-eurobonds/

Sikorski, R. 2011. I fear Germany's power less than her inactivity. *Financial Times*, November 28. Available online at http://www.ft.com/intl/cms/s/0/b753cb42-19b3-11e1-ba5d-00144feabdc0.html#axzz355KUI33Z

Springford, J. 2009. Strengthening the stability and growth pact with a common Eurozone bond. *CentreForum*, September. Available online at http://www.centreforum.org/assets/pubs/stability-and-growth.pdf

Walker, M. 2011. Eurobond debate rises in Germany, France. *Wall Street Journal*, August 16. Available online at http://online.wsj.com/news/articles/SB10001424053111903392904576510092321990596

Weidman, J. 2012. Croire que les Eurobonds résoundrant la crise est une illusion. *Interview with Le Monde*, May 25. Available online at http://www.lemonde.fr/economie/article/2012/05/25/jens-weidmann-croire-que-les-eurobonds-resoudront-la-crise-est-une-illusion_1707264_3234.html

Weimer, W. 2012. Hollande will den Schuldensozialismus. *Handelsblatt*, May 25. Available online at http://www.handelsblatt.com/meinung/kolumnen/weimers-woche/weimers-woche-hollande-will-den-schuldensozialismus/6674160.html

Zelizer, V. 1994. *The social meaning of money: pin money, paychecks, poor relief and other currencies*. Princeton: Princeton University Press.

Reforming the Bulgarian State of Knowledge: Legal Expertise as a Resource in Modelling States

OLE HAMMERSLEV

Department of Law, University of Southern Denmark, Odense, Denmark

ABSTRACT   The transformation of the Eastern European countries from communist states to EU members was supported by massive investments in Western discourses and social science knowledge and export programmes for these from the West to the East. In the West, and specifically in the US, a market for discourses and knowledge production professionalized and intertwined with institutions that exported specific forms of policy visions of US modes of the State. In the East, the importation of discourses and knowledge became pivotal in the struggles for power of modelling the state and its institutions, and thus as knowledge tools to guide and legitimize the path towards democracy and later towards membership of the EU. Based on the notion of co-production, this study focuses on how leading American and European lawyers, think tanks and different agencies were involved in the reorganisation of the Bulgarian field of power.

The EU enlargement towards Eastern Europe has often been characterised as one of the greatest achievements of the EU. In less than 20 years after the fall of the Berlin Wall and a divided Europe, even some of the poorest Eastern European former communist states had become members of the EU. The countries went from Communism to being integrated members of the EU in a process where not only state institutions, commerce, professional practices and norms underwent changes, but also knowledge, categories and understandings transformed towards a new reality. As Adler-Nissen and Kropp note in the introduction to this special issue, the integration process of the EU, and thus also the enlargement process, consisted of a *co-production* between specific agents' trajectories, investments and social scientific knowledge. It was not only the production of knowledge that was important, equally important was dissemination of knowledge and education of local agents to take part in promoting new possibilities of societal transformation. The integration of the Eastern European countries into the EU was not an inevitable process, but a process supported by a host of international organisations, think tanks, private foundations, law firms and universities that invested massively in export of discourses, policies and social and legal categories in order to assist the development towards a market economy and new forms of state power. Through new forms of knowledge and state practices, the intention was to rebuild the Eastern European states on the basis of democracy and a market economy protected by strong legal institutions. A telling illustration of the directions some of the Eastern European countries could have taken and of the overall dominating paradigm underpinning cultures, practices and interpretive frameworks in Eastern Europe is the events in Bulgaria after 1989. For the extraordinary party congress on 30 January 1990, a draft statute was prepared that suggested a de-Stalinization of the Bulgarian Communist Party. The leaders of the party urged 'a new type of contemporary Marxist party'. The draft documents suggested abandoning the *nomenklartura* system at all levels and replacing it with 'political pluralism, freedom of religion, a 'market-oriented economy within a socialist state' and the separation of legislative, executive, and legal powers'. (Report on Eastern Europe: Weekly Record of Events, 2 February 1990, 53). Within the party, several opinions existed about the direction the party and society should take. Some of the persons from the party told a press conference on 17 January 1990 that 'Bulgaria did not suffer so much from Socialism as from an underdevelopment of Socialism' (Report on Eastern Europe: Weekly Record of Events, 2 February 1990). Opposition parties and groups developed as well, with the Union of Democratic Forces as the strongest. However, the Communist Party had control of the press and thus, in order to be able to take part in public politics in general and in the round table talks in particular, the opposition parties demanded the rights and means to publish their own dailies and weeklies; they demanded office space, press facilities as well as broadcasting time on radio and television (Report on Eastern Europe: Weekly Record of Events, 2 February 1990, 52). The opposition parties tried to delegitimise the Communists and legitimise themselves as the natural heirs of power through publishing hitherto concealed knowledge about, for example, ecological disasters and human rights violations. And through new factual knowledge and claims to Western human rights concepts, the opposition tried to redefine and rewrite the conditions and history of the country. They attempted to produce knowledge based on a liberal paradigm and to get legitimate positions to write a new authentic history of the country and promote policy visions for apparently inevitable future developments. Moreover, opposition parties aimed at being able to distribute such knowledge. Changing the state of mind of the citizens, the countries' expert knowledge and the dispositions and habitual orientation of the experts in the countries was an enormous challenge, just as it was also a huge challenge to change their beliefs in state institutions. However, legitimate discourses, state models, law and new forms of expertise were to a large extent produced in Western fields of power and exported to the East, where they became part of the national struggles.

This article examines how the production and export of legal development programmes to Eastern Europe after 1989 were closely related to policy visions in the West by following the trajectories of different programmes on a micro-level. The article focuses on the programmes directed towards Bulgaria and illustrates how the programmes were imported in Bulgaria and used in a larger struggle in the field of state power.

First, the article introduces its methodological framework in which it uses the concept of co-production to examine the relation between knowledge production and state transformation. In order to get tools to examine the agents that produce such knowledge and state forms, it uses the Bourdieusian theoretical tools. Hereafter, there is a discussion on the transformation of the law and development movement, and the article examines how this transformation unfolded in parallel with the changes in Eastern Europe. Whereas US agents were crucial to the first developments, the EU invented their own programmes focusing on specific forms of knowledge and state transformation that also changed with the further developments of Eastern Europe. The last part of the article concerns these pan-European developments.

Methodology

A sizable body of literature examining the transformation of Eastern and Central Europe after the Cold War (Elster, Offe, and Preuss 1998; Keohane, Nye, and Hoffmann 1993) and the subsequent integration into the EU has emerged, and different theoretical schools have taken form following general theories of European integration (Rosamond 2000). Schimmelfennig focuses, for example, on rhetorical action and states' strategic use of norm-based arguments in the process of European enlargement (Schimmelfennig 2001, 48; Schimmelfennig and Sedelmeier 2005) and criticises much of the literature about European integration for ignoring that international organisations have taken part in the EU enlargement, even though he still focus on states as agents (Schimmelfennig, Engert, and Knobel 2006). The characteristics of such studies are — as others also point out (Mudge and Vauchez 2012; Vauchez 2011) — that they focus on states as rational agents and state leaders as driving forces for European integration and for the EU enlargement. Rather than affirming the 'internal' history of the European Union, this article adopts a Bourdieusian sociology that insists that 'the European field of power does not stop at the edge of the EU, but reaches beyond into a transnational space' (Cohen 2008, 113). Academic institutions, political associations, international organisations as well as think tanks, law firms, major corporations and professional groups both inside and outside of Europe struggle over the elaboration of the principles of vision and division that will shape the distribution of power in the EU (Arnholtz and Hammerslev 2013). Also historical materialist perspectives have examined the reasons for why Central and Eastern European countries applied for membership of an EU dominated by neo-liberalism (Bieler 2002; Holman 1993, 1998, 2001; Van Apeldoorn 2000, 2003; Van Der Pijl 2001). However, the studies tend to reduce the multi-dimensional interests of individuals to represent different fractions of economic capital. The Bourdieusian approach has clear parallels to those studies drawing on Foucault (Diez 2009) in an effort to understand how the European Union is inscribed with a purpose both by theoretical and political discourses. But rather than doing so by analysing apparently free-flowing discourses, attention is constantly paid to the producers, exporters and importers of discourse, law and knowledge and how their efforts are articulated within specific fields. The social production of the policies, law and knowledge are products of local and stiuated factors, as Adler-Nissen and Kropp argue in the introduction.

The article will utilise Jasanoff's framework of co-production to point to the relation between knowledge production and state formation as two interdependent areas (Jasanoff 2004). Both are formed of different agents entrenched in different social settings. Thus, the article focuses on how production of knowledge is 'incorporated into practices of state making ... and, in reverse, how practices of governance influence the making and use of knowledge' (Jasanoff 2004, 3). In a study of the transformation of an Eastern European country, the framework as laid out by Adler-Nissen and Kropp brings to the fore how the state and legal institutions were produced and developed in accordance with very specific conditions of possibilities of practices with expressions and comprehensions of legitimate development in larger societal contexts. Especially relevant are the principles of situatedness and contextualism because they help understand how legal expertise was produced and exported in one concrete situation closely related to the production of policy visions and were imported and used in larger battles of state power in another importing concrete situation. The principles are operationalised through the very basic notions of 'situation' and 'context', where situation concerns social — or objective — structures and context concerns symbolic forms such as law and policy visions. The focus on the progress of legal development programmes is an entrance to study the local Western production and local Eastern European import of law and legal expertise. Moreover, it is an entrance to study the context in which the legal programmes were developed in close relation to Western policy visions of state institutions and liberal markets.

Using the tools provided by Bourdieusian sociology in studies of transnational export of law and state models and of EU legal integration (Cohen 2007, 2011; Cohen and Vauchez 2007; Dezalay and Garth 1996, 2002, 2010; Vauchez 2010, 2011), the article can empirically study the agents and their use of different kinds of expertise and discourses to transform state and legal institutions. With such a focus, it becomes apparent that the transformation was related to various forms of social and cultural capital and that the changes and continuities of the Bulgarian state and legal institutions were closely related to foreign expertise, funding and actors. Similarly, the focus can show how a transnational field of state production and export of the legal assistance programmes had an impact on the local import of knowledge and expertise in the process of transforming the Bulgarian state. The Bulgarian state was thus transformed on the basis of international expertise, law and productions of legal capacity building.[1]

US Production and Export of Knowledge and Legal Expertise

It was not a coincidence that the American Bar Association (ABA) played an important role in the first transformation steps in Eastern Europe in the beginning of the 1990s. Since WWII, US lawyers have played a role in legal assistance programmes around the world. With the invention of the 'law and development movement' in 1950s and 1960s (Gardner 1980; Trubek and Galanter 1974), idealistic and entrepreneurial US lawyers tried to put law, legal institutions and legal expertise on the agenda to distribute legal institutions that could manage the economy and transform traditional societies. Law was seen as a tool to transform countries in Africa and Latin America into liberal capitalist and democratic states. The promotion was advanced by leaders of the ABA, leading US law schools, the American judiciary and the executive branch of the US government. These 'legal missionaries' were supported by private foundations and by the US government's aid programmes. In the 1980s, the law became a central part of policy-making 'heavily influenced by neo-liberal ideas about development', as Trubek and Santos (2006, 2) write. Law was seen as the foundation for market relations and as a way to control or diminish the state. As Trubek and Santos note 'attention shifted from the establishment of an administrative state to the core institutions of private law, the role of the judiciary in protecting business against the intrusions of government, and the need to change local laws to facilitate integration into the world economy' (Trubek and Santos 2006). Whereas the first movement of the 1950s and 1960s was rather small in scale, the movement of the 1980s not only expanded the number of projects, but they also became larger. With the fall of the communist regimes in Eastern Europe in the late 1980s and early 1990s, legal assistance programmes became even more important in the promotion of US policy visions (Carothers 2003).

However, even though the development of legal assistance programmes and the actual implementation of legal reforms are often considered and described as a rational process, it is more a loosely coordinated set of competing enterprises on an expanding market. One key institution in US exports of legal programmes has been the ABA, which revitalised its focus on legal development just after 1989 (Hammerslev 2010). The following section will examine the development of the legal programmes of the ABA.

American Lawyers' Promotion of Legal Institutions

In the US, the fabrication of post-Cold War legal assistance in the area of rule of law and judiciary was to a large extent the result of a private initiative taken by American commercial lawyers within the ABA. Using the ABA as a platform for their undertaking, Sandy D'Alemberte[2] and Homer Moyer[3] set up the organisation known as Central and East European Law

Initiative (CEELI), which was to provide legal assistance in Eastern Europe (Hammerslev 2007, 2010).

With a focus of the programmes on apparently universal claims of the rule of law, human rights and core legal institutions to protect the market and democratic institutions in Eastern Europe, CEELI would become one of the largest legal programmes in the world within 15 years.[4]

Drawing on their social and legal capital, the people behind CEEIL convinced the people in the US State Department dealing with Eastern European assistance that they were worth investing in. Based within the ABA, they had the network and legal expertise to promote constitutions, core institutions of private law and strong judiciaries to protect business and democratic developments, although they were not experts in local conditions in Eastern Europe.

Until then, the US government had focused primarily on weakening the strong political bureaucracies in Eastern Europe to oust the former communists from the field of power and replace them with reform-friendly forces. Officials from the US administration, government, judges and think tanks were training the opposition to the communists, and through funding and definition of research agendas, the US think tanks and NGOs could support local NGOs, think tanks and non-state institutions and direct their policy visions towards specific reform initiatives. These institutions could produce and import visions and discourses concerning apparently necessary reforms, concerning problems that had to be solved, and they could train other reform-friendly forces. The perspective was, in other words, to train, support and fund institutions and individuals who could fight their fights by strongly investing in making virtues of necessity. Moreover, the US government focused on privatisation and building up markets rather than supporting the growth of new state bureaucracies (Wedel 2001, 53). The focus of the US government was not on legal programmes, and it did not have any real strategy for rule-of-law programmes. Like the government, the National Endowment for Democracy (NED) and its agencies, all of which were key institutions in the task of training opposition groups to take up the fight against the former communists through new forms of expertise and practises, did not focus strongly on rule-of-law programmes, though it was 'one of the underpinnings of what we did … We worked on rules regarding democratic elections, representation etc. We tried to change the democratic rules', (Int. 112, Washington DC, 13 February 2006) as someone previously associated with the regime of NED expressed it.

CEELI — and the persons involved — became part of a larger US professional field consisting of US policy idea brokers and its trajectory corresponds with local structures of the field. The legal programmes were, however, considered disconnected from the policy contexts in which they were produced. Through law and legal training, it was possible to export programmes that aimed at transforming the Eastern European states away from new forms of Socialism and towards apparently inevitable developments as states based on market economy and the rule of law. An important part in the transfer of legal knowledge and practices was education of Eastern European lawyers, judges and statesmen, who were trained in the

USA to adopt legal practices that were in accordance with Western standards. In the process, various American and European legal experts from academia, the judicial branch and lawyers were involved at different levels and academics were often used to legitimise the reform programmes. One specific programme, CEELI, managed to set up was the 'Sisters' law school programme', in which around 2/3 of the law schools of the US took part in exchange programmes for Eastern European law students (Int. 116, Indianapolis, 15 February 2006).

To illustrate the context of how the legal programmes were produced and exported, as well as to illustrate how the local setting of the production was important for the way the export programmes worked, it is relevant to follow the trajectory of NED. NED was founded under former President Ronald Reagan to promote democracy globally. The people behind NED and the policy establishment in Washington came out of anticommunist policy in the USA in the 1950s. It is a core institution behind the transformation of Cold War activism into a professional field of international practices based on democracy, human rights and the rule of law (Dezalay and Garth 2002).

NED has promoted the production and export of specific forms of policy knowledge by supporting a wide range of professional idea brokers both nationally and abroad such as politicians, lawyers and not least what they call independent research centres. The latter work primarily in areas defined and funded by dominating agents and institutions. Such institutions work to promote ideas in the areas of public policy. The ideas are formulated in a scientific language in various scientific traditions — such as law, economics and political sciences — but the policy behind the ideas is hidden. As Nicolas Guilhot (2005, 87) notes on the basis of American research centres, funding, building institutions and training of professionals ensure that 'a significant control is exercised over the process by which policies are fabricated and circulated'. The scientific and 'independent' idea of production emphasises the universal need for a US policy industry. With this specific US model of promoting ideas, cultures, management techniques and ways of practices, funded by among others NED, the Washington policy community can extend its reach. Emanating from dominating institutions and people in Washington, this form of export opens new foreign markets for policy prescriptions which focus on public institutions and the market.

Turning towards Bulgaria and to how the US programmes were imported into another setting and used in another national battle of the field of power, NED managed to relate to and train a group of younger Bulgarian lawyers, some of whom went on to become prime ministers and presidents of the country and would be the driving force within the political field for investments in private law reforms and strong legal institutions. The Bulgarian NED-trained lawyers collaborated with the representatives of CEELI in Bulgaria in determining the priorities and focus areas in relation to the development of the rule of law and the independent courts. The Prime Minister of Bulgaria in the first non-socialist government, Philip Dimitrov, and former Minister of Justice, Svetoslav Louchnikov, are two examples of such persons. Alexander Djerov, who also was trained by NED, might exemplify the resources and impact of these legal key reformers. Alexander Djerov was born in 1929 in Sofia. He came from a famous law family; the grandfather had chaired the Supreme Court of Cassation and had been Minister of Justice three times. His father was one of the first lawyers in Bulgaria working in the field of finance law and commercial law. After the communist takeover, his father was deported to a small village. During Communism, Djerov started as 'an enemy of the state', but by drawing on the prestige of his family and social network, he managed to study at university. In 1989, he joined the Radical Democratic Party, again due to his social capital with the addition of cultural capital. In 1992, he became a professor of civil law. Djerov also practised civil and property law at the law firm he shared with his son. Just after 1989, he was in the USA on a study programme. Djerov was one of the founders of the private New Bulgarian University, which was created after the US model to oppose the previous communist domain of St. Kliment Ohridski University in Sofia. St. Kliment Ohridski University was considered 'a communist university ... that had too long been run by the communists, and the professors there had believed in Communism and taught in Marxism and Leninism. After 1990 the same persons are teaching there' (Int. 41, Sofia, 18 November 2004). The law faculty was 'infiltrated with the communist party', and they were appointed by the communist minister of justice, Yaroslav Radev, — who was the 'gatekeeper' to legal and state positions and who, as is often noted, was feared even by persons in the Communist Party. The New Bulgarian University was founded in agreement with the establishers and owners of the leading think tanks — people who also were or had been related to the establishment and continuation of George Soros' Open Society Institute and people who were mainly funded by various foreign institutions, especially USAID. At the same time, these people were professors at the New Bulgarian University. The New Bulgarian University did not set up a legal programme; it was more important with programmes that could take part in supporting the policy visions of market economy and the rule of law.

CEELI focused on programmes in a number of legal areas such as the constitution, legal education, judicial reforms, bar reforms, commercial law reforms and criminal law reforms. The focus on rule of law was very closely related to commercial law reforms and the development of market reforms to assist these countries on their way towards global economic integration. The new legal agenda, which went hand in hand with business interests, was invented in the legal field as neutral universals and was extended and imposed globally onto the political fields. The new agenda was imposed on the political agenda in the USA and Europe, and various governments, international institutions and philanthropic foundations began to focus on the rule of law and associated legal areas such as human rights, strong and independent courts and commercial law.

CEELI thus became part of a larger US production field of knowledge, discourses, policy visions and legal assistance. CEELI and the persons involved grew out of a specific US field, and their actions abroad were shaped by their national field. The particular US model of state, with its main focus on governance and civil society, was exported to Eastern Europe (and other places) via structural homologous agencies trained and supported by US agents to fight their fights through specific forms of knowledge and discourses. Despite the fact that Bulgaria reformed a lot of legal acts, CEELI (and later other international institutions) also contributed to educational and training programmes, which aimed at changing both the perspectives of the locals and the practices around the law and around legal institutions. A former liaison officer in Bulgaria noted that a lot of what he did, in fact, was to teach judges how to file and organise cases so it was possible better to adhere to precedents and thus establish an important element in the rule of law. With new court management systems, they aimed at changing the *practices,* so the practices corresponded to Western legal standards. The situation was, as was later reported, that there 'was near universal agreement that the company register and foreclosure processes (both of which require the approval of judges) were extremely corrupt ... More often, payments, favors, gifts, or pressure usually comes indirectly, through friends or acquaintances. In a paradigm mentioned repeatedly, a bribe is paid to a lawyer (not involved in the case) that is married to a judge ruling on the affected case. Again, opinions vary, but it is commonly reported that frequently judges act not for money but to do a favor for a friend or relative' (CEELI Judicial Reform Index (JRI) for Bulgaria 2002, 37).

CEELI also invented tools to assess the various legal institutions such as independent courts and the legal profession and wrote periodical reports, 'Reform Indexes', about the status of the Eastern European countries. The JRI, for example, is,

> a tool for assessing a cross-section of key factors for judicial reform in emerging democracies. In an era when legal and judicial reform efforts are receiving more attention than ever, the JRI is proving essential as CEELI, its funders, and the emerging democracies themselves target judicial reform programs and monitor progress as they work toward establishing accountable, effective, and independent judiciaries. (http://www.abanet.org/ceeli/publications/jri/home.html, 7 April 2006)

The JRI had — like other judicial assessment tools — some overall criteria that were developed over time. They were based on Western legal standards both as tools to monitor the legal development and as prescriptions of areas where reforms were needed. They were thus tools that helped the export of law and legal practices from one context to another. The EU Commission uses the Reform Indexes in the writing of country reports focusing on the developments in the countries on the doorsteps to the EU.

The Indexes are partly based on interviews with legal experts, with NGOs and with different governmental officers in Eastern Europe. Often these are the Westernised lawyers, judges and individuals working for NGOs funded by US money. They are often trained and educated by either CEELI or other American agencies. Most of these individuals were themselves a part of the Sofia establishment that advanced quickly in the legal field with the fall of the Zhivkov regime. However, local judges and local lawyers — whom Western assessors saw as being represented by the Sofia establishment — did not necessarily have the same concerns about the various sectors of the law. The locals did not possess the same forms and amounts of capital as their Sofia counterparts and felt that the reforms were an attack on them, their lifestyle and their way of practicing law and conducting business. Or as someone from one of the large Bulgarian cities noted: 'The problems are in Sofia, they do not correspond to the problems outside'. Another judge from a large city believed that 'the problems found by the elite in Sofia are overexposed. I would hope the EU Commission would, like you, go out to the provinces ... power is centralised in Sofia'. As the quotations illustrate, the assessment tools were used by certain groups in the Bulgarian legal field who supported reforms as they were imposed by the West against an increasingly marginalised groups of legal professionals.

With a body of prescriptive literature and semi-scientific reports in the one hand and with tools invented to assess the independence of the courts in Eastern Europe in the other, American lawyers managed to establish standards important for the evaluation of legal institutions globally — standards that also model legal institutions.

The legal principles of perception and appreciation were projected to an international level and were also imported into Eastern European countries by people working as Eastern European brokers of these ideas; people able to introduce such principles into the national battles of the field of power and use the international capital gained from the international investments in the national fields. The necessity of the development was inscribed in the habitus of people working both in the legal field and in the political field. This is illustrated by the following statement from a person with a Western master degree working for the Open Society Institute in Sofia: 'What we do is not really political. And we do not have a political agenda to follow'. Law became a legitimate and neutral way of transforming the State and the market.

EU Programmes and Expertise

In the EU, the co-production of knowledge and integration programmes followed another path than the American. As the following demonstrates, the EU's legal programmes were created in the bureaucratic field of the EU, namely in the Commission (Smith 2004; Smith and Timmins 2000). However, with hardly any expertise about the new situation in the Eastern European countries, the people who were to develop and administer the EU programmes had their background in development or in commerce and competition. In the absence of other expertise, they were inspired by EU programmes in Africa and the expertise that followed from such programmes. In the early stages of the Phare programme, the countries could apply for support for projects which they found necessary to rebuild their societies such as educational programmes, private sector restructuring and investment promotion. Legal reforms were a part of this. As one of the key persons in the Commission, who came from development and took part in the Eastern European programmes, noted 'we developed this type of aid based on individual projects as opposed to regional aid where you give the money to the government directly for agriculture assistance for instance' (Int. 123, Oxford 12 January 7). The assistance was what is termed *demand and market* driven. Private consultancies from the West took part in the big projects that were established (Wedel 2001).

When it became clear that the Eastern European countries were moving for membership of the EU, a group of people invested in a legal focus. In 1993, the Copenhagen European Council defined the criteria the Eastern European countries had to meet if they were to join the European Union: stable institutions guaranteeing democracy, the rule of law, human rights and respect for minorities; the economic criterion was a functioning market economy; and finally, the countries had to incorporate the Community *acquis* and had to adhere to the various political, economic and monetary aims of the European Union. Despite the vague criteria, which did not give specific instructions of institutional organisation, they institutionalised the cooperation and could be used by the EU as an instrument to put pressure on the Eastern European countries in relation to the reform of the countries. Therefore, the group adjusted the Phare programmes. As one of the key persons in the Commission told in an interview:

> And then we felt, now they have applied for membership, should we continue the programmes in the same manner? Or should we reverse the situation? We know in principle what should be good for you, what assistance you should receive, if you want to become member, we could tell you what we think your priorities should be. So we invented the accession partnership, which was an instrument whereby we would draw the priorities. And therefore we changed the way that the Phare programmes were driven: from demand-driven to accession-driven. You can also say that the EU promotion became legalised. The accession partnership gave us the possibility to say, 'Look do not take US experts in that field. Here is the priority, it is this EU legislation'. (Int. no. 118, Brussels, 23 February 2006)

The inventors used their strength to impose the rule-of-law agenda into the political field which became a core area of the assistance to Eastern Europe. With the rule-of-law agenda settled, legal expertise was needed in the Commission.

Another invention was the Twinning programmes, which are programmes supporting specific collaborations between a public institution in the recipient country and a similar institution in one of the EU's Member States. By inventing the new programmes, the Commission changed the ways of using experts and, more importantly, it could place a larger responsibility on the Member States for European integration. 'We saw that the area of public administration was extremely expensive, and we needed to draw on our expertise on the market. And they did not leave stable results, once the experts had left we did not get any local know-how to take on the reforms' (Ibid.).

This new legal turn of the assistance to Eastern Europe not only meant that new forms of assistance were invented, it also meant that the expertise that the Commission would rely on changed: 'Under the Phare programme, whenever there was a study that should be conducted, university teachers or experts from the audit companies wanted to do it; it had become a beautiful cake endless amount of studies. We wanted to get rid of all that as well. Twinning was a way to bring in practitioners, people who could do the job on the ground — bring them in the ministries. But of course the universities were not very enthusiastic about this. Just like the audit companies' (Ibid.). With the Twinning programme, state and legal (and other) bureaucrats were related and became committed to the development of the Eastern European countries. The Twinning programmes, which sent bureaucrats, judges, police officers — or in other words, state officials — to the countries to share their expertise and assist in reform, were also an invention to 'create networks and focus, not a private focus. And then, it might be possible to put political pressure from the members of the EU on the institutions in which the Twinning is', as one of the inventors of the programme told in an interview, before continuing 'by nature, the field of justice and home affairs is something the state is in charge of; it is not the market that changes the judiciary' (Ibid.).

Lamoureux, who had been one of the closest advisors to Delors and who knew the rules of the game, succeeded in ousting others who wanted to expand the programmes to softer areas such as civil society, unions and welfare states. Despite the resistance, especially from the UK, to the changes from market expertise to legal state expertise, Lamoureux won the battle. The legal assessment criteria of the legal reform programmes were decided progressively, mainly by a group of lawyers in the DG Enlargement in Brussels with the assistance of Justice and Home Affairs.

However, the US was still dominant in the area. They had educated the people the EU had to count on when it evaluated the Eastern European countries, just as CEELI had invented evaluation criteria and written country assessment reports on the various Eastern European countries, which the EU lawyers had to use. Thus, many of the criteria and evaluation priorities were set with inspiration from the work of CEELI.

Conclusion

I went to a cocktail party attended by the president's economic adviser. He was a Ph.D. in economics from the Karl Marx Higher Institute of Economics. He did really not know about how things worked. He and I were standing over a glass of wine and he was telling me about the mafia and about how the mafia had infiltrated Bulgaria. And I said I hear about it a lot, but I have personally not experienced the mafia. Oh, he said, I have just heard a story about a person, a young man, who had borrowed one million leva from a bank, and who went down to Greece and bought oranges. He came back and sold the oranges for two million leva and paid the bank back the loan. And made a profit of 200.000 leva. Can you think of anything more mafia-ish? And I just said in the US we would have given him a reward as businessman of the year. And this was the economic advisor to the president! (Int. 1, Colorado, 2 June 2004, see also (Meyer 1992, 1993a, 1993b).

The anecdote was told by an American lawyer and ABA CEELI liaison, who was in Bulgaria just after the changes in 1989. It illustrates the social catego-ries and the overall paradigm of social scientific knowledge of the time in Eastern Europe, which to a certain degree were changed within a limited time period despite efforts to base the developments in Bulgaria on more moderate forms of Socialism. However, the scholarly production supporting such categories diminished with the broader social developments and with the transformation of the state. A host of international experts, think tanks, institutions, private foundations, law firms etc. supported the development through policy visions produced in concrete situations in the West and exported to another concrete situation and very different setting in the East and through legal development programmes based on the neutrality of the law paved the way to liberal reforms. US agents and institutions invented education and training programmes as well as study tours to the US, and they posted Western volunteers, who could relate to Eastern European bro-kers, to support the cultivation of an opposition that could use US knowl-edge, policies and law to transform the national fields of power. Yet, the anecdote symbolises not only the social categories and specific knowledge paradigm of a public employee in Bulgaria in the very beginning of the 1990s, it also illustrates who was involved as a foreign expert to assist the transformation, namely American lawyers. This article has demonstrated how American lawyers took part in the co-production of Western expertise and promotion of state reforms in Eastern Europe in a context of a larger US policy field. The lawyers produced and exported knowledge and policies about state forms, law, market reforms and democracy that were based in a language of necessity hiding the different ways the Eastern European states could take. Moreover, they invented different assessment criteria that were used in the process to — in an allegedly neutral way — evaluate the progress of the Eastern European states and to give recommendations for future development. The programmes were invented in concrete situations in the USA by individual agents in a larger field of production of policy and legal reform programmes closely related to the academic environments.

The EU engagement in Eastern Europe developed over time but was gen-erally based on the expertise of persons in the EU Commission. Initially, the EU did not have expertise on Eastern Europe and had to rely on exper-tise from the market, where experts from universities and especially audit companies dominated. With the transformation of the Phare programme and with the invention of the Twinning programme, the assistance became legalised and the expertise could be found among practitioners in the Member States.

Following the trajectories of legal development programmes in the West, and based on the notion of situatedness as advanced by the sociology-of-knowledge approach, this article has exemplified how legal expertise has been produced in situated national fields, the very structure of which was exported through the funding of institutions, education and support of key agents etc. to other settings, but was transformed when it was used by importing brokers in other national fields with different power structures. Using the notion of contextualism, the article found that the development of legal programmes was intertwined with specific US and EU policy visions, and both policy visions and new legal acts and practices were in focus for the producers and exporters in the West.

Notes

1. The article is based on 155 interviews with key agents who have taken part in the transformation process. Moreover, it is based on policy reports, documents and other research. All interviews were conducted in confidentiality, and the names of interviewees are withheld by mutual agreement.
2. D'Alemberte is a lawyer with the firm of Hunton and Williams. He came from politics, where he was associated with a progressive group of prominent South Florida Democrats, who wielded influence over state policy and politics from the late 1960s. The group included long-term friends such as Janet Reno, as well as the late Governor Lawton Chiles. D'Alemberte received his juris doctor with honours from the University of Florida where he was named to the Order of the Coif and has studied at the London School of Economics and Political Science. He has been dean at the College of Law at the Florida State University and later president of Florida State University, with which he has had long family connections.
3. Moyer is a commercial lawyer working in the international department of the Washington law firm Miller & Chevalier, which specialises in tax, litigation and international disputes. The law firm took in Moyer from the US Commercial Department, where he had worked on international issues, to create an international department. A political appointee in both Democratic and Republican administrations, Moyer has served as General Counsel and Counsellor to the Secretary of the US Department of Commerce. Before government, he practised with Covington & Burling and served in the Office of the Judge Advocate General of the Navy, with collateral duty at the White House. He qualified at Yale Law School.
4. The board was made up of the likes of Max M. Kampelman, Justice O'Connor and Lloyd Cutler. Kampelman was a lawyer with the New York/Washington law firm, Fried, Frank, Harris, Shriver & Jacobson LLP. Alongside his association with the law firm, he has worked in US diplomacy and in related institutions such as Georgetown University's Institute for the Study of Diplomacy, the Woodrow Wilson International Center for Scholars and the think tank Freedom House. Justice O'Connor from Texas was nominated by Reagan for a position at the US Supreme Court, and received her degree from Stanford University. She is married to a commercial lawyer, who used to work for Miller & Chevalier, Washington (Homer Moyer's law firm). Lloyd Cutler was a commercial lawyer whom Clinton took in as legal adviser — albeit on unusual terms that allowed Cutler to remain as senior counsel at his law firm and to work for undisclosed private clients Nader and Smith (1996).

References

Arnholtz, J., and O. Hammerslev. 2013. Transcended power of the state: the role of actors in Pierre Bourdieu's sociology of the state. Distinktion: Scandinavian *Journal of Social Theory* 14, no. 1: 42–64.

Bieler, A. 2002. The struggle over EU enlargement: a historical materialist analysis of European integration. *Journal of European Public Policy* 9, no. 4: 575–97.

Carothers, T. 2003. *Promoting the rule of law abroad: the problem of knowledge*. Washington, DC: In Rule of Law Series.

Cohen, A. 2007. Who are the masters of the treaties? Law and politics in the birth of European constitutionalism. *Praktiske Grunde. Tidsskrift for kultur- og samfundsvidenskab* 1, no 2: 20–33.

Cohen, A. 2008. Transnational statecraft: leagal entrepreneurs, the European field of power and the genesis of the European constitution. In *Paradoxes of European legal integration*, eds. H. Petersen, A.L. Kjær, H. Krunke, and M.R. Madsen, 111–27. Aldershot: Ashgate.

Cohen, A. 2011. Bourdieu hits brussels: the genesis and structure of the European field of power. *International Political Sociology* 5, no. 3: 335–9.

Cohen, A., and A. Vauchez. 2007. Introduction: law, lawyers, and transnational politics in the production of Europe. *Law & Social Inquiry* 32, no. 1: 75–82.

Dezalay, Y., and B.G. Garth. 1996. *Dealing in virtue: international commercial arbitration and the construction of a transnational legal field*. Chicago, IL: The University of Chicago Press.

Dezalay, Y., and B.G. Garth. 2002. *The internationalization of palace wars*. Chicago, IL: University of Chicago Press.

Dezalay, Y., and B.G. Garth. 2010. *Asian legal revivals*. Chicago, IL: University of Chicago Press.

Diez, T. 2009. Michel foucault and the problematization of European governance. *International Political Sociology* 2, no. 3: 266–8.

Elster, J., C. Offe, and U.K. Preuss. 1998. *Institutional design in post-communist societies*. Cambridge: Cambridge University Press.

Gardner, J.A. 1980. *Legal imperialism: American lawyers and foreign aid in latin America*. Madison, WI: The University of Wisconsin Press.

Guilhot, N. 2005. *The democracy makers*. New York: Columbia University Press.

Hammerslev, O. 2007. Reform strategies around the Bulgarian judicial branch: social struggles converted into struggles about court reforms. In *Judicial reforms in central and eastern europe*, eds. R. Coman and J.-M. De Waele, 135–55. Brugge: Vanden Broele.

Hammerslev, O. 2010. The US and the EU in East European legal reform. In *Lawyers and the rule of law in an era of globalization*, eds. Y. Dezalay and B.G. Garth, 134–55. New York: Routledge.

Holman, O. 1993. Transnationalism in Spain: the paradoxes of socialist rule in the 1980s. In *Restructuring hegemony in the global political economy*, ed. H.W. Overbeek, 134–61. London: Routledge.

Holman, O. 1998. Integrating Eastern Europe: EU expansion and the double transformation in Poland, the Czeck Republic, and Hungary. *International Journal of Political Economy* 28, no. 2: 12–43.

Holman, O. 2001. The enlargement of the European Union towards central and Eastern Europe: the role of supranational and transnational actors. In *Social forces in the making of the new Europe: restructuring of European social relations in the global political economy*, eds. A. Bieler and A.D. Morton, 161–84. New York: Palgrave.

Jasanoff, S. 2004. The idiom of co-production. In *States of knowledge*, ed. S. Jasanoff, 1–12. London: Routledge.

Keohane, R.O., J.S. Nye, and S.E. Hoffmann. 1993. *After the cold war: international institutions and state strategies in Europe, 1989–1991*. Cambridge: Harvard University Press.

Meyer, W.D. 1992. *You listened and you cared: year one of the CEELI Liaison mission to Bulgaria*. Washington, DC: CEELI.

Meyer, W.D. 1993a. Bulgarian lawyers in transition. *The Journal of the Legal Profession* 18: 123–44.

Meyer, W.D. 1993b. Remnants of Eastern Europe's totalitarian past: the example of legal education in Bulgaria. *Journal of Legal Education* 43, no. 2: 227–45.

Mudge, S.L., and A. Vauchez. 2012. Building Europe on a weak field: law, exonomics, an scholarly avatars in transnational politics. *American Journal of Sociology* 118, no. 2: 449–92.

Nader, R., and W.J. Smith. 1996. *No contest: corporate lawyers and the perversion of justice in America*. xxviii, 427 p. New York: Random House.

Rosamond, B. 2000. *Theories of European integration*. Hampshire: Macmillan Press.

Schimmelfennig, F. 2001. The community trap: liberal norms, rhetorical action, and the eastern enlargement of the European Union. *International Organization* 55, no. 1: 47–80.

Schimmelfennig, F., S. Engert, and H. Knobel. 2006. *International socialization in Europe*. Hampshire: Palgrave Macmillan.

Schimmelfennig, F., and U. Sedelmeier. 2005. *The politics of European Union enlargement*. London: Routledge.

Smith, K.E. 2004. *The making of EU foreign policy*. New York: Palgrave Macmillan.

Smith, M.A., and G. Timmins. 2000. *Building a bigger Europe EU and nato enlargement in comparative perspective*. xiii, 184 p. Aldershot: Ashgate.

Trubek, D.M., and M. Galanter. 1974. Scholars in self-estrangement: some reflections on the crisis in law and development studies in the United States. *Wisconsin Law Review* 1062–102.

Trubek, D.M., and A. Santos. 2006. *The new law and economic development*. Cambridge: Cambridge University Press.

Van Apeldoorn, B. 2000. Transnational class agency and European governance: the case of the European round table of industrialists. *New Political Economy* 5, no. 2: 157–81.

Van Apeldoorn, B. 2003. The struggle over European order: transnational class agency in the making of 'embedded neo-liberalism'. In *State/space*, eds. N. Brenner, B. Jessop, M. Jones, and G. MacLeod, 147–64. London: Sage.

Van Der Pijl, K. 2001. What happened to the European option for Eastern Europe? In *Social forces in the making of the new Europe: the restructuring of European social relations in the global political economy*, eds. A. Bieler and A.D. Morton, 185–204. New York: Palgrave.

Vauchez, A. 2010. The transnational politics of judicialization: Van gend en loos and the making of EU polity. *European Law Journal* 16, no. 1: 1–28.

Vauchez, A. 2011. Interstitial power in fields of limited statehood: introducing a weak field approach to the study of transnational settings. *International Political Sociology* 5, no. 3: 340–5.

Wedel, J.R. 2001. *Collision and collusion: the strange case of western aid to Eastern Europe*. New York: Palgrave.

What is the Nature of the Relationship between Changes in European Higher Education and Social Science Research on Higher Education and (Why) Does It Matter?

ROSEMARY DEEM

School of Management & Principal's Office, Royal Holloway and Bedford New College, Egham, UK

ABSTRACT   The paper examines the relationship between changes in European higher education and social science research on this theme and why it matters. Higher Education (HE) research is a new field significantly assisted by European funding, the Bologna process and the massification of HE. The field is populated by many emerging researchers but few established academics. The paper examines the sub-field's characteristics including lack of theoretical/methodological consensus, co-production of the knowledge base and the differing micro and contextual backgrounds of emerging European HE researchers (drawing on a recent study). It considers three recent major European-funded HE research projects as examples of co-production, specifically looking at the kinds of knowledge produced and the strategies adopted to ensure that research outcomes permeate the policy process. It is suggested that the sub-field needs to develop a better infrastructure to support emerging researchers, but care needs to be taken not to impair their independence from European bureaucrats.

Introduction

The paper examines the nature of the relationship between changes in European higher education and social science research on higher education and why this matters. In so doing, it draws on a sociology of knowledge approach as outlined in the editors' introduction to this volume, particularly drawing on the principles of the symmetry of different knowledge claims, rejection of internal and external divisions between knowledge production and societal or economic developments, situatedness which emphasizes the micro-settings of scholars and academic departments and contexualism which suggests how national or regional cultures can shape knowledge debates. The paper relates the recent history of a relatively new sub-field of Education studies,[1] namely Higher Education (HE) research. This account enquires into the status of HE research (it isn't a close disciplinary community with high paradigmatic and methodological consensus), its legitimacy (which is as much in relation to practice as policy) and its connections to European education policy and practice. The paper deals with how HE research is generated and how EU bureaucrats may have accidentally helped develop a new type of researcher studying HE, one typically focused on teaching and learning, as well as a new type of HE in the aftermath of the Bologna process reforms to structures, systems and processes in higher education institutions. EU grant funding has played a part in the growth of HE research, but it is the Bologna transformation of European higher education and the massification of HE that has generated the most pressing questions for new researchers in the sub-field (Curaj et al. 2012; Corbett and Henkel 2013). Both the social context and the science have often been closely intertwined, in the tradition of co-production of knowledge (Jasanoff 2004), thus to a large extent blurring the internal and external elements of the sub-field. At the same time, the proliferation of research themes and inexperience of many HE researchers mean a high degree of contestation in the field (Bourdieu 1986, 1988) and a danger of overlooking the issue of symmetry in relation to past and present knowledge claims. Also, the prominence of European initiatives fuelling the sub-field's growth could lead to what Vauchez (2008), writing about the development of European Legal Studies, calls a 'weak' academic field, heavily dependent on EU bureaucrats and lawyers for its very existence, though it seems this is only partially true for HE research. As we will see later, the European HE sub-field is characterized by a large number of doctoral students and post-doctoral researchers, typically based in Education, Sociology, Public Administration, Economics or Management/ Business units, where HE is often a minority interest for a small number of established academics. Other emerging researchers may be focused on pedagogical research in their own subject, institutional research or working in a unit supporting the development of new academics' teaching skills. Thus, sources of legitimacy for and motivation to work in the field cross many local contexts. In addition, there are a very small number of established HE Research Centres in Europe that attract significant external research funding.

The knowledge produced in the field of HE is very varied. Some of it serves particular political and strategic interests or is funded directly from European sources (whether policy-focused or 'blue skies'), while other projects deal with practical demands (most usually related to teaching) at the coalface of higher education institutions. Although co-produced by practitioners and researchers, these projects are not directly related to the activities of EU bureaucrats, even though some pedagogic and curricular challenges arise from the consequences of the uneven imposition of the Bologna process (Curaj *et al.* 2012). Emerging researchers working in the HE sub-field may have no sense of being situated within a coherent academic community (Ashwin, Deem and McAlpine 2013) and their projects often reflect local conditions or practitioner challenges, not European concerns. The lack of agreement on key paradigms or methodologies means that in Bourdieu's terms (Bourdieu 1986, 1988), this is a highly contested field. It is not, however, the local or wider national context that gives rise to this, rather it is the wide range of disciplines that HE researchers come from. Emerging HE researchers are not always able to exploit the full potential of the knowledge they have created and may have naïve views about how to interact with the policy process (Ashwin, Deem and McAlpine 2013). All this is considered in the sections about the field and who undertakes HE research and in the final section of the paper where three large European HE projects are considered. But first, we turn to a description and analysis of the field of HE research as presently constituted.

Higher Education as a Field of Study

Higher education research is a fast growing area of study in Europe and elsewhere, including North America and Australasia (McFarlane and Grant 2012; Tight 2012). Its content is comprehensive, covering a wide range of matters from academic, student and leader/manager identities, institutions, systems, policies, cultures and discourses to teaching, learning and assessment practices and quality assurance mechanisms. The interest in cultures is particularly apposite as European higher education moves away from transmitting and interpreting national cultures (Delanty 2001; Clegg 2012) towards focusing on more global concerns. Not all HE research is social science-based because often HE researchers (especially newer recruits) have no background in social science. This does not matter if they are drawing on their own disciplinary traditions to support their investigations, but a minority claim to do social science without knowing the literature or understanding its methods.

The sub-field has been boosted in Europe and beyond as almost all signatory countries to the Bologna agreement are funding and supporting higher education research, whether directly or through publicly funded institutions. Much of this growth is linked to the massification of higher education, which has led to a search for the systemic, cultural, social, political, economic and organizational requirements of universities that are not elite research-intensive institutions and which may either be dual-intensive (focused on both teaching and research) or teaching-intensive (sometimes with a vocational focus). Undoubtedly, the expansion of European higher education has led to the growth of many more teaching-intensive institutions, perhaps because adding research is expensive. Improving teaching has become an important European-wide consideration (European

Commission 2013), leading to many institutionally-funded investigations as well as a mass of curriculum development, intervention and networking projects funded by the EU. Governments and higher educational institutions, not just in the European Higher Education Area but worldwide, have become very interested in how students learn, how they should be taught and how they can be assessed, widening socio-economic access to universities, analysing how higher education and economic development connect, considering how to exercise control over world league tables of universities and how and which quality evaluation measures should be applied to teaching and research. But as with its parent subject Education, which is itself arguably not a discipline but a multi-disciplinary subject (Deem 1996), higher education research has a complex and sometimes tenuous relationship to social science. Though it might seem self-evident that the study of higher education, as something so closely bound up with cultural, economic and social development, would have a close connection to social science, both this connection and the theoretical component of higher education research have been questioned (Tight 2004, 2014); Tight based his analysis on outputs published in major international HE research journals. Though most of HE research knowledge has a social science underpinning, those who carry out HE research come from diverse backgrounds, from doctoral students and post-doctoral fellows with a strong social science background embarking on a first career, to those whose first degree might have been in any discipline from physics to history and who have entered the field serendipitously as a second or third career, whether in academe, educational administration or institutional research. Where neither social science nor an alternative disciplinary base is evident, such as history or philosophy, there can also be questions about the quality and validity of the analyses produced.

The foci of higher education research are similarly diverse. One categorization suggests there is research *into* higher education (e.g. policy, organizational studies, academic identities or quality assurance/enhancement); academic development (which supports teaching staff in universities) plus disciplinary pedagogic research (Clegg 2012). Leaving aside that there might be both research *on* higher education and research *for* higher education (the latter often comprising institutional research and not necessarily adopting a critical approach), there are also those with no background in educational research but who work in higher education and have become interested in analysing some of the recent policy developments and organizational consequences through a polemical lens (Docherty 2011; Collini 2012). In Bourdieu's terms (Bourdieu 1986, 1988, 1993), higher education research is not just one contested field of cultural and knowledge production but several, with very different routes into them. Overlaying this is the division of academics into those who base their status and prestige on academic power 'founded on the accumulation of positions allowing control of other positions' (Bourdieu 1988, 73), such as acting as academic gate keepers, whether as recruiters of other academics or as editors and referees of academic publications and funding bodies and those who base their status and prestige on scientific research expertise and scientific prestige, which is 'founded on successful investment in the activity of research alone' (ibid., 74). In higher education research, it is arguable that both capitals are found within the same people but with the proviso that many researchers have little access to either. Yet Bourdieu's assumption was that those exercising academic power have different habituses and capital to those for whom scientific prestige is their main form of power. So it may be useful before going further to gain an understanding of who it is that actually carries out higher educational research and the extent to which researchers are reliant on EU bureaucrats, either directly or indirectly, for their research questions and funding.

Who is Conducting Higher Education Research?

In exploring the recent history of higher education research, one study talks of *forerunners,* mostly from sociology, psychology, philosophy or history who set the boundaries of the field and *pathtakers* who then develop these further (McFarlane and Grant 2012). But given Clegg's definitional work (2012) and my own view that HE research is really a series of contested sub-fields, things may be a little more complicated. Most of the major established HE researchers in Europe are drawn from the social sciences, mainly from sociology, public administration, economics, psychology, organizational studies, science studies or economics. Their bases include locations like the International Centre for Higher Education Research (IN-CHER), Kassel, Germany; the Finnish Institute for Educational Research (FIER) at Jyvaskyla in Finland, the Centre for Research on Higher Education Policies (CIPES) at Matosinhos in Portugal, the Centre for Higher Education Policy Studies (CHEPS) in Enschede, the Netherlands, the Centre for the Sociology of Organisations (CSO) at SciencesPo, Paris, France and until quite recently the Centre for Higher Education Research and Information (CHERI)[2] at the Open University in the UK . The members of these centres are closely networked with each other, mainly from Western Europe/Scandinavia, run or work in sizeable research centres, tend to dominate cross-national funding as well as major field conferences and are responsible for writing many of the European papers in the main international HE journals and in edited book collections. They are in frequent touch with policy-makers, both EU and others, often work closely with them and do consultancy around the world. They work through a variety of means, including through conferences and policy focused events, briefing papers, expert advisory groups, telephone calls, social media and conventional media interventions. They have strong links to North American and Australasian researchers amongst others. They are mostly members of a European group called the Consortium for Higher Education Researchers (CHER), which organizes an annual conference with a policy focus. But there is also a vast array of researchers working on their own or with a small number of colleagues, from Western, Middle and Eastern Europe, often researching teaching and learning and sometimes involved in European funded projects focused on curriculum development, interventions, networking, teaching and learning, student/staff exchange or conducting national/locally focused studies, sometimes for institutional purposes. A considerable number of such researchers are studying for a doctorate, often part-time or have recently completed one. There are also a few researchers for whom higher education is an arena that they work in only occasionally, with their main interests elsewhere.

Where do the early-career individuals come from? Research conducted with Lynn McAlpine and Paul Ashwin on the biographies, experiences, ambitions and policy interactions of a sample of 42 newcomers to HE research mainly based in Europe and interviewed during spring/summer 2012, throws some light on this. The vast majority (31 women, 11 men) were completing or had recently completed a doctorate in some aspect of HE. There were some sharp divides here between the researchers from mainland Europe who mainly entered higher education research at doctoral level after a bachelor's and Master's degree in social sciences and those (typically in the UK) who had first and master's degrees in a range of non-social science disciplines, whether STEM or Arts/Humanities and turned to higher education research (which might be a professional doctorate with a substantial taught component and a shorter thesis, usually practitioner or practice-focused or a conventional PhD) as a means to entering a second or third career. Some of the latter group were experienced higher education staff (including academics and student support or quality assurance administrators) or working in professional fields such as healthcare. We found that despite being well-positioned to observe recent HE policy developments, only a minority of our respondents — mainly those who had already been working in HE or a cognate field in a senior post prior to taking their doctorate or those who were in their first career but with experience of European policy networks such as ESIB (European Students Union) or NGOs — were really aware of how they might set out to influence policy decisions. So, though co-production through the growth of HE institutions and changes to how they operate via Bologna is stimulating much of the research, the feedback loop is not necessarily operating in the other direction for emerging researchers. The Bologna process may add legitimacy to the knowledge claims of newer researchers but the knowledge they create typically permeates practice rather than policy and only at a very local level.

In Europe, as already noted, there are also a number of well-established centres of HE research. Such centres are typically staffed by a mix of senior and mid to early career researchers, where experienced academics can mentor early career colleagues once the latter's doctorates are complete. But few of the researchers we interviewed were attached to such centres. This means that there is a new generation of higher education researchers who may not have anyone experienced in the subfields to assist them in their peregrinations around academe and HE policy networks. Nor will most of them end up in academic roles, as the number of new posts is affected by the global and Eurozone financial crises, though some may come to occupy hybrid academic/administrative posts in fields like student support or research management. We found that many of the newer researchers we interviewed had naïve views about policy and believed that when their current project was complete or when they were in a more senior post, then, it would be relatively easy to influence policy. On the other hand, this does suggest independence from EU bureaucrats or their national equivalent. With a small number of exceptions, only those who had done a doctorate as a route to or alongside an established post in HE or a cognate professional field, were knowledgeable about how policy networks operate and how to permeate these. We have drawn conceptually on work about policy influence in UK schools which examines the different relationships that those working in educational institutions establish with policy, broadly summarized as people being active policy actors or more passive subjects of policy (Ball *et al.* 2010; Ball, Maguire, Braun, *et al.* 2011; Ball, Maguire, Hoskins, *et al.* 2011). Well over half of our sample fell into the latter category, though quite a few had the desire to become 'future influencers' of policy. But how, if at all, does HE research permeate the policy sphere? Does the co-production process help this or is being a new researcher in a 'weak' and heavily contested sub-field just too challenging for it to work effectively? This is explored in the next section.

How Does Research on Higher Education Affect Policy on and Practice in European Higher Education?

There are a number of ways in which HE research can shape policy, from basic research dissemination via email, websites, social media and e-journals, researchers being members of expert panels commissioned by policy-makers, contributions to public or debate on a topic, framing the decisions leading to policy, including the so-called evidence-based policy-making (Clegg 2005; Walter, Nutley and Davies 2005), through to changing the decision-making mechanisms of the policy-making processes, reshaping the cultures and practices of organizations and so on. The co-production of knowledge occurring when academics work with practitioners and policy-makers (Jasanoff 2004) is also much in evidence, whether by the established elite in big projects or at a more micro-institutional level by much less experienced researchers. Being in a local or national social context where big changes are happening to higher education as a result of Bologna-initiated changes to structures, credit frameworks, types of degrees, student and staff mobility and quality assurance processes, has had a formative effect on European higher education research. There are some very major aspects of European HE that have been particularly shaped by HE research. These include detailed and comprehensive studies of student mobility (e.g. Kelo, Teichler and Wächter 2006; Rizva and Teichler 2007), involving student exchange schemes such as Erasmus from 1987 onwards. Student mobility arguably preceded Bologna by many decades or even centuries but has also been a hallmark of both recent European higher education and the Bologna process and a strong driver of shared credit frameworks and common degree cycles and levels. A further key aspect of Bologna has been establishing common quality assurance mechanisms for teaching across the European Higher Education Area and research on quality assurance of teaching and learning has become a major field in itself, with whole journals devoted to it. There have been a number of large EU-funded projects on this topic (e.g. Eggins 2014) which have both documented and contributed to European HE policy on quality assurance mechanisms and practices. International League Tables and university rankings have been another field where HE research has made a significant impact on what happens in Europe, as in the European Commission sponsored 'Multi Rank' project (Van Vught and Ziegele 2010, 2012) described later in the paper.

But, as shaping policy works as much or more through networks (van Waarden 2006) as through sifting new evidence and ideas, so in the case of research, it is not just the data themselves (which inevitably in the social sciences are often tentative and provisional) which provide the impetus to change. In fact, this is rarely the case. Policy-makers and politicians don't tend to look around for new ideas by reading the evidence, they look for evidence that fits what they have already decided to do and often these days that is as likely to be on social media, particularly Twitter, as in policy briefings, at expert panel meetings or through policy-maker and practitioner-focused publications. Policymakers may on occasions commission a project (the EC 'Multi-Rank' project is one of these) rather than looking at what has been done already. Furthermore, though a lot of 'policy borrowing' and 'policy copying' certainly exist across different EHEA systems, this is often based on short visits by policy-makers and politicians to the system concerned rather than on research.

So, if we apply this to higher education, then those with established networks in policy communities, such as members of the well-known European HE research centres, are more likely to be on the inside track in relation to European policy and indeed more likely to be funded to do policy-relevant research than anyone else. Both Bourdieu's types of capital, academic and scientific converge into policy influence as gatekeepers and researchers combine resources. At local level, some of the many other higher educational researchers, if they have the right kinds of networks (social and academic capital), and can get funding for research (scientific prestige) or work through personal sponsorship (academic capital, which is often gendered), may come into their own. However, this can be serendipitous, as someone's work coincides with the area policy-makers are tackling and is well-disseminated beyond learned journals or has non-academic involvement built into the research design. This is confirmed by our current work with newer researchers, not just those in the UK, many of whom aspire passively to influence policy but have no idea how to achieve this. They may well have some influence locally but their reach beyond that is likely to be small. So, in a field like higher education research, the voice of the few well-established, well-networked researchers prevails on the European stage and de facto much funding (both policy-focused and 'blue skies') will also flow to those researchers. This has the effect of ensuring a certain degree of both conservatism and uniformity, and similar theoretical and methodological underpinnings in what is done and recommended. Whilst not merely serving the bureaucrats, such researchers are much closer to them than the emerging researchers, who are largely exploiting the changes to the HE social context that the Bologna process has made possible. In the broader context of higher education, there is also another problem with the potential effects of research on policy and practice. Even at the organizational level, universities themselves are often reluctant to take seriously the work done by higher education researchers (Deem 2006) because their senior teams dislike their organizations being held up as objects for research, despite the importance of academic research in general as a core activity to many institutions. This may, of course, say something about the way in which senior teams in universities operate (Organisation for Economic Co-operation and Development 2006; Deem 2009, 2012) and the horizons and visions they have for the future (Huisman, De Boer and Bótas 2012). In the next section, the focus shifts to reviewing some of the reforms that have already taken place in European higher education, in this case through the Bologna process, which have fuelled many of the research topics currently being investigated in the HE field, thus vividly demonstrating the effect of the social context on knowledge production.

Bologna and Changes to European Higher Education

The project of European coherence in higher education is arguably and largely being pursued at a transnational level through the Bologna process bureaucratically and not always with the benefit of sustained research evidence. But at the national and local levels, the many research projects and academic papers on the implementation of Bologna (Wihlborg and Teelken 2014) or on other issues thrown up by the Bologna process (Corbett and Henkel 2013), are more likely to have an effect and one which is independent of the bureaucrats, whilst still engaging with Bologna-related themes. Since the initial Bologna agreement was signed in 1999, many of the larger elements of Bologna, such as the three cycles of higher education, student and staff exchange and mobility, ECTS credit transfer and the wide availability of the Diploma Supplement and recognition of systems of quality assurance, have been achieved in principle in the majority of signatory countries, to the extent that there is acceptance of their importance and considerable numbers of countries have reformed their structures and co-operated in quality assurance (EACEA 2012). On the other hand, student and staff mobility rates are still quite low (ibid.) relative to EU expectations, and individual systems of higher education in the European Higher Education Area (EHEA) vary widely in terms of their governance (for example, who appoints or elects rectors and which external stakeholders sit on governing boards or councils), their academic, legal and financial autonomy, their cultures and their support for lifelong learning, as well as how they have implemented the first two cycles of higher education and the flow between these. Of course, there has been much research on the various elements of the Bologna agreement, some by the big players, or by a range of other both financially and academically independent researchers (Wihlborg and Teelken 2014), but it is unclear how much effect this knowledge has had on the overall implementation process, despite its evident co-production. This suggests that HE research does not fit neatly into Vauchez's 'weak' field category since it is not solely dependent on European bureaucrats and policy-makers for its existence in the way that European legal studies is. The field of HE research is alive and well globally as well as in Europe and in addition, national policies and the day-to-day challenges of HE teachers, researchers and leaders in different national systems are, if anything, a larger stimulus for HE research than European funding or bureaucratic foci and concerns. Many of the topics of HE research in Europe are not dissimilar to those which are pursued by researchers in countries which are not signatories to Bologna, as a glance at the last two years' submissions to and publications in top journals in the HE field suggests.[3] Doing research *for* rather than *on* policy is in any case challenging. Those who run higher education systems tend to want positive recognition of their reforms and changes, not academic criticisms of their failings, but they may nevertheless from time to time alight on or commission research which meets their requirement for a scientific backing to decisions already made or about to be made.

Bologna implementation was arguably not helped by the global financial crisis from 2008 onwards or by the related Eurozone crisis, both of which sent several European public higher education systems into crisis mode. As the level of private higher education funding in the EHEA rises, even in those countries which have had relatively little privatization so far, it is questionable how much further progress Bologna will be able to make towards a uniform system of HE. It may be that some of the next areas of development in higher education lie outside the scope of Bologna. Indeed, some innovations with a research base seem initially to have passed Europe by; thus whilst the US launched its MOOCS (Massive Open Online Courses) some years ago, Europe was slower to do so (though the UK Open University-based FutureLearn has now been set up to do this). MOOCs on higher education topics would be a significant if partial contribution to one of the more elusive elements of Bologna, namely lifelong learning. In the next section, I look at three examples of recent large funded projects on higher education carried out and funded in Europe and the extent to which the social science knowledge generated has contributed through these to the development of European higher education and whether those involved are too closely tied to bureaucratic concerns. These projects are in part themselves an example of Jasanoff's (2004) co-production of knowledge, in this case alongside policy-makers and of Vauchez's (2008) idea of how a weak field might operate, working alongside and closely tied to European bureaucrats, but the three project rationales and genesis differ considerably.

Three European HE Research Projects

In this section, I look briefly at three European HE projects funded in last few years that are concerned with the challenges and features of current and future European higher education. The first of these is the European Commission-funded UMap and Multirank project (Van Vught and Ziegele 2010), running from 2005 to 2010. This project involved a number of the elite group of European educational researchers including CHEPS at the University of Twente and also the Centre for Higher Education in Germany which is more of a think tank than a standard research group but which had already been devising an alternative ranking system for Germany and Austria higher education. Multirank and UMap have always had a practical rather than theoretical focus (Van Vught and Ziegele 2010):

> The U-Map project is the third phase of a research project on developing a European Classification of Higher Education Institutions. The first two phases produced a set of principles for designing the classification as well as a draft of a multi-dimensional classification including an appropriate set of dimensions (the areas in which institutions will be classified) and indicators to measure them. In this phase we evaluate and fine-tune the dimensions and their indicators and bring them into line with other relevant indicator initiatives, all of this in a process of stakeholder consultation and discussion that has been a hallmark of the project since its inception in 2005.

Ranking and league tables are a big concern for European universities and the European Commission as well as many other HE systems and policymakers (Hazelkorn 2011). The two dominant sets of international league tables, the Shanghai Jiao Tong table, which mostly focuses on research and the Times Higher Education ranking, which is broader but uses proxies for teaching quality and has some other problematic features such as stakeholder reputation ranking, do not always feature European universities at the highest level, particularly the Jiao Tong listings (whose development was funded by the Chinese government). So, whilst the EC want to develop a set of classifications using a more complex set of factors, making allowances for significant institutional variation is evident. Although social science expertise about universities as organizations and how to classify them internationally has fed into the projects, Multirank itself seems to have arisen far more from the demands of European politicians and policymakers than from social science itself, as most of the literature critiques league tables rather than seeking to emulate them, though it is true that the Multirank project does that to an extent too. The co-production of knowledge in this project could be seen as somewhat lop-sided. The EC adopted Multirank as of December 2012 (see http://www.u-multirank.eu) and so presumably hopes that it will in time take its place alongside the Times Higher and Jiao Tong league tables of universities. But of itself, this exercise does not contribute to the improvement and development of European higher education. Indeed, it may serve to exacerbate the differences between the elite universities and other institutions of higher education. However, maybe it is better to get social scientists to develop something rather than leave it to the private sector? The Times Higher League Table has strong links with Thomson publishers who run the Science and Social Science Citation Indexes and own many of the journals in those indices and Jiao Tong relies a lot on citation data. The Multi-Rank project has also led to more conventional outputs such as books (Van Vught and

Ziegele 2012). But does this trend to commissioned research and co-production of knowledge suggest that the use of social science knowledge and expertise in policy comes at a price to academic freedom? This would be an example of HE research as a 'weak' field (Vauchez 2008).

The second project considered here was a scoping exercise funded by the European Science Foundation 'Higher Education in Europe Beyond 2010: Resolving Conflicting Social and Economic Expectations (2005–2007)' and was part of the ESF's 'Forward Look' programme. A main aim was to develop an academic agenda for future higher education research. The same elite group of researchers were involved in the project as in other major European studies of higher education. It was led by John Brennan of the Centre for Higher Education Research and Information in the UK (the Centre, based at the OU, has now closed) with Jurgen Enders from CHEPS, University of Twente, the Netherlands, Christine Musselin from SciencesPo in France, Ulrich Teichler from INCHER at the University of Kassel, Germany, and Jussi Valimaa of FIER at the University of Jyvaskyla in Finland from 2006 to 2007. As well as reviews of existing research, the project also held workshops with other researchers in the field and focused on a number of themes including: higher education and the needs of the knowledge society; higher education and the achievement or absence of equity and social justice; higher education and its communities; the steering and governance of higher education and finally the differentiation and diversity of institutional forms and professional roles (Brennan *et al.* 2009). After this, ESF developed a new programme of research, the EUROCORES. The latter also involved national research councils, but it was not surprising that several of the projects in the subsequent EuroHESC programme went to those who had done or were linked to those who had undertaken the initial scoping exercise. This project and the programme that followed were undoubtedly fused with elements of blues skies social science research, but apart from a small number of early career higher education researchers who worked on some of the projects as research assistants, it did not build any significant new social science capacity but relied on existing networks and researchers. If we are to work towards a stronger higher education system in Europe, we need to also think about building serious capacity in higher education research alongside this elite group. In scattered fields of researchers, those with the most academic and scientific capital tend to dominate. Only a few of the Centres in the core group of European social scientists actually also teach higher education topics at undergraduate or masters level, so the research does not always even permeate teaching.

The final project is one on university autonomy which was in two parts, the first starting in 2009 and the second in 2010 and which was also ostensibly a very applied project more akin to Multirank than to 'Higher Education in Europe beyond 2010' and another example of co-production. The funding came from the European Universities Association (a Europe-wide university mission group) and the European Commission's Lifelong Learning Programme, but a number of individual universities also assisted the study. The project initially explored the complexities of university autonomy, which is often treated in the literature as though it were a single and easily identifiable phenomenon, and then moving onto classify European universities by country on the basis of a fourfold typology of dimensions of autonomy: organizational, financial, staffing and academic autonomy, in 26 European countries. Each dimension is divided into different indicators. A scorecard for each dimension gives a percentage score to each national system and adding them together, classifies them into four groups with different levels of autonomy. Unlike Multirank, this project is not aimed at developing a new league table but is intended to inform higher education policy in each country and to create a debate about university autonomy at system and European level (Estermann, Nokkala and Steinel 2011). At least one of the researchers who worked on the project was a relative newcomer to higher education research and Estermann was a professional administrator. Unlike Multirank, the conceptual framework from this study can be applied to other empirical work, including individual universities, so its existence has not only contributed to a Europe-wide debate about university autonomy, but also to the furtherance of an area of higher education research in its own right. However, interestingly, it too is an example of co-production of knowledge alongside policy-makers and other potential users of that knowledge. All three projects show how difficult it is to separate the internal from the external architects of social science research but equally demonstrates how this co-production may produce knowledge which is less critical than it might be if it operated entirely outside the EU context.

Why Does All This Matter?

The paper has explored, in an attempt to map the development of a new sub-field which has operated within the social context of the Bologna reforms, the content conditions and growth of European higher education research knowledge and issues of symmetry around different knowledge claims, who undertakes this research and their backgrounds (situatedness), the national systems they work within (contextualization) the extent of co-production of knowledge, the merging of internal and external divisions in knowledge creation and how established academics and bureaucrats can often be intertwined, how higher education research seeks to have an effect on policy-making (such as in the fields of student mobility, quality assurance of teaching and learning and league tables/rankings) and the naïvete of some of the more junior proponents of HE research in this regard. The paper has also summarized some of the major changes taking place in European higher education as a consequence of the Bologna agreement (not all of them on the basis of research evidence) and three recent funded projects on higher education themes which were very much related to wider European policy themes, albeit in different ways. As noted at the beginning of the paper, European higher education research covers many themes but also has a tenuous relationship with social science, since emerging researchers may have little or no grounding in this but rather come with more practical concerns from a wide range of disciplines. This adds to the lack of paradigmatic and methodological agreement in the field. Furthermore, though higher education research is burgeoning, much of the growth is in relatively new researchers who lack the experience, networks and other aspects of academic and scientific capital that more senior higher education researchers have but do have the advantage that they are not advancing the requirements of bureaucrats and are often genuinely independent researchers. The pyramid of researchers is far from top-heavy numerically, but in practice most of the researchers who conduct significant social science research in the sub-field are a tightly-knit network who come from a small number of research centres in Western European countries and who are well networked into policy communities too. This has consequences for the kind of research that is done, its theoretical underpinnings and methodologies and its future sustainability, particularly where it is not linked to undergraduate or masters teaching. It also has consequences for the future development of European higher education. The skillful use of social science in relation to researching and shaping higher education policy-making and policy reform in Europe does matter because otherwise the policy-makers will have everything their own way but perhaps the diversity in its focus, methodologies and theoretical perspectives at lower levels, though in some ways a weakness, means the knowledge produced is more detached from bureaucratic concerns and perhaps more critical than it can be at the level of more established researchers.

As we have seen in the paper, the implementation of the Bologna process is still far from complete and there are many new challenges ahead, particularly in respect of the current financial crisis in the Eurozone, which is likely to bring more private higher education and less government influence over what happens to HE systems and institutions. The 'public' systems of higher education in the European Higher Education Area still have very many differences, yet the amount of genuinely comparative research on European higher education is quite small. This is despite many previous EU funded collaborative projects in various versions of the Framework programmes, Socrates, Tempus, etc. All too often, the results of such funding have largely vanished, leaving little or no mark on either social science or higher education, except very locally. In addition, there are too few mechanisms for putting together the accumulated knowledge of many individual projects other than systematic literature reviews, which are quickly outdated and may be of limited interest to policy-makers. There is little flow into the established centres of higher education research from the wider reservoirs of newer higher education researchers and in fact more of the current centres may themselves disappear as funding becomes harder to obtain. So whilst it has been argued that HE research in Europe is only in part a 'weak' field dependent on EU bureaucracy for its survival since newer researchers are more independent, its health is not secured because research capacity at the bottom of the ladder is not necessarily being retained and the knowledge produced is not often feeding into policy, partially because of the lack of awareness of how to do this.

It is undoubtedly important that social science continues to inform the development of European higher education systems and their institutions, but it is also important that such inputs are critical and do not just serve the interests of bureaucrats. Using a sociology of knowledge approach to this theme has allowed the skewed pyramid of European HE research to become more visible and has shown the complexities of the micro and social contexts in which such knowledge is co-produced and the variation in whether HE research is tied to bureaucratic concerns or to the day-to-day challenges of practitioners. The use of the sociology of knowledge approach, which is different to that used in most other accounts of the growth of HE research, has also suggested that distinguishing between internal and external drivers of research is unhelpful and that all knowledge claims need to be acknowledged.

In conclusion, both academic and scientific capital in the subfields of European higher education research remain locked into a small number of locations and those who are part of the research elite are not necessarily opening up policy networks to newcomers, yet these networks and co-production of knowledge would benefit considerably from permeation by a plurality of different kinds of higher education research. Equally, the freedom of emerging HE researchers to investigate any topic they wish is worth preserving, since it ensures they are free from being pressurized into only researching phenomena created by EU bureaucrats, which Vauchez (2008) notes is one feature of a weak discipline. The story of European HE research has until now largely remained untold within the field of European studies, yet as this paper has demonstrated, what happens to the co-production of higher education research knowledge is very important to Europe's future.

Acknowledgements

An earlier version of this paper was presented at the 'Making Europe: The Social Sciences and the Production of European Integration' workshop, University of Copenhagen, 4–5 February 2013. I am grateful to the anonymous referees and participants in both the Copenhagen workshop and those at the September 2014 Joint Network 22 (HE) of the European Conference on Educational Research (ECER) and Society for Research into Higher Education workshop 'European Higher Education — Exploring Effective Strategies for Turbulent Times' held at the University of Porto, Portugal, for their helpful comments on the paper.

Notes

1. This ambiguity between whether Higher Education research is a sub-field or a sub-discipline relates to a wider debate about the status of Education as a discipline or subject. It may be best characterized as a subject because its proponents come from a wide range of disciplines and there is no paradigmatic agreement between different academics within the field. This is reflected in Higher Education research too.
2. CHERI closed in summer 2011 and its staff have now dispersed.
3. Confidential communication to the author.

References

Ashwin, P., R. Deem, and L. McAlpine. 2013. Newer researchers in European higher education creating new knowledge in a climate of austerity; policy actors or policy subjects? Unpublished paper presented to the Consortium of Higher Education Researchers Conference, Lausanne. September & currently under review.

Ball, S., M. Maguire, A. Braun, and K. Hoskins. 2011. Policy actors: doing policy work in schools. *Discourse* 32, no. 4: 625–39.

Ball, S., M. Maguire, A. Braun, K. Hoskins, and J. Perryman. 2010. *Policy actors/policy subjects peopling policy*. http://www.ioe.ac.uk/Policy_actors_policy_subjects_peopling_policy.pdf.

Ball, S., M. Maguire, K. Hoskins, and A. Braun. 2011. Policy subjects and policy actors in schools: some necessary but insufficient analyses. *Discourse* 32, no. 4: 611–24.

Bourdieu, P. 1986. The forms of capital. In *Handbook of theory and research for the sociology of education*, ed. J.G. Richardson, 241–58. New York: Greenwood Press.

Bourdieu, P. 1988. *Homo academicus*. Cambridge: Polity Press.

Bourdieu, P. 1993. *The field of cultural production*. Cambridge: Polity Press.

Brennan, J., J. Enders, C. Musselin, U. Teichler, and J. Välimaa. 2009. *Higher education looking forward: relations between higher education and society*. Strasbourg: European Science Foundation.

Clegg, S. 2005. Evidence-based practice in educational research: a critical realist critique of systematic review. *British Journal of Sociology of Education* 26, no. 3: 415–28.

Clegg, S. 2012. Conceptualising higher education research and/or academic development as 'fields': a critical analysis. *Higher Education Research & Development* 31, no. 5: 667–78.

Collini, S. 2012. *What are universities for?* London: Penguin.

Corbett, A., and M. Henkel. 2013. The Bologna dynamic: strengths and weaknesses of the Europeanisation of higher education. *European Political Science* 12: 415–23.

Curaj, A., P. Scott, L. Vlasceanu, and L. Wilson, eds. 2012. *European higher education at the crossroads: between the Bologna process and national reforms*. Dordrecht: Springer.

Deem, R. 1996. Educational research in the context of the social sciences: a special case? *British Journal of Educational Studies* XXXXIV, no. 2: 141–58.

Deem, R. 2006. Changing research perspectives on the management of higher education: can research permeate the activities of manager-academics? *Higher Education Quarterly* 60, no. 3: 203–28.

Deem, R. 2009. Leading and managing contemporary UK universities: do excellence and meritocracy still prevail over diversity? *Higher Education Policy* 29, no. 1: 3–17.

Deem, R. 2012. The twenty-first-century university: dilemmas of leadership and organizational futures. In *The Global University: past, present, and future perspectives*, eds. A. Nelson and I. Wei, 105–32. New York: Palgrave MacMillan.

Delanty, G. 2001. *Challenging knowledge: the university in the knowledge society*. Buckingham: Open University Press.

Docherty, T. 2011. *For the university: democracy and the future of the institution*. London: Bloomsbury Academic.

Education, Audiovisual and Culture Executive Agency, Eurostat, Eurostudent. 2012. *The European higher education area in 2012*. http://www.ehea.info/Uploads/(1)/BolognaProcessImplementationRe port.pdf.

Eggins, H., ed. 2014. *Drivers and barriers to achieving quality in higher education*. Dordrecht: Springer.

Estermann, T., T. Nokkala, and M. Steinel. 2011. *University autonomy in Europe II: the scorecard*. Brussels. http://www.eua.be/Libraries/Publications/University_Autonomy_in_Europe_II_-_The_Score card.sflb.ashx.

European Commission High Level Group on the Modernisation of Higher Education. 2013. *Improving the quality of teaching and learning in Europe's higher education institutions*. Luxembourg: Publications Office of the European Union.

Hazelkorn, E. 2011. *Rankings and the reshaping of higher education: the battle for world-class excellence*. Basingstoke: Palgrave.

Huisman, J., H. De Boer, and P.C.P. Bótas. 2012. Where do we go from here? The future of English higher education. *Higher Education Quarterly* 66, no. 4: 341–62.

Jasanoff, S. 2004. *The co-production of science and the social order*. New York: Routledge.

Kelo, M., U. Teichler, and B. Wächter. 2006. Toward improved data on student mobility in Europe: findings and concepts of the Eurodata study. *Journal of Studies in International Education* 10, no. 3: 194–223.

McFarlane, B., and B. Grant. 2012. The growth of higher education studies: From forerunners to pathtakers. *Higher Education Research & Development* 31, no. 5: 621–4.

Organisation for Economic Co-operation and Development. 2006. *Four future scenarios for higher education*. Paris. http://www.oecd.org/document/8/0,3343,en_2649_35845581_37031944_1_1_1_ 1,00.html.

Rizva, B., and U. Teichler. 2007. The changing role of student mobility. *Higher Education Policy* 20: 457–75.

Tight, M. 2004. Research into higher education — an a-theoretical community of practice? *Higher Education Research and Development* 23, no. 4: 398–412.

Tight, M. 2012. *Researching higher education*. 2nd ed. Maidenhead: Open University Press.

Tight, M. 2014. Discipline and theory in higher education. *Research Papers in Education* 29, no. 1: 93–110.

Van Vught, F., and F. Ziegele. 2010. Design and testing the feasibility of a multidimensional global university ranking: final report. http://ec.europa.eu/education/higher-education/doc/multirank_en.pdf.

Van Vught, F., and F. Ziegele, eds. 2012. *Multidimensional ranking: the design and development of U-multirank*. Dordrecht: Springer.

Vauchez, A. 2008. The force of a weak field: law and lawyers in the government of the European Union (For a renewed research agenda). *International Political Sociology* 2, no. 2: 128–44.

van Waarden, F. 2006. Dimensions and types of policy networks. *European Journal of Political Research* 21, no. 1–2: 29–52.

Walter, I., S. Nutley, and H. Davies. 2005. What works to promote evidence-based practice? A cross-sector review. *Evidence and Policy* 1, no. 3: 335–64.

Wihlborg, M., and C. Teelken. 2014. Striving for uniformity, Hoping for Innovation and Diversification: a critical review concerning the Bologna Process - providing an overview and reflecting on the criticism. *Policy Futures in Education* 12, no. 8: 1084–100.

The Creation of a European Socio-economic Classification: Limits of Expert-driven Statistical Integration

ETIENNE PENISSAT* & JAY ROWELL**

*CNRS, Centre for Study and Research in Administration, Politics and Society, University of Lille, Lille, France;
**CNRS, Society, Actors and Government in Europe Research Centre, University of Strasbourg, Strasbourg, France

ABSTRACT   Since the 1990s, the European Union has sought to create a harmonised socio-economic classification scheme which symbolically unifies the social structures of the 28 member States in a common tool of description. Relying heavily on expert networks, this project, with numerous potential policy applications, has so far failed to come to fruition. After examining the scientific networks and institutional resources of an initial model which was at the centre of discussions for nearly ten years, the article explores the reason for its ultimate failure. Combining science studies and a political sociology approach, the article highlights the effects of conflicting legitimacies within expert networks, the lack of diversified institutional resources and contacts of the dominant experts, the poor fit of sociologically based methods to an EU administrative culture more focused on knowledge based on economic methodologies, and the lack of a wider European debate and mobilisation on inequalities which, in national histories, were key to the creation of national socio-economic classification schemes.

Since the mid 1990s, the political project of the European Union has been increasingly shaped by statistical tools. Statistical categories provided institutions and actors with uniform descriptive languages and categories, and the importance they have steadily acquired can be seen as a means to manage the increasing diversity of the EU following enlargements and

127

expansion into new policy areas. Statistical indicators deployed by the EU have several functions: setting tangible targets and monitoring national policy convergence in the run-up to the Euro or the enforcement of budgetary discipline; relying on statistical information to improve the quality of decisions; using ex-post and ex-ante evaluation to increase output legitimacy; providing the empirical basis for new forms of policy coordination such as benchmarking or the open method of coordination (Arrowsmith, Sisson, and Marginson 2004; Büchs 2007; Dehousse 2011); and making the activities of EU institutions more transparent to citizens, and more objective (Porter 1995) and predictable (Power 1999) to stakeholders.

Social statistics have been integral to this broad trend and were an essential element in the institutionalisation of European social policies which did not command many of the traditional tools of EU regulation. The development of social policies in the EU therefore required a determined effort to equip policies with common definitions and statistical indicators. This process is in many ways comparable to the role played by statistics in the emergence of modern States where control over the production, the circulation and the use of statistical knowledge was essential to the extension and the consolidation of modern bureaucracies (Brian 1994; Desrosières 1998; Tooze 2001). The process of totalisation and simplification of complex realities through statistical measurement allows for comparisons, the identification of problems and, more broadly, it symbolically unifies territories, social groups and practices within a single polity (Bourdieu 1993). Knowledge instruments do not just capture a pre-existing reality. Despite their apparent scientific objectivity, they are by no means politically or socially neutral (Lascoumes and Le Gales 2007). Instead, they have transformative effects on their objects through selection and categorisation (Goody 1986) that simplify and translate a variety of people, things and practices into categories that can be acted upon by bureaucracies. Therefore, knowledge instruments contain a performative and symbolic dimension (Austin 1962) and as indicators they construct abstractions such as inflation, unemployment or social groups as tangible realities (Desrosières 1998). This has historically involved the enrolment of scientific knowledge (Hacking 1990; Jasanoff 2004; O'Connor 2001), and the EU is no exception.

In a polity where 'evidence-based policy-making' built on different forms of quantification has become a central catchword, insights provided by the sociology of science could provide useful tools to study relationships between scientific knowledge and bureaucratic power as well as the various dynamics involved in the selection of pertinent knowledge in the forging of new categories and scales of policy intervention. To study these processes more closely, we will focus on an ongoing project to construct a harmonised European socio-economic classification (ESeC) scheme entitled ESeC and recently renamed European Socio-economic Groups.[1] Since 1999, Eurostat and DG Research have funded a series of studies, working groups and task forces principally composed of academic sociologists and representatives of national statistical offices to operationalise the goal to construct a classification scheme. However, despite the scientific and technical legitimacy of the involved experts and the availability of a classification system in use for over

20 years in comparative research, the project has still to come to fruition.[2] European bureaucracies which could imaginably have a strong interest in this powerful analytical tool revealing inequalities in a variety of areas (health, consumption, employment, education, culture, etc.) have not shown much interest or even awareness of the project.

To unravel these puzzles, our analytical framework mobilises several guiding principles of science studies outlined in the introductory chapter. First, statistical instruments are objects which combine scientific methods and categories with bureaucratic practices and imperatives and thus can only be studied by combining internal and external approaches to knowledge production. This implies not only taking into account validity claims within scientific communities, but also considering social and institutional contexts which shape representations, expectations and interests (Bourdieu 1991) which can hinder or facilitate circulations of knowledge between academic and bureaucratic fields. Second, the situated approach (Abbott 1999; Camic 1995) focusing on contextualised configurations of actors, the resources they mobilise, as well as controversies is useful to reconstruct the internal dynamics of expert groups which frame solutions for bureaucracies. In order to understand the conditions in which knowledge produced in expert circles generates wider beliefs in their validity, circulates and becomes integrated in policy-making, a third and final principle of recent science studies can be mobilised for the benefit of EU policy studies: symmetry. By studying this largely failed attempt at institutionalising new categories of knowledge and action into European public policy, we may get new insights into the conditions which promoted the successful circulations between European institutions and academic disciplines. As research on European statistical objects such as indicators on social inclusion (Atkinson *et al.* 2002), homelessness (Brousse 2005), benchmarking in research policy (Bruno, Jacquot, and Mandin 2006) or Eurobarometer (Aldrin 2011) have shown, statistical instruments deployed by the EU are often co-constructions between academic experts and European bureaucracies (Kassim and Le Galès 2010). Bureaucracies, themselves often in competition, identify and capture available knowledge instruments to further their own objectives. In this transactional dynamic, it is important to ascertain the sociological and institutional properties and interests of bureaucrats in order to understand why they select certain available knowledge instruments and experts, rather than others. Conversely, the ability of academic experts to translate their expertise into categories and procedures which are both understood and perceived as useful depends largely on their familiarity with bureaucratic logics and the diversity of their social capital.

Taking into account the sociological and institutional structuring of the European field (Georgakakis and Rowell 2013) appears all the more important, as professional interests, representations and anticipations are largely structured by their participation in their respective fields (Bourdieu 1998). In this sense, the conceptualisation of Europe as a 'weak field' facilitating (but sometimes hindering) the occupation of multiple institutional positions or career moves from one field to another appears beneficial (Mudge and Vauchez 2012; Vauchez 2008). This line of research has demonstrated that the relative permeability of the European field allowed for the multipositioning of lawyers in academia, politics and EU institutions which was conducive to a circulation of knowledge and legitimacy between the emerging EU institutions and some academic scholars. As we will demonstrate, the weak connections between the academic sociologists promoting ESeC and the Brussels bureaucracy, as well as the cognitive dissonance between sociological tools of measurement and established knowledge instruments based on economic theories embedded in existing policy frames, greatly hindered the institutionalisation of ESeC.

Using this analytical framework, we retrace in the first section the various stages of harmonising socio-economic categories which began in the late 1990s. In doing so, we show that the initial political impetus was relatively weak and that the momentum of the project was largely maintained by a network of sociologists around John Goldthorpe who sought to 'outsource' data collection to Eurostat. In the second section, we examine the controversies which opposed this group of sociologists to statisticians led by the French INSEE (National Institute of Statistics and Economic Studies). These controversies, as well as the bureaucratic capital held by INSEE, tended to 'renationalise' a classification scheme which had been used for over two decades in international comparisons. By making visible a series of 'anomalies' which were not adequately described by the 'standard' theory, to use Kuhnian terminology (Kuhn 1962), these statisticians were able to weaken the foundations of one of the prerequisites to the successful institutionalisation of European categories: beliefs in its ability to accurately measure and compare across member States. We will then examine the sociological and institutional context which appears to have hindered the circulation and the institutionalisation of this tool despite its many potential uses in policy-making.

ESeC Between Bureaucratic Impulsion and a Scientific Enterprise

The emergence of limited, yet institutionalised European policy competencies in employment, social inclusion, lifelong learning and the fight against discrimination brought with them the need to develop statistical indicators. This process gave increased prerogatives to Eurostat vis-à-vis national statistical institutes (Sverdrup 2005) and resulted in the harmonisation of statistical tools through the increasing standardisation of EU surveys (Elissalt 2001; Nivière 2005), a convergence of definitions and statistical categories, and the elaboration of new indicators to measure to identify best practices.

The first mentions of a ESeC date to seminars organised by the Mondorf group (1995–1996), which brought together members of Eurostat and the directors of social statistics services of national statistical offices. Without being central in the discussions, the desirability of a ESeC figured in Eurostat reports defining the strategy for producing common European variables (Everaers 1998; Østby et al. 2000). The first in-depth report was commissioned in 1999 from a recently retired General Inspector of INSEE who had previously worked for Eurostat, Bernard Grais. In his exploratory report, Grais justified its utility in the following terms:

> Socio-professional classifications have long demonstrated their analytical capacity and represented an essential element in national statistical integration. A harmonised European classification could play the same unifying role by providing a common language in order to improve the integration of social statistics into the Community, horizontally in each Member State, and vertically at the European level. (Grais 1999)

If this quote underscores the potential of the instrument as an analytical tool as well as a lever for European integration, its commissioning owes much to the behind-the-scenes activity of the British and French national statistical offices. Both countries had a strong tradition in this area and their representatives, on temporary postings to Eurostat, sought to promote their statistical tools as a model for European harmonisation. The Grais report compares the different existing national classification schemes in order to identify points of convergence and divergence as a starting point for further work.

After the initial report, Eurostat published a call for tenders to define recommendations for setting up a European classification system. The British Office of National Statistics won the contract in 2001 and sub-contracted the report to a group of sociologists from the University of Essex (David Rose and David Pevalin) and an economist from the University of Warwick (Peter Elias). This group had played a leading role in the 2001 reform of the British social class scheme. These social scientists were recognised experts in statistical classifications and the study of social mobility and stratification. Their 2001 report did not follow the direction of the Grais report which recommended a search for common ground among existing national classifications (Rose, Pevalin, and Elias 2001). Instead, it proposed a prototype largely inspired by the British sociologist John Goldthorpe's classification scheme and argued that it was validated by years of comparative academic research. However, Eurostat did not immediately pursue the project and it was DG Research, with which this group of sociologists had strong ties over a number of years, which picked up the project and put together a consortium to pursue the project two years later. Between 2003 and 2006, the consortium, composed of representatives from seven universities and several national statistical offices, was provided with 800,000 to refine the prototype and undertake validation tests. The final report (Harrison and Rose 2006) confirmed the theoretical orientations of the 2001 report and it appeared at the time that the scientific legitimacy of the Goldthorpe scheme would allow it to be confirmed as a new tool at the disposal of European policymakers. In order to understand why this tool appeared as the only way to harmonised statistics, but also why it was vulnerable to controversies which tended to 'renationalise' its claims to universal validity (as we will see later), we will examine the consolidation and institutionalisation of a knowledge instrument which was forged in a specific national context in the 1970s before its construction as a theoretical scheme with universal application in the following decades.

The authority which the sociologists commanded in the 2000s was built on a long experience in statistical classification and on the density of a scientific network built around John Goldthorpe since the 1970s. After a series of widely read qualitative research publications on the transformations of the working class in Britain in the 1960s, Goldthorpe switched to quantitative research and constructed his first classification scheme, entitled the 'Goldthorpe classes' in the mid-1970s, on the basis of a large survey on social mobility and class in the UK. Composed of seven classes, the classification scheme is inspired, but it does not totally overlap with status hierarchies developed in earlier research on social prestige; the 'Hope–Goldthorpe scale' (Goldthorpe and Hope 1974). This initial classification scheme was developed in the context of an intense debate in sociology on social mobility, with mainly American conceptions based on status and prestige in a fluid conception of social mobility on the one side and researchers such as Goldthorpe who reasoned in terms of distinct social groups or classes on the other. While distancing himself from a Marxist class conception, Goldthorpe also rejected a representation of society in terms of continuous positions with great fluidity, as class barriers remained central to political debates in the UK of the 1970s, and the upward mobility of the working class a central political question.

The Goldthorpe classes were first mobilised in comparative research at the end of the 1970s (Erikson, Goldthorpe, and Portocarero 1979). From then on, the classification, also known as EGP following the names of the three authors, would engage in an international 'career', structuring an increasingly dense and diversified network of sociologists. What started as a tool to measure social mobility in the UK in the context of specific scientific and political debates would become a codified and routinised tool for international comparison benefitting from several forms of institutionalisation. Together with the German sociologist and specialist in social mobility and education, Walter Müller, Goldthorpe headed a vast comparative project launched in 1984: *Comparative Analysis of Social Mobility in Industrial Nations* (CASMIN), which included 10 European countries as well as Australia and the United States. The project ended with an influential publication: *The constant flux: a study of class mobility in industrial societies* (Erikson and Goldthorpe 1992). The diffusion and institutionalisation of the tool was also based on the density and the mobilisation of the network of researchers who adopted it in their research. The Committee on Social Stratification and Mobility of International Sociological Association played an important structuring role, and Goldthorpe was the vice president from 1974 to 1982 before becoming president. Together with Karl-Ulrich Meyer, in 1984 Goldthorpe also founded one of the first European sociological journals, *The European Sociological Review,* which became a platform for publishing quantitative comparative research. Finally, the sociologists also created a foundation, the European Consortium for Sociological Research in 1991, serving as a structure to promote the discipline within the European Commission, as well as funding projects and training researchers in statistical methods. The strength of this network and its institutional surface allowed it to obtain a succession of large European framework grants and to play an important role in the 2001 creation of the European Social Survey funded by the EU but driven by academic research.

At the beginning of the 2000s, EGP was well established in countless scientific publications, was used by a number of prestigious sociologists from many European countries, and had benefitted from institutionalisation in national as well as professional institutions. ESeC, as it appeared in the 2001 and 2006 reports, was therefore not the result of a distillation of common denominators of existing national classifications. It was rather a 'capture' of an existing instrument promoted by a network of prominent and highly internationalised sociologists.

In order to understand the controversies which blocked its adoption by the EU, it is necessary to briefly present Goldthorpe's classification scheme and ESeC. In the original model, individuals are allocated to one of nine socio-economic groups by applying two criteria: market situation and work situation. Labour market experience was seen to be capital in determining life chances and was considered to be relatively homogeneous within each class and different from one class to the other in terms of revenues and their progression, consumption, educational choices, health, values, political behaviour, etc. The model was relatively empirical and pragmatic in the 1970s, but at the beginning of the 1990s, as he sought to intensively diffuse his model, Goldthorpe theoretically formalised the class scheme. Market situation and work situation were collapsed into one concept, 'employment relations' (Erikson and Goldthorpe 1992). Directly inspired by this model, ESeC created 10 groups and operated an initial distinction between employees, employers and the self-employed. Employees were broken down by differentiating the degree of subordination with their employer. This conception, establishing hierarchical differences based on the degree of autonomy in the workplace, is implicitly built on the model of large organisations characterised by a pronounced division of labour. To a certain extent, it also takes the viewpoint of the employer by drawing on the principal–agent literature. ESeC is presented by its promoters as a purely theoretical construction using categories which are simple to manipulate and which authorise the assignation of class positions based on professions and hierarchical positions. For these promoters, ESeC is constructed by and for scientific comparative research, it is built on a conversion matrix with the International Standard Classification of Occupations (ISCO), but it requires the collection of other variables such as company size and the number of workers supervised in the workplace.

Representing European Social Groups: Social and Institutional Determinants of Scientific Controversies

Despite the legitimacy of the tool and the domination of the 'Goldthorpian' sociologists within the 2003–2006 consortium, the internal controversies cast doubt on the ability of the tool to accurately reflect social structures in all member States. Although the controversies centred on definitional or methodological issues, they were structured by struggles to impose the legitimate form of expertise, and they reflected differing institutional interests and national representations of how to correctly reflect social stratification.

The work of the consortium, spanning over three years, included 90 persons, but the central core was composed of about 20 sociologists and statisticians from national statistical offices. The principal protagonists were: David Rose (UK) who headed the consortium,[3] aided by Eric Harrison, Peter Elias (UK),[4] Christopher Whelan (Ireland),[5] Robert Erikson (Sweden), Walter Müller (Germany), Anton Kunst (Netherlands),[6] Antonio Schizzerotto (Italy),[7] and Dominique Goux, Pierre Biscourp, then Cécile Brousse (INSEE) for France. Erikson and Müller were the most prominent academics involved; the former in part due to his proximity with Goldthorpe and through his presence on the European scene. The latter directed the Mannheim Centre for European Social Research, played an important role in the conception of German statistical tools and was an active participant in the revision of the international education classification; ISCED. The academics were exclusively masculine and from Western Europe, with only one representative from Southern Europe. All were sociologists with the exception of Peter Elias, an economist, and Anton Kunst, a demographer. Most were towards the end of distinguished careers, with the exception of Kunst and Harrison, and were members of the same scientific networks: ISA, members of the editorial committee of the *European Sociological Review*, the CASMIN project and participants in the FPRD projects. Most had extensive experience in expert committees of the European Commission, and several played important roles in revisions of statistical categories in national or international institutions.

The backgrounds of the French participants diverge considerably. They were not academics, but civil servants and statisticians with a background in economics. The uncontested monopoly the INSEE holds on socio-economic classifications in France and the relative weakness of quantitative sociology in France explains why INSEE represented France rather than academics. These professional and sociological differences between academic sociologists and statisticians, primarily from INSEE, are essential to understanding the controversies which punctuated the work of the consortium.

During internal debates, the promoters of ESeC mobilised a series of claims to reinforce beliefs that the tool produced knowledge which was both universal (i.e. European) and valid. ESeC is a classification based on an unique and distinctive criteria (employment relations), making it possible to test and to potentially invalidate, but which provides unequivocal results. The second argument, close to the first, was that the routine use of the model in international comparative research made it ready to use. 'It could travel' as Goldthorpe wrote (Goldthorpe 2000). Finally, and this argument is less used, but perhaps decisive, the statistical methods underpinning the classification justify its use. The multidimensionality of the French INSEE classification or the British Social Classes in use until 2001 combines employment status, the position in the organisation, the status of the employer (private or public) and qualifications, making statistical tests based on regressions impossible, as one is uncertain of what is actually being measured: employment position, qualifications or revenues (Goldthorpe 2002, 187–189). Regression techniques dominate in many academic disciplines, while multiple-factor analysis is marginal in international publications. This helps explain why the sociologists so vigorously opposed proposals from Eurostat or INSEE statisticians to include skills and qualifications in a harmonised European classification.

Most of the internal controversies were initiated by the French statisticians. They admitted the 'national' character of their own classification and did not present it as a viable alternative. Their criticisms of the ESeC prototype initially focused on several aspects. First, the labels of the Goldthorpe classes were criticised for their abstraction (e.g. 'higher and lower salariat' or 'routine occupations'), thereby raising the problem of the social resonance of categories which made little sense in the different national contexts. Second, they criticised, without success, the claim that socio-economic positions could be adequately captured without including the distinction between private or public employers, skills or wealth. Once this battle was lost, worried that the British model would become generalised and weaken the French classification which had existed since 1954, INSEE representatives changed strategies and played to their comparative advantage by steering the debate away from theoretical questions to 'technical' problems of implementation where their cards were stronger.

From 2005 on, the new representative of INSEE used 'technical' knowhow in validation tests to raise two essential objections. The first concerned the volatility of results depending on the wording of questions used to ascertain the size of the employer and the level of supervision; questions which were key to the assignment of individuals to the different classes of salaried employees. Here, the use of a convention of three or 10 employees per employer generated huge shifts from one category to another. The phrasing of the question on supervision again produced huge movements from one class to another, as a study carried out by INSEE demonstrated by showing that size of the class 6 of 'supervisors' varied from 30% of the active French population when the question was phrased: 'Does your work include the supervision of at least three other persons'? (question used to construct ESeC), to only 7% when the more restrictive ILO survey question was asked: 'Is supervision your principal function'? Furthermore, Walter Müller raised the problem of the translation of the question in the Labour Force Surveys of Eurostat and its potential effects on the comparability of data (Müller *et al.* 2006). In Germany: 'Are you in a supervisory position'? In Italy: 'Are you responsible for the coordination of the work of other employees'? In the UK: 'In your work, are you formally responsible for the supervision of other employees'?

A second series of controversies also undermined beliefs in the ability of ESeC to correctly capture social stratifications across Europe. Debate arose on the centrality ascribed to supervision rather than qualifications, most notably in Germany and France where qualifications are much more essential to defining employment status than in the UK (Müller *et al.* 2006). Working with Swedish data, the sociologist Michael Tahlin presented a paper to the consortium claiming that employment relations actually measure, without saying so, differences in qualification (Tahlin 2007). More disturbing was the fact that the validation tests revealed that ESeC was poorly equipped to capture socio-economic stratification in Eastern and

Southern Europe. A Greek geographer, Thomas Maloutas, argued in a discussion paper that a classification scheme invented in a (British) context in which 90% of the population was salaried, predominantly in large organisations, had limited validity in countries in which small businesses and a large agricultural sector dominate (Maloutas 2007).

These controversies revealed underlying oppositions of professional expertise and interests as well as national political and scientific traditions. Ultimately, these debates were a reflection of struggles for the authority to impose the legitimate 'visions of the divisions of the social world' (Bourdieu 1980). ESeC was based on the supposed capacity of a theoretical model to generate equivalencies between a variety of national socio-professional structures. However, the controversies revealed some implicit 'national biases' built into the model at its inception, which had been neutralised over the decades by the collective scientific enterprise of theorisation and through the routinisation of comparisons.

From a sociology of science perspective, the lack of scientific and methodological consensus within the community of experts undoubtedly weakened beliefs in the validity of the scheme proposed by the Goldthorpian sociologists. Doubts on the robustness of ESeC categories proved to be decisive for Eurostat officials and for national statistical officers of countries who were not familiar with the instrument and whose professional ethos of precision led them to question the pertinence of variables which appeared so dependent on the wording of questions and on national contexts. In a tight budgetary context, increasing the number of core variables placed extra burdens on national statistical institutes and risked lowering survey response rates by lengthening the list of core variables. In addition, personal contacts which the INSEE statisticians enjoyed at Eurostat were also undoubtedly capital in blocking the officialisation of the 'British' scheme in 2006 and the commissioning of a new round of studies in 2011 awarded to a group of national statistical institutes headed by INSEE. The remit of the group, which finished its work in May 2014, was to propose a new, simplified classification scheme based on the reformed ISCO 2008 categories; a scheme which did not require any additional core variables in the European Labour Force Survey.

To understand why Eurostat or other Commission DGs failed to commit more resources to the project to push it to fruition, we will widen the scope of enquiry to look at the more structural obstacles to the institutionalisation of this knowledge tool.

Contextual Obstacles to the Institutionalisation and Circulation of Knowledge Instruments

Despite the scientific authority of the sociologists in the consortium and their classification scheme, there appears to have been little political impetus from DGs such as Employment, Health, or Culture and Education, even though social inequalities play an important role in determining behaviour and outcomes in their policy areas. Over more than 15 years, Eurostat has failed to conclude decisively or commit significant internal resources to the project. Only one Eurostat statistician was in charge of the project on a part-time basis and work was consistently sub-contracted. In interviews, Eurostat officials bluntly stated that the project was never high on the list of priorities.[8]

How can we make sense of the hiatus between the centrality of numbers in the public discourse of the EU and the relatively weak implication of EU bureaucracies in creating this potentially powerful analytical tool? Here, our attention will move from the producers and production of knowledge in confined expert circles to the study of its reception in segments of the EU Commission. Due to the fact that the project has so far failed to find broader support, it was by definition impossible to trace the circulation of knowledge from one arena or set of actors to another. However, by taking up the symmetry principle presented in the introduction by comparing with documented cases where the collaboration between academic experts and the Commission succeeded, we can make some sound hypotheses on the configurations which are more or less conducive to the bureaucratic institutionalisation of knowledge tools originating in the academic sphere.

It is striking that little attention was given, either by Eurostat or by academic experts, to spell out the potential uses of the tool to end-users in the Commission. Contrary to other indicators which can be used directly to measure performance or outcomes in benchmarking procedures, socioeconomic classifications do not by themselves represent a target or objective for policy-making. They only reveal their potential when put into relation with indicators measuring other 'problems' on the institutional agenda. As such, in many national contexts socio-economic classifications have proved to be a powerful analytical tool in sociology, public debate and policy-making, for example in understanding inequalities in cultural practices, employment, school performance, health indicators and morbidity, political behaviour and so forth. Their potential uses in policy-making include targeting populations for policy measures and more generally measuring the effects of policy in terms of unequal outcomes or access to material or symbolic goods.

Part of the answer to the puzzle undoubtedly lies in the fact that the expert academics formed a homogenous group whose professional interests mainly remained imprisoned in the logics of the academic field. Due to their weak disciplinary diversity (nearly all are sociologists), institutional contacts (centred mainly on DG Research) and thematic diversity (social mobility with little expertise on health, consumption, education or employment), the academics were unable to promote their tool to potential users in the Commission. Contrary to the British economist, Tony Atkinson, who headed the team that conceptualised indicators for the MOC Inclusion and who had been cultivating relations to top civil servants of the Commission since the 1970s, or the close relationship and shared interest in the institutionalisation of Eurostat between Jacques-René Rabier and Ronald Inglehart (Aldrin 2011), the academic sociologists of the consortium had few contacts in the Commission other than DG Research or Eurostat:

We never had a direct line to the Commission. That I remember. T. would write to people in the Commission, mainly at Eurostat. It was very much a statistical exercise really, rather than a policy one or a broader scientific one. It was quite narrow. You develop a classification, get national statistical offices to test it, then Eurostat would take it. But there was never anything in a straight line selling it in terms of impact, policy usage, no, I don't remember having contact with particular DG's. We did produce, and that's in the book, and was presented in Bled, sort of what K. and the Rotterdam guys did on health. You know good kind of socially useful illustrations. [...] There was no other flow.[9]

The lack of diversified social capital in the Commission made it difficult for them to integrate potential uses other than scientific research into their reasoning. In their debates with statisticians, they mainly sought to maintain a scientific orthodoxy of their model in order to fulfil the goal of having long series of tailor-made statistical data in all EU countries for use in their scientific research and academic debates.

The failure to make connections takes on a less strategic and more structural aspect when the homogeneity of the academic sociologists is put into relationship with the sociological profiles and bureaucratic interests of the potential end-users in 'social' DGs. A survey from 2008 (Kassim *et al.* 2013), corroborated by other studies (Georgakakis and de Lassalle 2007), documents the predominance of top Commission officials with degrees in economics within the DGs whose perimeter of action theoretically would include questions of social equality. In DG Employment, for example, nearly all division heads and a majority of unit heads were trained in economics. The reflex of trained economists when thinking about social inequalities (if at all), ingrained during their studies and through indicators used in academic literature, is to use income inequalities, or in a more human capital approach, educational attainment. These indicators, which were harmonised in the early 2000s, are perceived to be straightforward and simple (even if their measurement and comparison across countries is complicated), and correspond both to professional norms of how inequalities should be measured and norms of 'evidence-based policy making' within the Commission where DG ECFIN plays a leading role in defining the types of legitimate knowledge.[10] The vision of society is structurally a sociological insofar as their professional training and practice leads them to think of the European population either in terms of geographically based aggregates (national or regional) or in terms of the sociologically decontextualised individual of econometric models in which the individual, equipped with an economic rationality, is thought to respond predictably to sanctions or rewards produced by public policy (i.e. benefit or welfare traps, active social policy, fiscal stimulation, etc.). What was lacking was both a common language and a set of cognitive tools bringing together bureaucrats and academic experts pursuing distinct, yet complimentary interests (Aldrin 2011). In the case of ESeC, a majority of civil servants were certainly receptive to the logic and power of numbers, but they were unable to make sense of the aggregated sociological categories of ESeC or see their potential.

In contrast to gender, age, handicap, immigrant status or territorial inequalities, the sociological conception of socio-economic inequality has not been constructed as a subject of political preoccupation at the European level. Evaluating social inequalities of 'life chances' based on socio-economic categories is simply put a type of knowledge which is unfamiliar to EU civil servants and, in contrast to the other forms of institutionalised inequality and their measurement, there was no active interest group such as the European Trade Union Confederation putting pressure on the Commission or feeding a public debate. Wider social mobilisation of interest groups and public debates appear thus to be a final and important condition to the successful institutionalisation of knowledge instruments in Europe, where advances in harmonising employment statistics, social exclusion or homelessness echoed important public debate in Europe. A series of seminal works in national contexts also underscores the importance of wider public debate in generating and stabilising measurement tools: the links between the debates on eugenics and the creation of statistical knowledge in Britain between 1865 and 1930 (MacKenzie 1981), the conceptualisation of poverty in the United States (O'Connor 2001), and the invention of social class classifications in the UK (Szreter 1996) or in France (Desrosières and Thévenot 1988). In these cases, the inscription of categories of vision and division of society into official statistics and bureaucratic logics was supported by mobilised collective actors and connected to broader debates: the position, size and role of the working class; the official recognition of new social groups; the size and the contours of the social and economic elite; the logics of social reproduction and the justification of differential social status; the question of the porosity of frontiers between social classes, and so on. There are neither collective-bargaining mechanisms on the European scale, nor is there a European debate on the causes or consequences of socio-economic inequalities; however, powerful these determinants may still be in determining life chances in education, cultural practice, health or economic outcomes.

Conclusion

The EU as a whole, and the Commission in particular, claims to base policy-making on 'evidence' in an effort to improve efficiency, transparency and legitimacy by mobilising the power of numbers. As in science studies, we took the claim that 'evidence' is essential to European policy-making seriously by studying struggles to define the validity and methodology of knowledge claims. The integration of 'exterior' contexts (institutional, sociological and political) to understand successful and unsuccessful attempts to transform scientific knowledge into bureaucratic tools places the European discourse on the objectivity of statistical evidence in a more political light. As administrative expertise and capacity is limited, the EU has relied largely on outsourcing expertise and capturing knowledge tools developed in other social fields (Gornitzka and Sverdrup 2011). However this 'capture' of outside knowledge is by no means politically neutral, as it involves the selection of particular forms of expertise and knowledge instruments dependent on budgetary and institutional constraints, as well as on professional expectations, shared conceptions of the legitimate visions and divisions of the social order, and the congruence of knowledge tools with pre-existing policy frames.

By mobilising a set of analytical principles borrowed from the sociology of knowledge (situatedness, symmetry, combining 'internal' and 'external' dynamics to understanding controversies) and combining these with more structural sociological approaches in EU Studies (Fligstein 2009; Georgakakis and Rowell 2013; Kauppi and Madsen 2013; Vauchez and De Witte 2013), we have proposed a methodological framework which could usefully contribute to EU policy research by empirically hardening constructivist perspectives (Rowell and Mangenot 2010). The symmetry argument was used to highlight the conditions of the successful institution-alisation of knowledge instruments by identifying some of the obstacles to circulations between academic and bureaucratic fields which our case study revealed. These included professional, institutional and national cleavages within the expert community, but also the porosity between the academic and bureaucratic fields, the existence of divergent, but compatible interests, and the way in which academic tools are presented as useful and easy to understand for civil servants with backgrounds in economics. The advan-tage of working on a sequence of events marked by controversy and hesita-tion was that it made a series of structural and local oppositions visible for observation. While successful operations of knowledge production, selec-tion, codification and institutionalisation give less empirical purchase, the methodological toolbox presented in this paper provides some avenues to explore 'successful' cases, not only in social policy, but also in economic policy, where the cognitive categories provided by statistical indicators appear as objective and apolitical cornerstones of European public policy. Finally, the findings indicate that what many have interpreted as the neo-liberal bias in the EU is not sufficiently explained by the asymmetry between positive and negative integration, the aggregation of national pref-erences or the political values of European civil servants. When looking at the statistical categories used to equip EU social and anti-discrimination policies and comparing these to the failed attempt to institutionalise ESeC, one can understand that statistical categories are not just neutral recordings of social reality, but they are also vehicles which institutionalise certain visions of society and political orientations to the exclusion of others. EU statistics and support and recognition for interest groups institute social groups such as women, the youth, senior citizens, ethnic or national minor-ities or the handicapped for measures relating to discrimination. Indicators on employment, poverty or education mobilise indicators on revenues and educational attainment to target territories and the most vulnerable in soci-ety for policy measures largely built on reinforcing individual human capi-tal. While anti-discrimination policies institute social groups, existing social policy indicators are centred on the individual and do not provide the pos-sibility to question relationships between socio-economically defined groups such as social mobility or differences in life chances in a broad range of fields of human activity affected by public policies. This is a reflec-tion of the decline of a class-based social critique in European societies, the lack of collective actors mobilised around these themes on the European scene, and also the predominance of policy frames and instruments informed by economic knowledge which have become sociologically embedded into European institutions.

Funding

This work was supported by the French National Agency for Research (ANR EUREQUA).

Notes

1. The empirical basis of this article relies on private archives belonging to members of the different consortiums and working groups, a reading of scientific literature and 'grey' literature written by European institutions and the scientific experts involved in the different stages of the project, a reconstruction of the social and professional trajectories and networks of the promoters and protagonists of this knowledge instrument, and finally semi-directive interviews with these same actors.
2. A final report by the ESSnet group headed by statisticians from the French INSEE between 2011 and 2014 was sent to Eurostat on 30 May 2014 and presented a less ambitious model largely based on the ILO's International Standard Classification of Occupations. At the time of writing, there was no official decision to implement and a socio-economic classification therefore remained the last of the major indicators of social Europe defined in the late 1990s which had yet to be implemented (unemployment, employment, revenues, educational attainment, poverty, homelessness, etc.).
3. Rose is a specialist in the construction of socio-economic classifications and he headed the team which revised the official British social class scheme between 1993 and 2001 which derived from Goldthorpe's class scheme.
4. An economist specialised in work and training, Elias is a specialist in the development of statistical tools, most notably ISCO.
5. Trained at the LSE, Whelan is a sociologist specialised in social mobility, social inequalities and poverty. He has been part of the social mobility network since the 1980s.
6. The most peripheral member of the network, Kunst is much younger (PhD in 1997), and is a demographer by training, specialised in socio-economic inequalities with regard to health issues.
7. Sociologist of social mobility, Schizzerotto is a highly recognised international scholar and was one of the most active academics in the creation of the European Social Survey.
8. Interviews at Eurostat in Luxembourg, 12 December 2011 and in Paris on 18 November 2011 with the former director of social statistics at Eurostat.
9. Interview with a former member of the Consortium, 11 December 2012.
10. Interviews with two heads of Unit, DG ECFIN, and three heads of Unit in DG EMPL in 2009 and 2010.

References

Abbott, A. 1999. *Department & discipline, Chicago sociology at one hundred*. Chicago, IL: University of Chicago Press.

Aldrin, P. 2011. The Eurobarometer and the making of european opinion. In *Perceptions of Europe. A comparative sociology of european attitudes*, eds. D. Gaxie, N. Hubé, and J. Rowell, 17–34. Colchester: ECPR Press.

Arrowsmith, J., K. Sisson, and P. Marginson. 2004. What can 'benchmarking' offer the open method of co-ordination? *Journal of European Public Policy* 11, no. 2: 311–28.

Atkinson, T., B. Cantillon, E. Marlier, and B. Nolan. 2002. *Social indicators*. Oxford: Oxford University Press.

Austin, J.L. 1962. *How to do things with words*. Cambridge: Harvard University Press.

Bourdieu, P. 1980. L'identité et la représentation. Éléments pour une réflexion critique sur l'idée de région. *Actes de la recherche en sciences sociales*, no. 35: 63–72.

Bourdieu, P. 1998. *State nobility: elite schools in the field of power*. Cambridge: Polity.

Bourdieu, P. 1991. *The political ontology of Martin Heidegger*. Stanford, CA: Stanford University Press.

Bourdieu, P. 1993. Esprits d'Etat. Genèse et structure du champ bureaucratique. *Actes de la recherche en sciences sociales*, no. 96–97: 49–62.

Brian, E. 1994. *La mesure de l'Etat. Administrateurs et géomètres au XVIIIe siècle*. Paris: Albin Michel.

Brousse, C. 2005. Définir et compter les sans-abri en Europe: enjeux et controverses. *Genèses*, no. 57: 48–71.

Bruno, I., S. Jacquot, and L. Mandin. 2006. Europeanization through its instrumentation: benchmarking, mainstreaming and the open method of co-ordination ... toolbox or Pandora's box? *Journal of European Public Policy* 13, no. 4: 519–36.

Büchs, M. 2007. *New Governance in European social policy*. Basingstoke: Palgrave.

Camic, C. 1995. Three departments in search of a discipline: localism and interdisciplinary interaction in American sociology, 1890–1940. *Social Research* 62, no. 4: 1003–33.

Dehousse, R. 2011. *The community method. Obstinate or obsolete*. London: Palgrave Macmillan.

Desrosières, A. 1998. *The politics of large numbers: a history of statistical reasoning*. Oxford: Oxford University Press.

Desrosières, A., and L. Thévenot. 1988. *Les catégories socioprofessionnelles*. Paris: La Découverte.

Elissalt, F. 2001. La statistique communautaire au tournant du XXIème siècle. *Courrier des Statistiques*, no. 100: 41–51.

Erikson, R., and J. Goldthorpe. 1992. *The constant flux. A study of class mobility in industrial societies*. Oxford: Clarendon Press.

Erikson, R., J. Goldthorpe, and L. Portocarero. 1979. Intergenerational class, mobility in three Western European societies: England, France and Sweden. *The British Journal of Sociology* 30, no. 4: 415–41.

Everaers, P. 1998. *A framework for harmonisation: key social indicators, core variables and a framework for the joint use of administrative sources, register and survey data*. Luxemburg: Eurostat.

Fligstein, N. 2009. *Euroclash; the EU, European identity and the future of Europe*. Oxford: Oxford University Press.

Georgakakis, D., and M. de Lassalle. 2007. Genèse et structure d'un capital institutionnel européen. *Actes de la recherche en sciences sociales*, no. 166–167: 38–53.

Georgakakis, D., and J. Rowell (eds.). 2013. *The field of Eurocracy. Mapping EU actors and professionals*. Basingstoke: Palgrave Macmillan.

Goldthorpe, J. 2000. *On sociology, numbers, narratives and the integration of research and theory*. Oxford: Oxford University Press.

Goldthorpe, J. 2002. On official social classifications in France and in Britain. *Sociétés Contemporaines* 45–46, no. 1: 187–9.

Goldthorpe, J., and K. Hope. 1974. *The social grading of occupations: a new approach and scale*. Oxford: Clarendon Press.

Goody, J. 1986. *The logic of writing and the organization of society*. Cambridge: Cambridge University Press.

Gornitzka, A., and U. Sverdrup. 2011. Access of experts: information and EU decision-making. *West European Politics* 34, no. 1: 48–70.

Grais, B. 1999. *Les nomenclatures socio-économiques (CSE) utilisées dans la statistique officielle des États membres de l'Union Européenne. Report to Eurostat*.

Hacking, I. 1990. *The taming of chance*. Cambridge: Cambridge University Press.

Harrison, E., and D. Rose. 2006. *The European Socio-economic Classification (ESeC), Draft User Guide*.

Jasanoff, S. 2004. *States of knowledge: the co-production of science and the social order*. London: Routledge.

Kassim, H., and P. Le Galès. 2010. Exploring Governance in a multi-level polity: a policy instruments approach. *West European Politics* 33, no. 1: 1–21.

Kassim, H., J. Peterson, M.W. Bauer, S. Connolly, R. Dehousse, and L. Hooghe. 2013. *The European Commission of the twenty-first century*. Oxford: Oxford University Press.

Kauppi, N., and M. Madsen (eds.). 2013. *Transnational power elites: the new professionals of Governance, law and security*. London: Routledge.

Kuhn, T.S. 1962. *The structure of scientific revolutions*. Chicago, IL: University of Chicago Press.

Lascoumes, P., and P. Le Gales. 2007. Introduction: understanding public policy through its instruments? From the nature of instruments to the sociology of public policy instrumentation. *Governance* 20, no. 1: 1–21.

MacKenzie, D. 1981. *Statistics in Britain, 1865–1930: the social construction of scientific knowledge.* Edinburgh: Edinburgh University Press.

Maloutas, T. 2007. *Socio-economic classification models and contextual difference.* A look at the *European Socio-economic classification* (ESeC) from the south european angle, Discussion Paper Series, 13. Thessaly: University of Thessaly.

Mudge, S., and A. Vauchez. 2012. Building Europe on a weak field: law, economics, and scholarly avatars in transnational politics. *American Journal of Sociology* 118, no. 2: 449–92.

Müller, W., H. Wirth, G. Bauer, R. Pollak, and F. Weiss. 2006. ESeC — Kurzbericht zur Validierung und Operationalisierung einer europäischen sozioökonomischen Klassifikation. *ZUMA-Nachrichten* 30, no. 59: 111–9.

Nivière, D. 2005. Négocier une statistique européenne: le cas de la pauvreté. *Genèses*, no. 58: 28–47.

O'Connor, A. 2001. *Poverty knowledge. Social science, social policy, and the poor in twentieth-century U.S. history.* Princeton, NJ: Princeton University Press.

Østby, L., P. Everaers, S. Gassemyr, and L. Mejer. 2000. *Harmonisation of recommended core units, variables and classifications.* Luxemburg: Eurostat.

Porter, T. 1995. *Trust in numbers. The pursuit of objectivity in science and public life.* Princeton, NJ: Princeton University Press.

Power, M. 1999. *The audit society.* Oxford: Oxford University Press.

Rose, D., D. Pevalin, and P. Elias. 2001. *Towards a European socio-economic classification: final report to Eurostat of the expert group.* London, Colchester: ONS and ISER, University of Essex.

Rowell, J., and M. Mangenot (eds.). 2010. *A political sociology of the European Union. Reassessing constructivism.* Manchester: Manchester University Press.

Sverdrup, U. 2005. *Administering information: Eurostat and statistical integration.* Arena Working paper. Oslo: Centre for European Studies, University of Oslo.

Szreter, S. 1996. *Fertility, class and gender in Britain 1860–1940.* Cambridge: Cambridge University Press.

Tahlin, M. 2007. Class clues. *European Sociological Review* 23, no. 5: 557–72.

Tooze, A. 2001. *Statistics and the German state, 1900–1945: the making of modern economic knowledge.* Cambridge: Cambridge University Press.

Vauchez, A. 2008. The force of a weak field: law and lawyers in the Government of the european union (for a renewed research agenda). *International Political Sociology* 2, no. 2: 128–44.

Vauchez, A., and B. De Witte (eds.). 2013. *Lawyering Europe. European law as a transnational social field.* Oxford: Hart Publishing.

Sociology of Knowledge and Production of Normative Power in the European Union's External Actions

IAN MANNERS

Department of Political Science, University of Copenhagen, København K, Denmark

ABSTRACT   The article focuses on the entanglement between the EU's attempts to construct its external actions in global politics and research on the EU as a global actor. The article argues that both the development of EU external actions and the sociology of knowledge production surrounding the analysis of these actions suffer from unnecessary dichotomisation. Advocates and analysts of the EU's normative power have argued that the separation of norms and interests, both in terms of policy-making and policy analysis, is impossible. In contrast, advocates and analysts of the EU as a 'normal power', a great power pole in the coming multipolar world, have dichotomised the advocacy of policy-making and the analysis of knowledge production of EU external actions. The article sets out, through an examination of the interlinking of policy-making and policy analysis, how such false dichotomies weaken the sociology of knowledge about the EU and the production of the EU's external actions. The article uses an analytical means of illustrating the deep interdependencies between the sociology of knowledge and production of the EU's external actions. This application illustrates how ideas about external actions are spread from the study of normative power to other normative frameworks, and from analysts to policy-makers in the field of EU external actions. The article concludes that strategic dichotomisation and social diffusion are integral to the social sciences and the production of European integration in making Europe 'normal'.

Introduction: Sociology of Knowledge and Production

> If the normative and the structural are to be combined, the synthesis should follow E. H. Carr in taking knowledge and power and values and interests as two sides of the same (social reality) coin. Inching toward a synthesis, thus, would consist of, for example, studying the normative foundations of power—Ian Manners' concept of 'Normative Power' shows the way. (Adler, Buzan, and Dunne 2005, 197–198)

> The existence of a normative power suggests that there are other entities that do not fulfil the same defining criteria. Implicitly these 'normal' actors are pragmatic and materialist in their aims and policy orientations, or they are normative in nature but do not possess sufficient of whatever is needed to enforce their preferences. (Wood 2009, 116)

Why are the sociology of knowledge about the EU as a global actor and policy production of the EU's external actions always talked about in dichotomous terms of one approach 'versus' another? Why, for example, is it value-neutral political science to argue that the EU does and should act as a self-interested, security maximising 'normal power', while it is normative political science to argue that the EU does and should act to reconcile concerns for the self with concerns for others through cosmopolitical 'normative power'? And finally, why is it routinely assumed that EU external policy analysis and policy-making are not co-constitutive of each other as policy fields???

This article sets out to address these questions by tracking some of the trends in the sociology of knowledge and production of EU external action that have evolved over the past two decades since the normative power approach (NPA) first started to question them. As Emanuel Adler, Barry Buzan and Tim Dunne, three of the world's leading international relations (IR) scholars, recognised in 2005 (above), the NPA studies the normative foundations of power through a synthesis of historically dichotomised approaches of structural IR (interests and power) and normative IR (values and knowledge). The dichotomisation of structural IR from normative IR leaves the question of how to understand the interrelationships between material and non-material forms of power broadly unanswered. As Steve Wood argued in 2009 (above), such dichotomisation has become so popular than many seek to claim that 'normative power' should be separated from 'normal power' in analytical terms. The application of Adler-Nissen and Kropp's (2015) principle of symmetry to such dichotomisations illustrates how such 'facts' are taken as beliefs to be explained socially.

A close reading of two of the earliest normative power papers (Manners 2000, 32, 2002, 239) makes clear how any and all attempts to dichotomise the study of normative from normal are untenable—if normative power is the ability to shape normality, then the study of normal cannot avoid an understanding of normative power. Advocates and analysts of the EU's normative power have argued that the separation of norms and interests, both in terms of policy-making and policy analysis, is impossible (Manners

2011, 243; Diez and Manners 2007, 18). As Rosamond (2014, 136) notes, 'reducing the adjudication of the liberal credentials of an external intervention to strategic vs. normative motivations is—at one level—a false dichotomy'. In contrast, advocates and analysts of the EU as a 'normal power', a great power pole in the coming multipolar world, have dichotomised the advocacy of policy-making and the analysis of knowledge production of EU external actions (Pacheco Pardo 2012; Youngs 2004a). The article sets out, through an examination of the interlinking of policy-making and policy analysis, how such false dichotomies weaken the sociology of knowledge about the EU and the production of the EU's external actions. To clarify, 'false dichotomies' refers to attempts to falsely dichotomise between the sociology of knowledge about EU external actions vs. the production of policies about EU external actions; between value-neutral positive vs. normative political science; and between normative power vs. normal power.

To study this interlinking of policy analysis and policy-making, the article illustrates the deep interdependencies between the sociology of knowledge and production of the EU's external actions. Here, the article has similarities to Rosamond's (2015) contribution on the deep entanglement of theories and policies in the early European Commission. This application illustrates how ideas about external actions are spread from the study of normative power to other normative frameworks, and from analysts to policy-makers in the field of EU external actions. The article concludes that strategic dichotomisation and social diffusion are integral to the social sciences and the production of European integration in making Europe 'normal'.

The Study of Normative Power and Diffusion into Other Normative Frameworks

As discussed extensively elsewhere (Manners 2013a, 306–307, 2014, 2015), the past 15 years have seen a gradual increase of knowledge and production around the idea of normative power. Over a dozen volumes have been published on the subject, including Adler *et al.* (2006); Lucarelli and Manners (2006); Sjursen (2006); Laïdi (2008a, 2008b); Tocci (2008); Aggestam (2008); Gerrits (2009); Kissack (2010); Manners (2010b); Sicurelli (2010); Whitman (2011); Kavalski (2012); Woolcock (2012); Nicolaïdis and Whitman (2013); Voloshin (2014); Björkdahl *et al.* (2015). As discussed in Manners (2013a, 308–309), the social sciences have many different understandings of 'normative power', but the NPA found in Manners (2000, 2002) was the first to develop the idea of normative power to understand the EU in global politics. The following analysis of diffusion in the scholarly community demonstrates the merits of the principle of situatedness set out by Adler-Nissen and Kropp (2015) where situations shape the practice and institutionalisation of ideas of normative power into other normative frameworks.

Normative Power in the Scholarly Community

An approximate search of Google Scholar references and Google web page references per year illustrates this gradual increase in knowledge production. As the first chart on Google Scholar references illustrates below, there has been a steady increase in references per year to normative power since 2000, with a take-off in 2005–2006. The chart also shows that the number of scholarly uses of the term 'normative power Europe' is almost double the number of scholarly references to the 2002 Journal of Common Market Studies article. Furthermore, the chart illustrates the extent to which there is increasingly a much wider use of the terms 'normative power' plus 'European Union', without specific reference to either the JCMS article or the term 'normative power Europe'.

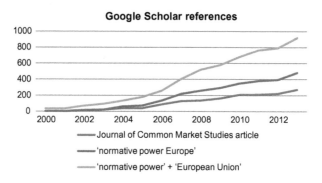

The second chart on Google web search hits (below) illustrates the extent to which there has been a steady increase in web pages references to normative power, with a later take-off in 2007–2008. The chart also shows that the use of the term 'normative power Europe' is almost double the use of the Journal of Common Market Studies as a reference. More interestingly, the chart also illustrates the much more widespread use of the terms 'normative power' plus 'European Union' without reference to either the JCMS article or the term 'normative power Europe'. This second chart also suggests there has been a second increase in the use of the terms 'normative power' plus 'European Union' since 2010, as witnessed in the blogosphere.

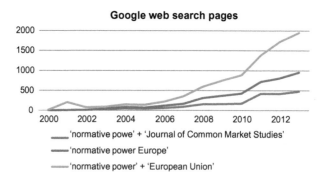

Taken together, the two charts suggest a gradual increase in the use and diffusion of ideas of normative power, first into scholarly references, then into the wider web. The two charts also illustrate the much wider use of the terms 'normative power' plus 'European Union' without reference to the JCMS article. Furthermore, after the web take-off of 2010, the terms 'normative power' plus 'European Union' are almost twice as common in the wider web than they are in scholarly references. Thus, the two charts suggest that the idea of normative power increasingly has wider resonance beyond academic debates.

Normative Power Diffusion into Other Normative Frameworks

Equally interesting as the increase in books, scholarly references and web pages, is the way in which the idea of normative power has diffused into other normative frameworks, as five examples illustrate. This short discussion illustrates very well Adler-Nissen and Kropp's (2015) principle of contextualism where all knowledge is produced in relation to other knowledge claims. The first case of normative power diffusion starts with a June 2002 UACES seminar at the University of London where Richard Youngs was introduced to the idea of normative power. On the basis of this encounter and being given two preliminary drafts of what were to become Manners (2002) and Manners and Whitman (2003), Youngs (2004b) writes a Foreign Policy Centre working paper on 'Engagement: Sharpening European Influence' (see also Youngs 2004a). In the paper, Youngs (2004b, 3–5) transforms the idea of normative power into that of 'transformative power'. Working in the London-based EU milieu at the same time as Youngs, both Heather Grabbe (2004, 2006) and Mark Leonard (2005a, 2005b) draw on normative power in their work. As Leonard asserts, citing Youngs (2004b) paper, 'We can see that a new kind of power has evolved … Europe's power is a 'transformative power' (Leonard 2005a, 5). Similarly, Grabbe (2006, 46, 50, 63, 67) writes of the EU's transformative power in terms of 'normative pressures' and 'normative institutional structure'. By 2009, the normative power of the EU's transformative power is found in the research programme on 'The Transformative Power of Europe: The European Union and the Diffusion of Ideas' at the Free University of Berlin (Börzel and Risse 2009).

The second case starts with a September 2002 workshop at the University of Warwick where Zaki Laïdi was first introduced to the idea of normative power. Laïdi's engagement with normative power has been important for French audiences with the publication of *La norme sans la force. L'énigme de la puissance européenne* (Laïdi 2005). Subsequent publications in French, for example Petiteville (2006), Manners (2007), Laïdi (2009a) and Saurugger (2010), contributed to the diffusion of ideas of normative power. Laïdi's subsequent publications in English pushed the idea of normative power further into the public and policy-making spheres (see Laïdi 2008a, 2008b, 2008c, 2009b). The third case was about the theoretical and ethical basis of normative power and began with a 2005 conference at the Swedish Institute for International Affairs, Stockholm, organised by Lisbeth Aggestam. The resulting publication focussed on making a distinction between the procedural notion of a 'normative heading' and the more problematic notion of 'ethical foreign policy' (Manners 2006a, 116–7). The second meeting was a workshop on 'ethical power' held at Chatham House (formerly the Royal Institute for International Affairs), London, which led to a special issue of *International Affairs* edited by Aggestam

(2008; see also Manners 2008). This diffusion of ideas of normative power in engagements with ethical theory has proved fruitful in terms of connecting to international political theory (Aggestam 2009, 2013).

The fourth case moves closer to the policy institutes of Brussels with a joint EU Framework Programme funding bid on normative foreign policy led by Nathalie Tocci, together with Thomas Diez, Dietrich Jung and myself during 2007. Without EU funding, the project was anchored at the Centre for European Policy Studies (CEPS) in Brussels where Tocci brought together in-house scholars, together with contributors from the USA, Russia and India. The final product was a first attempt to comparatively analyse five global actors—the EU, USA, Russia, India and China using a normative power framework (see Tocci 2008; Tocci and Manners 2008). The fifth case is the diffusion of ideas of normative power into the concept of 'normative institutionalism' through studying the ways in which substantive and procedural norms of the EU shape EU foreign policy (Thomas 2011, 4). Using March and Olsen's idea of a normative institutionalist approach, Thomas takes the ideas behind normative power such as theories of social learning and normative persuasion and turns them into positivist-like hypotheses. This normative institutionalist variant of the NPA illustrates how ideas of utilitarian and social norms (Manners 2000, 27–30, see also Manners 2013a, 312–313) can be operationalised to study the power of EU norms.

What this brief review of five of the ways in which the idea of normative power has diffused into other normative frameworks illustrates is that a sociology of knowledge of EU external actions reveals a whole series of false dichotomies. Strangely, what these five cases of scholarship reveal, despite the similarity between the works, are widespread attempts to misrepresent and then deny these similarities. In other words, the sociology of knowledge of EU external actions is built on attempts to dichotomise normative power from transformational power, norm power, ethical power, normative foreign policy and normative institutionalism. This is strange because of their shared origins in social theory, the similar mechanisms of norm diffusion and the coincidence of interest in the power of ideas. The negative effects of such dichotomised sociology of knowledge are manifold, leaving most observers and many participants confused over the realities and implications of such approaches. Equally problematic is the relative lack of knowledge accumulation which such dichotomisation renders improbable. Here, there are similarities with Penissat and Rowell's (2015) contribution on the limits of expert integration and the role of context in understanding the lack of wider European debate on the idea of normative power.

The Advocacy of Normative Power and Diffusion into the Policy-making Field

Whereas the knowledge and production of normative power and EU external actions have been widely discussed in the academic field, there has been far less consideration given to the policy-making field. This is probably because it is far harder to trace and track normative power in the policy-making field. As Adler-Nissen and Kropp (2015) argue, the analysis of the diffusion of normative power into the policy-making field illuminates the principle of rejecting the internal/external division by looking at how scholarly production is entangled with broader societal and economic developments. Three strategies will analyse this diffusion by focusing on policy advocacy, news media and EU institutions.

Normative Power in the Policy-making Community

The diffusion of ideas of normative power into the *policy-making community* can be examined by looking at the Nordic, pan-European and Brussels EU policy communities. An approximate search of Google web references per year illustrates this gradual increase in knowledge production and diffusion between policy centres and communities. As the first chart on Google web search Nordic policy community references illustrates below, there had been a steady pattern of web references per year from 2000 to 2006. From 2006 to date, there has been an increase in web pages per year at the Danish Institute for International Affairs (DIIS) and the Finnish Institute for International Affairs (FIIA). There are a number of reasons for the diffusion of ideas of normative power into Nordic policy centres and policy community. First, I was a visiting researcher at the Copenhagen Peace Research Institute (COPRI) during 2000–2001 and then head of the EU unit at the Danish Institute for International Studies (DIIS) during 2006–2009. Second, the Nordic peace studies institutes (COPRI, SIPRI, PRIO and TAPRI), and the Nordic international studies institutes (DIIS, SIIA, NUPI and FIIA) have been linked by close formal and informal patterns of research cooperation, facilitating the diffusion of ideas. Furthermore, from 2005 to 2013, DIIS, SIIA and FIIA shared membership of the EU FP6 'EU-Consent' network of excellence (2005–2009) and the EU FP7 'LISBOAN' Erasmus academic network. This cooperation led to a series of exploratory workshops in Helsinki, Stockholm and Oslo on EU foreign policy, funded by the joint committee for the Nordic research councils. The roles of Thomas Diez (COPRI); Hiski Haukkala (FIIA) and Hanna Ojanen (FIIA/SIIA) in Finland; Pernille Riker (NUPI) and Nina Græger (NUPI) in Norway; Lisbeth Aggestam (SIIA), Mark Rhinard (SIIA) and Björn Fägersten (SIIA) in Sweden have all been important in this diffusion.

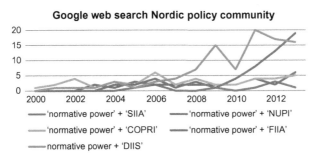

A second search looks at three pan-European policy communities (below) —the European Policy Institute Network (EPIN), the Trans-European Policy

Studies Association (TEPSA) and the European Council on Foreign Relations (ECFR). While there has been a small number of hits per year on Goole web searches for 'normative power' plus EPIN or TEPSA, it is hits on 'normative power' plus ECFR that have taken off since 2010. EPIN and TEPSA have both been important facilitators of the diffusion of ideas of normative power because of membership of DIIS in both, along with CEP and Notre Europe in EPIN, as well as FIIA and SIIA in TEPSA. For example, the joint TEPSA and NIIR-Clingendael conference in Brussels (May 2009) on the EU's normative power in the new global order was important because it brought scholars (such as Richard Youngs and Lisbeth Aggestam) with representatives of policy centres, together with EU policy-makers (such as Robert Cooper and Richard Wright)—see Gerrits (2009).

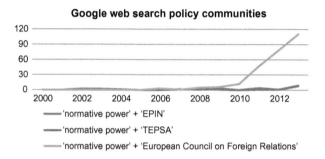

A third Google web search (below) illustrates the way in which there has been a steady increase per year of web pages referring to both Brussels pol-icy centres (either CEPS or EPC) and 'normative power' since 2004, with a take-off in 2006–2007. The chart also shows the extent to which references to 'normative power' plus CEPS start earlier and are more numerous than references to 'normative power' plus EPC. The role of Natalie Tocci (CEPS/IAI), Michael Emerson (CEPS), Rosa Balfour (EPC) and Antonio Missiroli (EPC/EU Institute for Security Studies [EU-ISS]) has been impor-tant in this diffusion—see (Balfour 2006; Missiroli 2000; Tocci 2008).

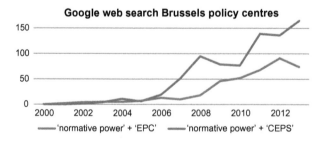

These three patterns of Nordic, pan-European and Brussels policy centres and communities suggest that while policy analysts and policy-makers were initially inionly mildly exposed to ideas about normative power, from 2005 onwards the diffusion of ideas intensified. The processes that facilitate this diffusion are multi-dimensional involving all six mechanisms of norm diffusion. The three main processes involve (i) the free flow of ideas between scholarship, policy communities and policy-makers; (ii) the role of scholarship in training new generations of policy-makers who entered EU foreign service during the 2000s; (iii) the less-free flow of personnel between academia, policy institutes and EU employment.

Normative Power in News Media

The second approach is to understand the diffusion of ideas of normative power in *news media* by looking at international news media, as is accessible via LexisNexis. The main venue for the informational diffusion of ideas of normative power has been the *Financial Times*, although this has had perverse effects in wider policy-making circles. Writing in 2008, Zaki Laïdi argued 'How Europe can shape the global system' (*Financial Times*, 1 May 2008). Laïdi argued that with the end of the unipolar moment, the rise of China, Brazil and India, and with no chance of the EU becoming a super-federal state:

> The only credible scenario for Europe lies in its 'normative power'—promoting standards that are negotiated and legitimised within international institutions. Norms aim to discipline the behaviour of state and non-state actors. To be efficient, those norms should rely on soft and hard mechanisms of enforcement. Of course, those norms could be biased in favour of the dominant powers, as some developing countries argue. There is a risk, for example, that stringent environmental rules in Europe will hurt the development of some exporting countries that have lower standards. That is why norms need legitimacy and mechanisms of compliance that allow weaker countries to have a say. The World Trade Organisation's dispute settlement system is one example of a relatively un-biased enforcement process. (Laïdi 2008c)

The article began a protracted discussion in the *Financial Times* between Laïdi and journalist Philip Stephens regarding the idea of normative power. The perverse effects of this exchange can be seen in the abstract above: (i) that normative power is the power of European norms; (ii) that the practice of European norms should rely on soft and hard mechanisms; and (iii) that the WTO's dispute settlement mechanism was an example of normative power in action (Laïdi was special advisor to Pascal Lamy when he was EU trade commissioner between 2000 and 2004). Following the Russian invasion of Georgia, Stephens retort to Laïdi argued in September 2008 that 'Mr Putin's invasion of Georgia has already provided a brutal demonstration of the limits of Europe's normative power. Subsequent negotiations with Moscow have served only to underline the latter's disdain for anything but force' (Stephens 2008). Here, the first confusion between the Laïdi and Stephens' position, that normative power is the power of European norms, and the NPA position that an understanding of how physical force, material incentives, and normative justification are enacted in practice is critical to understanding normative power, not simply the absence of force. In this respect, the Laïdi position is very similar to that of Börzel and Risse's reading of 'transformative power' as norm power, rather than normative power. As Laïdi responded, 'the only influence [the EU] commands is a normative one, a capacity to shape the world through the diffusion of norms in global regulation—finance, environment, food security, and so on. This is far from negligible, but cannot make up for the lack of strategic power' (Laïdi 2009b). What is interesting about Stephens subsequent articles on normative power over the past five years is that they appear to both consolidate and advocate normative power:

> Barack Obama's administration seems to have understood the importance of what the political scientists call 'normative' power. States are strong when others want to imitate them. For some that means an admiration for US democratic values, for others enthusiasm for America's cultural and economic vibrancy. (Stephens 2009)

> There was a brief period during the 1990s—after its dismal failure in the Balkans—in which Europe seemed to have found its role. The spread eastwards of western democracy and market economics provided it with a different model of influence. The US had the military muscle; but the European Union was emerging as a "normative" power —shaping events by example rather than coercion. (Stephens 2010a)

> There is nothing wrong in setting an example—political scientists call it 'normative power'. As Mr Barroso gave his address, Hillary Clinton was setting out an alliance-building approach to the shifting power balance. The US secretary of state recalled the words of Dean Acheson: 'The ability to evoke support from other' is 'quite as important as the capacity to compel'. (Stephens 2010b)

> The first instinct is to celebrate the way globalisation lifts hundreds of millions of people out of poverty; the second to fret whether the rebalancing of global power will usher in a new era of might is right in IR. Even Europeans, who have come to look at the world through normative lenses, are beginning to think that soft power may sometimes need a hard centre. (Stephens 2014)

As Europe's only moderately transnational newspaper, these discussions and (mis)understandings of normative power are important, particularly given Philip Stephens' high profile in international journalism. What is also clear is that ideas of normative power have diffused into wider international public spheres over the past six years, with references found in over 70 different news media according to LexisNexis. Most of the news media are European based, but a significant proportion is outside of Europe. A small sample of four different news sources illustrates the diffusion of the idea of normative power.

An editorial from *The Frontier Post* in Pakistan from May 2011, in the context of the Arab uprisings, illustrates the importance of normative power for those witnessing Turkey's 'source of inspiration' in terms of democratisation and socio-economic transformation:

Alienating Turkey from the EU track because of political short-sightedness of some member states will not only discourage millions of people who see Turkey as a 'beacon of democracy' and 'source of inspiration' for their own development and democratisation, but will also damage the credibility of the Union that aspires to be a normative power embracing and promoting universal values of democracy, cultural diversity and pluralism. It is for the EU to decide whether to become a genuine global power or not. (Frontier Post 2011)

A syndicated report by Simon Tay carried in Hong Kong's *South China Morning Post* and Thailand's *The Nation* in July 2011, sets out how South China Sea tensions at the ASEAN regional forum should be addressed through normative power:

Asean as a group must think not only about balancing power with power, even as it reaches out to the US. While the US military presence has been a factor for stability, the urgent need is to develop norms and habits for peaceful co-operation. Asean, with neither the capacity nor ambition for military assertion, must develop itself as a normative power. (Tay 2011)

A more recent article by Charlemagne in *The Economist* in March 2012 discusses the problems of EU foreign policy in the context of the global financial and Eurozone crises:

The problem runs even deeper. The EU's claim to importance is that, as the biggest market in the world, it matters. As an example of peaceful integration, it is a 'normative power', able to set a magnetic example of co-operation. But what kind of normative power can the EU wield if its biggest project, the euro, is seen to be in danger of collapse?

Finally, a reflection on the EU and climate change by Helmut Anheier and Alexander Ruser in *European Voice* in November 2013:

The European Union became the pioneer of global climate protection with its ratification of the Kyoto Protocol in 1997 and subsequent legislation at the European level. The role of environmental leader fitted a political Union that also thinks of itself as a community of values. The EU still likes to portray Europe as a normative power, as a supranational showcase able and willing to lead the world in climate protection.

What these few examples, together with a much broader array of references in international media suggest is that the idea of normative power has become widely diffused in news media. In particular, references in articles from the *Financial Times*, *The Economist* and *European Voice* indicate that European and Brussels-based policy-makers are exposed to ideas about normative power.

Normative Power in EU Institutions

The third and final approach is to understand the diffusion of ideas of normative power in **EU institutions** by looking at public debates as found on the European Commission (ec.europa.eu) and European Parliament (www.europarl.europa.eu) websites. As the introduction article by Adler-Nissen and Kristoffer Kropp suggested, the idea of normative power has been taken up by former Commission President José Manuel Barroso as illustrated by a number of his interviews, articles and speeches. As part of the recognition of the 50-year anniversary of the Treaty of Rome, Barroso was invited to read and reflect upon the five most significant academic publications of the previous decade. Barroso's reading of the idea of normative power appears to be formative, as his subsequent speeches reveal. In his interview, Barroso identifies a number of key principles from the 2002 normative power article as being particularly important, including human rights and the environment:

> We are one of the most important, if not the most important, normative powers in the world. Look, for instance, even beyond the case that he talks about: the death penalty. The candidate countries were adapting their norms to our norms. There is not another case, I'm sorry, where the United States or China or Russia, has been able to have so many other countries following their patterns. (Barroso in Peterson 2008, 69)

Two years later, writing in *The Guardian* in 2010 prior to the Eurozone crisis, Barroso argues that the EU's strength in a post-crisis world lies in its normative power, or as he put it, the power of its values (echoing Laïdi's, and Börzel and Risse's interpretations of normative power):

> It is often said that the EU's comparative advantage lies in its normative power, or the power of its values. I think this is right. In a post-crisis world, when people are looking for new ways to ensure their well-being, peace, and prosperity, the European experience has a great deal to offer. (Barroso 2010)

In a 2012 speech at Princeton University, Barroso sought to argue that the EU was an indispensible partner for the USA. But in a twist, he argued that normative power required both an effective foreign policy (soft power) and a credible defence capability (hard power):

> The world needs a European Union that is ready to complement the effectiveness of its foreign policy with a credible defence capability because there is no normative power without both soft and hard power. (Barroso 2012, 5)

But Barroso was not the only Commissioner to advance the idea of normative power. Former MEP, Commissioner and Italian Trade and Foreign Minister Emma Bonino was an advocate of normative power, largely because it resonated with her position on human rights. To recognise the 50th anniversary of the Treaty of Rome, Bonino was invited to contribute to a joint European Commission and Financial Times 'views and visions' media publication:

> An EU capable of acting as a normative power and a major player on the global scene is a basic prerequisite if our goal for the EU is to secure peace, maintain stability, foster economic prosperity and preserve our lifestyle over the next 50 years. It will require both institutional change in the short term and the rise of a genuine political community to be governed by a directly accountable, legitimate European leadership in the medium to long term. To have the former without the latter would be unrealistic. (Bonino 2007)

The idea of normative power is also to be found in the European Parliament, particular in the activism and speeches of MEP Jacek Saryusz-Wolski. As well as an influential member of the Committee on Foreign Affairs and Vice-President of the EP, Saryusz-Wolski is Member of the Board of TEPSA. After joining the EP in 2004, Saryusz-Wolski acted as rapporteur on the EP's response to Council's Annual Report on CFSP discussed 2008. It is worth noting that both Javier Solana (High Representative CFSP) and Günter Verheugen (Vice-President of the Commission) participated in the debate and responded to Saryusz-Wolski's points. When debating his report, Saryusz-Wolski argued that the EU's role as a peace-maker needed to include both the normative power of freedom, democracy and human rights promotion, as well as developing capabilities for physical force projection:

> The European Union should continue its role as peace-maker and mediator, a soft power helping to stabilise, reconstruct and reform, a supplier of assistance and humanitarian aid, as a normative power, value-projecting and promoting democracy, freedom and human rights, but at the same time we should complement the soft dimension with a harder one by developing the ESDP dimension and our military capabilities to be prepared for power projection also. (Saryusz-Wolski in European Parliament 2008)

More specifically, during a debate with European Commissioner Karel De Gucht on the 2010 EU–China summit, MEP Monika Flašíková Beňová suggested that EU relations with China go beyond security and economic interests to include the idea of normative power regarding IR and human rights:

> The entire tense dynamic of EU-China relations arises from the fact that, apart from mutual pragmatic, strategic and geopolitical interests, the EU is attempting to exert influence on China from the position of a normative power. Hence, the Union not only needs China on account of its security and economic interests, but also needs China to support and implement the ideas of the Union regarding international relations and human rights. (Flašíková Beňová in European Parliament 2010)

Finally, Jacek Saryusz-Wolski and Pier Antonio Panzeri's EP resolution on the European Neighbourhood Policy in 2013 argued that the EU should enact normative power with citizens in the Eastern Partnership region through the promotion of democracy, rule of law and human rights:

> Recommends that the Union should: (c) encourage those citizens to advance the values the EU is based upon—namely democracy, the rule of law and respect for human rights and fundamental freedoms—through their commitment to promote them, thus making them the main source of normative power transformation. (European Parliament 2013)

Taken together, these brief examples of policy-makers in the European Commission and European Parliament discussing and advocating ideas of normative power suggest that by 2007 the diffusion of normative power had moved beyond scholarly fields, policy communities and news media to reach policy-makers. While there is a large literature illustrating how normative power is used by EU actors in policy-making, it is a qualitatively different task to demonstrate how ideas of normative power lead directly to policy outcomes. A number of illustrations suggest how links between scholarly fields, policy communities, news media and policy-making work for the diffusion of EU norms within ideas of normative power.

The case of the EU-ISS helps illustrate these links, beginning with the October 2002 publication of Chaillot Paper No. 55 on *What model for CFSP?* containing a section on 'Models for the EU's international role' (Ehrhart 2002, 10–14) taken from Manners 2002. It is possible to trace how this paper contributed to the spread of ideas of normative power within the EU-ISS and its closely associated CFSP policy-making community. The idea of normative power has subsequently featured in 5 more Chaillot Papers, 3 ISS Analyses, 2 ISS Occasional Papers, and an ISS Brief. More importantly, the idea of normative power featured in the two widely read reports edited by EU-ISS director Álvaro de Vasconcelos—*What ambitions for European defence in 2020?* (de Vasconcelos 2009), and *A strategy for EU foreign policy* (de Vasconcelos 2010). It is worth noting that contributors to these reports included Javier Solana, Catherine Ashton, Nicole Gnesotto, Tomas Ries (Director of SIIA), MEP Jacek Saryusz-Wolski, Alexander Stubb (Finnish Foreign Minister), Alexander Weis (Chief Executive of the European Defence Agency) and Richard Wright (European Commission/EEAS).

Other examples growing out of the case of the EU-ISS include ideas of 'human security', and in particular 'sustainable peace' evolving both within and without the European Commission, the EU-ISS and office of the High Rep. since 2003. As documented elsewhere, interpretations of human security (freedom from fear and freedom from want) and sustainable peace (addressing the causes and symptoms of conflict and violence) can been seen linking together the idea of normative power with scholarly fields, policy communities, news media and policy-making (Manners 2006b, 2006c, 2006d, 2013b; see also Kaldor 2012; Martin 2011; Martin and Kaldor

2009). Drawing on the scholarship of Thomas Diez and Michelle Pace, it is possible to identify the impact of EU normative power on conflict transformation in cases such as Cyprus and Palestine (Diez and Pace 2011). As Diez went on to argue, the greatest impact of ideas of normative power is discursive in their ability to set the limits of EU actions (Diez 2014). More specific examples identified by EU officials include European Commission DG Trade's support for Fair Trade policies (Manners 2010); the advocacy of the European Parliament and Jacek Saryusz-Wolski's Committee on Foreign Affairs for the creation of a European Endowment for Democracy; and the explicit inclusion by the European Commission's DG Research of a funding call for the study of normative power in 'Europe's contribution to a value-based global order and its contestants in the FP8—Horizon 2020 Work Programme.

What these brief cases suggest is that ideas of normative power circulating amongst EU-scholars involved in policy advice (such as Mary Kaldor), together with EU think tanks (such as the EU-ISS), have actively contributed to EU policy formulation by the High Rep. and the Council. But they also argue that the greatest impact of ideas of normative power is as discursive practice that sets the limits of EU actions. So the final question to be discussed is how to understand the relationships between scholarly fields and policy fields, and hence between the sociology of knowledge and the production of EU external actions.

Conclusion: Strategic Dichotomisation and Social Diffusion

> Exporting the EU model as a normative power may not be possible, but it still represents an approach that in its own ways has scored significant successes (including the enlargement of the EU). Increasing the peaceful pursuit of fundamental values in international relations would greatly stabilize the global system as it would reduce the likelihood and severity of conflicts. (WEF Global Agenda Council Reports 2010, 326)

The 2010 report of the World Economic Forum's Global Agenda Council on the 'Future of the European Union' (above) illustrates the dense interplay between scholarly and policy-making fields, and how ideas of normative power are diffused into global politics. As founder and executive chairman of the World Economic Forum, Klaus Schwab put it the report is about 'bringing together the best minds and foremost experts, the Summit on the Global Agenda is the starting point for global efforts to redesign our international system according to the needs of the twenty-first Century' (WEF Global Agenda Council Reports 2010, 5). What is interesting for the argument put forward here is that the members of the 'Council on the Future of the European Union' include a mixture of scholars, policy centre staff and policy-makers, some of which have been discussed here. Among the members were academic scholars—Timothy Garton Ash (University of Oxford); directors of EU policy centres Daniel Gros (CEPS), Charles Grant (CER), Mark Leonard (ECFR), and Jean Pisani-Ferry (BRUEGEL); EU policy-makers Klaus Gretschmann (Council of Ministers), Silvana Koch-Mehrin (MEP), and Jürgen Stark (ECB); and former Commissions and national Ministers Emma Bonino and Ana Palacio. Equally interesting is that the 'Forum Lead' on the Council was Stephen Kinnock, son of former European Commissioner Neil Kinnock and former MEP Glynnis Kinnock, and partner to Helle Thorning-Schmidt (Prime Minister of Denmark).

While the exact mechanisms of how diffusion from scholarly fields to policy-making fields take place remain complex, evidence suggests that the six mechanisms of norm diffusion play a role (see Manners 2000, 35–36, 2002, 244–245, 2006b, 184, 2006d, 76–81, 2007, 46–47, 2013a, 314–319). *Contagion* across the scholarly, internet, media, policy communities and policy-making circles since 2006 is important. As the discussion of diffusion into other normative frameworks, including the CER, FPC, ECFR, Free University of Berlin, Sciences Po Paris, and beyond has illustrated contagion mechanisms cut across the academic, policy analysis and policy-making communities. *Informational diffusion* in the form of academic papers, policy reports, news media articles and policy debates has played a role, as the example of the EU-ISS has illustrated. *Procedural relationships* introduced by EU consultation practices, educational practices and careers of scholars into policy-makers emerge as important. The EU educational centres of excellence such as the European University Institute near Florence, and College of Europe at Bruges and Natolin, have all served as procedural mechanisms through which scholars, analysts and policy-makers have been introduced to ideas of normative power. The role of *transference* in the form of both funding for research programmes such as EU-Consent and LISBOAN, as well as policy advice back into EU institutions, is clearly visible. Beyond these transference mechanisms, the joint activities of European policy institutes such as the annual *Think Global—Act European* report edited by the Notre Europe—Jacques Delors Institute illustrate how member states' publicly funded policy centres contribute to the diffusion of ideas of normative power. The *overt presence* of scholars in policy centres, policy analysts in policy debates and former scholars/policy analysts in policy-making roles has also proved significant. As discussed in this article, the overt roles of scholar/analysts such as Richard Whitman (RIIA/University of Kent), Mark Leonard (CER/EPC/ECFR), Antonio Missiroli (EPC/EU-ISS), as well as policy-makers such as José Manuel Barroso, Emma Bonino and Jacek Saryusz-Wolski have all been important in diffusing ideas of normative power. Finally, the role of the *cultural filter,* shaping how scholars, policy analysts and policy-makers alike (re)interpret the idea of normative power for strategic and/or cultural reasons is clearly critical in the diffusion of normative power. The importance of the agency of other actors in relations with the EU is critical in understanding the role of the cultural filter in the study of normative power. The systematic study of the cultural filter and the adoption, adaptation, resistance or rejection of norms and/or normative power by other political actors ensures that the study of the EU as a global actor moves from the social theory of the twentieth century to a more critical social theory in the twenty-first century (on the cultural filter see

Björkdahl *et al.* 2015; Kinnvall 1995, 61–71; Manners 2002, 245). As the discussion of normative vs. normal power suggests, the academic and policy communities tend to take a position on the idea of normative power depending on their strategic/cultural reading of whether the EU is or should be mimicking the great power trends of multipolar politics. This cultural filter of nineteenth century great power politics, twentieth century multilateral politics or twenty-first century global interdependence is clearly very powerful.

The 15-year diffusion of ideas of normative power briefly discussed here illustrates the importance of both 'strategic dichotomisation' and 'social diffusion' in understanding false dichotomies in the sociology of knowledge and production of the European Union's external actions. In the introductory discussion, the article sets out how strategic dichotomisation is a scholarly career strategy with intellectual consequences, as the five examples of normative power diffusion into other normative frameworks (Section 'The Advocacy of Normative Power and Diffusion into the Policy-making Field') have illustrated. What the social diffusion of ideas of normative power into other frameworks, as well as beyond the scholarly community, demonstrates is that social diffusion is a social science norm. While both strategic dichotomisation and social diffusion are to be found throughout the scholarly, policy analytical and policy-making worlds, they are both 'normal' practices and make Europe 'normal' in the sense of social practice. Most importantly, for those engaging in these normal social practices, both the strategic dichotomisation of 'normative power' vs. 'normal power' and social diffusion of policy knowledge and production are normative processes with normative consequences for EU external actions. Only by adopting a self-consciously reflexive sociology of knowledge approach to our understanding of the idea of normative power can we understand the power that these normative process and consequences have for the knowledge and production of normative power in the European Union's external actions.

References

Adler, E., B. Buzan, and T. Dunne. 2005. Forum afterword. *Millennium: Journal of International Studies* 34: 195–9.

Adler, E., B. Crawford, F. Bicchi, R. Del Sarto, eds. 2006. *The convergence of civilizations: constructing a mediterranean region*. Toronto: University of Toronto Press.

Adler-Nissen, R., and K. Kropp. 2015. A sociology of knowledge approach to European Integration. *Journal of European Integration* 37, no. 2: 155–73.

Aggestam, L. 2008. Introduction: ethical power Europe? *International Affairs* 84, no. 1: 1–11.

Aggestam, L. 2009. The world in our mind: normative power in a multi polar world. In *Normative power Europe in a changing world*, ed. A. Gerrits, 25–36. The Hague: Netherlands Institute of International Relations, Clingendael.

Aggestam, L. 2013. Global norms and European power. In *Routledge handbook on the European Union and international institutions: performance, policy, power*, eds. K.E. Jørgensen and K.V. Laatikainen, 457–71. London: Routledge.

Anheier, H., and A. Ruser. 2013. The affordability of climate protection. *European Voice*, 21 November 2013.

Balfour, R. 2006. Principles of democracy and human rights: a review of the European Union's strategies towards its neighbours. In *Values and principles in European Union foreign policy*, eds. S. Lucarelli and I. Manners, 114–29. London: Routledge.

Barroso, J.M. 2010. Europe's rising global role. *The Guardian*, 3 January 2010.

Barroso, J.M. 2012. Speech by President Barroso at Princeton University: 'European Union: an indispensable partner'. Princeton University, 27 September 2012. http://europa.eu/rapid/press-release_SPEECH-12-650_en.pdf

Björkdahl, A., N. Chaban, J. Leslie, and A. Masselot, eds. 2015. *Importing European Union norms: conceptual framework and empirical findings*. New York: Springer.

Bonino, E. 2007. It is time to act as one. European Union: The next fifty years. *Financial Times*, http://europa.eu/50/news/views/071109_en.htm 13 (accessed 9 November 2007).

Börzel, T., and T. Risse. 2009. *The transformative power of Europe: the European Union and the diffusion of ideas*. KFG Working Papers. Research College, The Transformative Power of Europe. Berlin: Freie Universität Berlin, 1.

Charlemagne. 2012. Tough talk, no strategy: Europe needs to do more than respond to every problem with fresh sanctions. *The Economist*, 3 March 2012.

Diez, T. 2014. Setting the limits: discourse and EU foreign policy. *Cooperation and Conflict* 49, no. 3: 319–33.

Diez, T., and I. Manners. 2007. Reflecting on normative power Europe. In *Power in world politics*, eds. F. Berensoetter and M.J. Williams, 173–88. London: Routledge.

Diez, T., and M. Pace. 2011. Normative power europe and conflict transformation. In *Normative power Europe: empirical and theoretical perspectives*, ed. R. Whitman, 210–25. Basingstoke: Palgrave.

Erhart, H.-G. 2002. What model for CFSP? Chaillot paper. Paris: EU Institute for Security Studies, no. 55, 1 October 2002.

European Parliament. 2008. *Debates—2006 annual report on the implementation of the European security strategy and ESDP*, Brussels. 4 June 2008.

European Parliament. 2010. *Debates—council and commission statements on the EU-China summit*, Brussels. 21 September 2010.

European Parliament. 2013. *Resolution on the European neighbourhood policy: towards a strengthening of the partnership*, Brussels. 23 October 2013.

Frontier Post. 2011 Turkey's EU mission a source of inspiration. *The frontier post*, 21 May 2011.

Gerrits, A. ed. 2009. *Normative power Europe in a changing world: a discussion*. The Hague: Netherlands Institute of International Relations Clingendael.

Grabbe, H. 2004. *The constellations of Europe: how enlargement will transform the EU*. London: Centre for European Reform.

Grabbe, H. 2006. *The EU's transformative power: Europeanisation through conditionality in central and eastern Europe*. Basingstoke: Palgrave.

Kaldor, M. 2012. The EU as a new form of political authority: the example of the common security and defence policy. *Global Policy*, 3, no. 1: 79–86.

Kavalski, E. 2012. *Central Asia and the rise of normative powers: contextualizing the security governance of the European Union, China, and India*. London: Continuum/Bloomsbury Academic.

Kinnvall, C. 1995. *Cultural diffusion and political learning: the democratization of China*. Lund: Lund University Press.

Kissack, R. 2010. *Pursuing effective multilateralism: the European Union, international organisations and the politics of decision making*. Basingstoke: Palgrave.

Laïdi, Z. 2005. *La norme sans la force. L'énigme de la puissance européenne* [The norm without the force: the enigma of European power]. Paris: Presses de Sciences Po.

Laïdi, Z. 2008a. *EU foreign policy in a globalized world. Normative power and social preferences*. London: Routledge.

Laïdi, Z. 2008b. *Norms over force*. Basingstoke: Palgrave.

Laïdi, Z. 2008c. How Europe can shape the global system. *Financial Times*, 1 May 2008.

Laïdi, Z. 2009a. L'Europe, puissance normative international [Europe: international normative power]. In *Politiques européennes*, ed. R. Dehousse, 227–42. Paris: Presses de Sciences Po.

Laïdi, Z. 2009b. Why Obama does not want a multipolar world order. *Financial Times*, 4 December 2009.

Leonard, M. 2005a. *Europe's transformative power*. London: Centre for European Reform. http://www.cer.org.uk/publications/archive/bulletin-article/2005/europes-transformative-power

Leonard, M. 2005b. *Why Europe will run the 21st century*. London: Fourth Estate.

Lucarelli, S., and I. Manners, eds. 2006. *Values and principles in European Union foreign policy*. London: Routledge.

Manners, I. 2000. *Normative power Europe: a contradiction in terms?* Working paper 38/2000. Copenhagen: Copenhagen Peace Research Institute.

Manners, I. 2002. Normative power Europe: a contradiction in terms? *JCMS: Journal of Common Market Studies* 40, no. 2: 235–58.

Manners, I. 2006a. European Union, normative power and ethical foreign policy. In *Rethinking ethical foreign policy: pitfalls, possibilities and paradoxes*, eds. D. Chandler and V. Heins, 116–36. London: Routledge.

Manners, I. 2006b. Normative power Europe reconsidered: beyond the crossroads. *Journal of European Public Policy* 13, no. 2: 182–99.

Manners, I. 2006c. European Union 'normative power' and the security challenge. In *Security and democracy in the European Union*, eds. C. Kantner, A. Liberatore, and R. Del Sarto, Special Issue of European Security, 15, no. 4: 405–21.

Manners, I. 2006d. The symbolic manifestation of the EU's normative role in world politics. In *The European Union's roles in international politics: concepts and analysis*, eds. O. Elgström and M. Smith, 66–84. London: Routledge.

Manners, I. 2007. L'identité internationale de l'Union européenne: un pouvoir normatif dans le jeu politique mondial [The international identity of the European Union: a normative power in global politics]. In *Europe, puissance tranquille? Rôle et identité sur la scène mondiale* [Europe: tranquil power? Role and identity on the global scene], ed. B. Adam, 33–49. Brussels: Editions Complexe.

Manners, I. 2008. The normative ethics of the European Union. In *Special issue on ethical power Europe?* ed. L. Aggestam. *International Affairs* 84, no. 1: 45–60. doi: 10.1111/j.1468-2346.2008.00688.x

Manners, I. 2010a. 'Free and fair trade' and 'fair trade' in the European Union, paper presented to Jean Monnet Centre of Excellence Workshop on 'Diverging Paradigms on EU Trade Policy', Leuven, 16–17 December.

Manners, I. ed. 2010b. Virtual special issue on normative power. *Journal of European Public Policy*. http://www.tandf.co.uk/journals/access/rjpp.pdf

Manners, I. 2011. The European Union's normative power: critical perspectives and perspectives on the critical. In *Normative power Europe: empirical and theoretical perspectives*, ed. R. Whitman, 226–47. Basingstoke: Palgrave.

Manners, I. 2013a. Assessing the decennial, reassessing the global: understanding European Union normative power in global politics. In Special issue on normative power Europe, eds. K. Nicolaïdis and R. Whitman. *Cooperation and Conflict*, 48, no. 2: 304–29.

Manners, I. 2013b. European [Security] Union: bordering and governing a secure Europe in a better world? *Global Society* 27, no. 3: 398–416.

Manners, I. 2014. Theories and myths of European foreign policy. In *Handbook of European politics*, ed. J. Magone. 877–91. London: Routledge.

Manners, I. 2015. The European Union in global politics: normative power and longitudinal interpretation. In *Research methods in European Union studies*, eds. K. Lynggaard, I. Manners, and K. Löfgren. Basingstoke: Palgrave.

Manners, I., and R. Whitman. 2003. The 'difference engine': constructing and representing the international identity of the European Union. *Journal of European Public Policy* 10, no. 3: 380–404.

Martin, M. 2011. Human security and the search for a normative narrative. In *Normative power Europe: empirical and theoretical perspectives*, ed. R. Whitman, 187–209. Basingstoke: Palgrave.

Martin, M., and M. Kaldor, eds. 2009. *The European Union and human security: European external interventions and missions*. London: Routledge.

Missiroli, A. 2000. Italy. In *The foreign policies of European Union member states*, eds. I. Manners and R. Whitman, 97–104. Manchester: Manchester University Press.

Nicolaïdis, K., and R. Whitman, eds. 2013. Special issue on normative power Europe. *Cooperation and Conflict* 48, no. 2 167–329.

Pacheco Pardo, R. 2012. Normal power Europe: non-proliferation and the normalization of the EU's foreign policy. *Journal of European Integration* 34, no. 1: 1–18.

Penissat, E., and J. Rowell. 2015. The creation of a European socioeconomic classification: limits of expert-driven statistical integration. *Journal of European Integration* 37, no. 2: 281–97.

Peterson, J. 2008. José Manuel Barroso: Political Scientist, ECPR Member. *European Political Science* 7: 64–77.

Petiteville, F. 2006. *La politique internationale de l'Union européenne* [The international politics of the European Union]. Paris: Presses de Sciences Po.

Rosamond, B. 2014. Three ways of speaking Europe to the world: markets, peace, cosmopolitan duty and the EU's normative power. *The British Journal of Politics & International Relations* 16, no. 1: 133–48.

Rosamond, B. 2015. Performing theory/theorizing performance in emergent supranational governance: the 'Live' knowledge archive of European Integration and the early European Commission. *Journal of European Integration* 37, no. 2: 175–91.

Saurugger, S. 2010. *Théories et concepts de l'intégration européenne* [Theories and concepts of European integration]. Paris: Presses de Sciences Po.

Sicurelli, D. 2010. *European Union's Africa policies: norms, interests and impact.* Farnham: Ashgate.

Sjursen, H. ed. 2006. *Civilian or military power? The European Union at a crossroads.* London: Routledge.

Stephens, P. 2008. A new president and a wake-up call for the west. *Financial Times*, 12 September 2008.

Stephens, P. 2009. A friendless Russia is held hostage to Putin's vanity. *Financial Times*, 21 August 2009.

Stephens, P. 2010a. A neuralgic Europe trails petulantly in America's wake. *Financial Times*, 22 January 2010.

Stephens, P. 2010b. Europe daydreams its way to Japanese irrelevance. *Financial Times*, 10 September 2010.

Stephens, P. 2014. How the best of times is making way for the worst. *Financial Times*, 28 March 2014.

Tay, S. 2011. Calm the waters. *South China Morning Post and The Nation*, July 2011.

Thomas, D. 2011. *Making EU foreign policy.* Basingstoke: Palgrave.

Tocci, N. ed. 2008. *Who is a normative foreign policy actor? The European Union and its global partners.* Brussels: CEPS.

Tocci, N., and I. Manners. 2008. Comparing normativity in foreign policy: China, India, the EU, the US and Russia. In *Who is a normative foreign policy actor? The European Union and its global partners*, ed. N. Tocci, 300–29. Brussels: CEPS.

de Vasconcelos, Á. ed. 2009. *What ambitions for European defence in 2020?* Paris: European Union Institute for Security Studies.

de Vasconcelos, Á. ed. 2010 *A strategy for EU foreign policy.* Paris: European Union Institute for Security Studies Report no. 7, June 2010.

Voloshin, G. 2014. *The European union's normative power in Central Asia: promoting values and defending interests.* Basingstoke: Palgrave.

Whitman, R. ed. 2011. *Normative power Europe: empirical and theoretical perspectives.* Basingstoke: Palgrave.

World Economic Forum. 2010. Global agenda council reports. Geneva: WEF. http://www.weforum. org/pdf/globalagenda2010.pdf

Wood, S. 2009. The European Union: a normative or normal power? *European Foreign Affairs Review* 14, no. 1: 113–28.

Woolcock, S. 2012. *European Union economic diplomacy: the role of the EU in external economic relations.* Farnham: Ashgate.

Youngs, R. 2004a. Normative dynamics and strategic interests in the EU's external identity. *Journal of Common Market Studies* 42, no. 2: 415–35.

Youngs, R. 2004b. Engaging: sharpening European influence. In *New terms of engagement*, ed. R. Youngs, 1–14. London: The Foreign Policy Centre.

Index

Contributing authors are only included in the index where their work is discussed by other contributing authors.

Page numbers shown in bold typeface refer to information in tables.

The entry commencing 'St.' is arranged in the index as if spelt 'Saint'.

For Product Safety Concerns and Information please contact our EU
representative GPSR@taylorandfrancis.com Taylor & Francis Verlag GmbH,
Kaufingerstraße 24, 80331 München, Germany

Batch number: 08158490

Printed by Printforce, the Netherlands